CHOCTAW BY BLOOD ENROLLMENT CARDS

1898-1914

VOLUME VI

TRANSCRIBED BY

JEFF BOWEN

NATIVE STUDY
Gallipolis, Ohio
USA

Originally published:
Baltimore, Maryland
2015

Reprinted by:

Native Study LLC
Gallipolis, OH
www.nativestudy.com

Library of Congress Control Number: 2020911767

ISBN: 978-1-64968-009-9

Made in the United States of America.

This series is dedicated to
Mike Marchi,
who keeps my spirits up.

CREEK CENSUS.

SECOND NOTICE.

Members of the Dawes Commission will be present at the following times and places for the purpose of enrolling Creek citizens, as required by Act of Congress of June 10, 1896:

At Muskogee, Nov. 8 to 30, 1897, inclusive.
At Wagoner, Nov. 8 to 13,   "   inclusive.
At Eufaula, Nov. 8 to 13,   "   inclusive.
At Sapulpa, Nov. 15 to 20,   "   inclusive.
At Wetumpka, Nov. 15 to 20,   "   inclusive.
At Okmulgee, Nov. 22 to 30,   "   inclusive.

All persons who have not heretofore enrolled before the Dawes Commission should appear and enroll. Parents and guardians can enroll their families and wards.

TAMS BIXBY,
FRANK C. ARMSTRONG,
A. S. McKENNON,
THOS. B. NEEDLES,
Commissioners.

The above illustration is similar in nature to what was found throughout Indian Territory for different tribes as far as postings on bulletin boards, public centers, or wherever they could be read so people would be notified of where and when they needed to be for enrollment with the Dawes Commission.

This is a picture of the Dawes Commission at Camp Jones in Stonewall, Indian Territory on September 8, 1898.

The images below are of two of the original cards given on the microfilm. The cards given in this book have been formatted to fit on one page and still give all the information found on the original cards.

Choctaw Nation   Choctaw Roll

Choctaw Nation   Choctaw Roll

Introduction

This series of Choctaw Enrollment Cards for the Five Civilized Tribes 1898-1914 has been transcribed from National Archive Film M-1186 Rolls 39-46.

The series contains more than 6100 Choctaw enrollment cards. All of the cards list age, sex and degree of blood, the parties' Dawes Roll Numbers, and date of enrollment by the Secretary of Interior for each person. The contents also give the enrollee's parents' names as well as miscellaneous notes pertaining to the enrollee's circumstances, when needed. Most entries indicate whether or not a spouse is an Intermarried White, with the initials I.W.

Enrollment wasn't as simple a process as most would think just by going through these pages. The relationships between the Five Tribes and the Dawes Commission were weak at best. There were political battles going on between the tribes and the U.S. Government as it was, but the struggles didn't stop there. Each tribe had its own political factions pulling it from every direction. On top of everything else, people from every corner of the United States were trying to figure how to get in on the spoils (Money and Land Allotment) by means of political favor. Kent Carter, author of *The Dawes Commission*, describes the continuous effort required to enroll the different tribes and the pressure the Commission incurred from people all over the country who tried to insinuate themselves into the equation:

"In May 1896 the Dawes Commission Returned To Indian Territory for its third visit, establishing its headquarters at Vinita in the Cherokee Nation. It now had to process applications for citizenship in addition to negotiating allotment agreements; these circumstances make the narrative of events more confusing because the commission attempted the two tasks concurrently. The commissioners resumed making their usual speeches to tribal officials and public gatherings to promote negotiations, but now they inevitably had to respond to questions about how the application process for citizenship would work. They also began receiving letters from people all over the United States asking how they could 'get on the rolls' so they could 'get Indian land'."[1]

For the actual process of Choctaw enrollment, "A commission was appointed in each county of the Choctaw Nation under an act of September 18 to make separate rolls of citizens by blood, by intermarriage, and freedmen; it was to deliver them to recently elected Chief Green McCurtain by October 20, but he rejected them even before they were completed because of charges that people were being left off for political reasons. On October 30, the National Council authorized establishment of a five-member

---

[1] *The Dawes Commission* by Kent Carter, page 15, para. 1

commission to revise the rolls within ten days and then directed McCurtain to turn them over to the Dawes Commission on November 11, 1896. The Choctaws hired the law firm of Stuart, Gordon, and Hailey, of South McAlester to represent the tribe at all proceedings held by the Dawes Commission,"[2] another indication that throughout the Commission's efforts there was always controversy between the tribes and the negotiators.

When completed, this multi-volume series will contain thousands of names, all of them accounted for in the indexes carefully prepared by the author. Hopefully this work will help many researchers find their ancestors and satisfy the questions that so many have had about their Native American heritage.

Jeff Bowen
Gallipolis, Ohio
NativeStudy.com

---

[2] *The Dawes Commission* by Kent Carter, page 16, para. 5

Choctaw By Blood Enrollment Cards 1898-1914

RESIDENCE:	Jackson	COUNTY.	**Choctaw Nation**				Choctaw Roll	CARD NO.	
POST OFFICE:	Crowder, I.T.						(Not Including Freedmen)	FIELD NO.	**1501**

Dawes' Roll No.	NAME		Relationship to Person	AGE	SEX	BLOOD	TRIBAL ENROLLMENT		
							Year	County	No.
15400	1 Crowder, Bolden	31	First Named	28	M	1/4	1896	Jackson	2795
15401	2 " William T.	4	Son	1	"	1/8			
15402	3 " Silvey E	3	Dau	2mo	F	1/8			
15403	4 " Allie Bama	1	Dau	5mo	F	1/8			
	5								
	6								
	7								
	8	ENROLLMENT							
	9	OF NOS. 1 – 2 – 3 – 4 HEREON APPROVED BY THE SECRETARY							
	10	OF INTERIOR May 9, 1904							
	11								
	12								
	13								
	14								
	15								
	16								
	17								

TRIBAL ENROLLMENT OF PARENTS

	Name of Father	Year	County	Name of Mother	Year	County
1	Thos C. Crowder	1896	Jackson	Flora Crowder	Dead	Cherokee Roll
2	No 1			Emma Crowder	1896	Non Citz
3	No 1			" "	1896	" "
4	No 1			" "	1896	" "
5						
6	No.1 on 1885 Choctaw Census Roll, Kiamitia Co. No 582, as Boland					
7	Father on Choctaw Card 1456(?)					
8	No 1 on 1896 roll as Boland Crowder					
	None of above applicants applied as Cherokees, nor are they on					
9	Mother of No1 was a Cherokee		Cherokee rolls; see letter of Cherokee land office			
10				of December 12, 1903.		
	No2 Affidovit[sic] of birth to be supplied. Recd May 17/99					
11	No.4 Enrolled Sept 4, 1901.					
12	Marriage certificate of parents of children on this card filed Sept 26, 1901					
13						
14					#1 & 2	
15				Date of Application for Enrollment	5/9/99	
16				No 3 enrolled Nov. 1/99		
17	P.O. Boswell I.T. 5/4/04					

1

Choctaw By Blood Enrollment Cards 1898-1914

RESIDENCE: Towson COUNTY. **Choctaw Nation** Choctaw Roll CARD No.
POST OFFICE: Doaksville, I.T. *(Not Including Freedmen)* FIELD No. **1502**

Dawes' Roll No.	NAME		Relationship to Person	AGE	SEX	BLOOD	TRIBAL ENROLLMENT		
							Year	County	No.
4210	1 Pritchard, Lizzie	34	First Named	31	F	1/4	1896	Towson	10347
4211	2 " Cora	13	Dau	10	"	1/8	1896	"	10350
4212	3 " Frank	8	Son	5	M	1/8	1896	"	10352
4213	4 " Nora ~~DIED PRIOR TO SEPTEMBER 25, 1902~~		Dau	3	F	1/8	1896	"	10351
4214	5 Peeler, Valley	17	Son	14	(x) ~~M~~ F	1/8	1896	"	10348
4215	6 " Mary	15	Dau	12	F	1/8	1896	"	10349
4216	7 Pritchard, Lewie G.	1	Son	1mo	M	1/8			
I.W. 177	8 " William E.		husband	45	M	I.W.	1896	"	14936

(x) 7/2/1915 Sex of No.5 changed from "M" to "F" per
10 Dept authority of June 29, 1905(See Dept Letter No 4438-1915)

11
12   ENROLLMENT
       OF NOS. 123456 and 7 HEREON
13   APPROVED BY THE SECRETARY
       OF INTERIOR Dec. 12, 1902
14
15   ENROLLMENT
       OF NOS. ----8---- HEREON
16   APPROVED BY THE SECRETARY
       OF INTERIOR Jun 13, 1903
17

TRIBAL ENROLLMENT OF PARENTS

	Name of Father	Year	County	Name of Mother	Year	County
1	Brit Willis	Dead	Non. Citz	Margaret Willis	Dead	Towson
2	William E. Pritchard	1896	" "	No 1		
3	" " "	1896	" "	No 1		
4	" " "	1896	" "	No 1		
5	R.E. Peeler	Dead	" "	No 1		
6	" "	"	" "	No 1		
7	Wm E Pritchard		" "	No 1		
8	James Pritchard	Dead	non citizen	Eliz Pritchard	1896	non citizen

9 No8 on 1896 Choctaw census roll as Wm E. Pritchard
10 No8 transferred from Choctaw card #D.150. See decision of May 1, 1903
11   Husband of No1 William E Pritchard on
12   Card No D.150.
13   No7 Born April 3, 1902, enrolled May 19, 1902
         ~~No4 died Aug. 22, 1900, proof of death filed Dec. 5, 1902.~~
14 No.4 died Aug 22, 1900. Enrollment cancelled by Department July 8, 1904.
15   For child of Nos. 1 and 8 see N.B. (March 3, 1905) #1218.
16
17 P.O. Fort Towson I.T. 4/22/05

Date of Application for Enrollment. 5/9/99

Choctaw By Blood Enrollment Cards 1898-1914

RESIDENCE:	Kiamitia	COUNTY.						
POST OFFICE:	Antlers, I.T.							

Choctaw Nation

Choctaw Roll *(Not Including Freedmen)*

CARD NO.

FIELD NO. **1503**

Dawes' Roll No.	NAME	Relationship to Person	AGE	SEX	BLOOD	TRIBAL ENROLLMENT		
						Year	County	No.
4217	1 Gibson, Willie E. 51	First Named	48	M	Full	1896	Kiamitia	4826
4218	2 " Siney 51	Wife	48	F	"	1896	"	4827
4219	3 " Elias 20	Son	17	M	"	1896	"	4838
4220	4 " Isaac 10	Son	7	M	"	1896	"	4839
see 1708 VOID	5 Adams, Missie	S Dau	19	F	"	1896	"	360
4221	6 Frazier, James 26	S Son	23	M	"	1893	"	P.R. 234
	7							
	8	ENROLLMENT						
	9	OF NOS. 1 2 3 4 and 6 HEREON APPROVED BY THE SECRETARY						
	10	OF INTERIOR Dec. 12, 1902						
	11							
	12							
	13							
	14							
	15							
	16							
	17							

TRIBAL ENROLLMENT OF PARENTS

	Name of Father	Year	County	Name of Mother	Year	County
1	Solomon Gibson	Dead	Jacks Fork	Salena Gibson	Dead	Kiamitia
2	Tobias Frazier	"	Jackson		"	Jackson
3	No 1			Agnes Gibson	"	Kiamitia
4	No 1			No 2		
5	Solomon Adams	Dead	Jackson	No 2		
6	Davis Frazier	"	"	No 2		
7						
8	No6 on 1893 Pay roll, Page 28, No 234, Kiamitia County					
9	No5 transferred to Choctaw Card #1708 with her					
10	husband Silas E Cole, January 3, 1901. Evidence of marriage filed with Choctaw case #1708					
11	Nos 1 and 2 are divorced					
12						
13						
14					Date of Application for Enrollment.	
15						
16					5/9/99	
17						

3

Choctaw By Blood Enrollment Cards 1898-1914

RESIDENCE: Jackson   COUNTY.   **Choctaw Nation**   Choctaw Roll   CARD NO.
POST OFFICE: Crowder, I.T.   (Not Including Freedmen)   FIELD NO. **1504**

Dawes' Roll No.	NAME		Relationship to Person	AGE	SEX	BLOOD	TRIBAL ENROLLMENT		
							Year	County	No.
I.W. 636	1 Brown, John T.	36	First Named	32	M	I.W.			
4222	2 " Frances	21	Wife	18	F	1/4	1896	Jackson	2821
4223	3 " Ella May	3	Dau	3mo	F	1/8			
	4								
	5								
	6	ENROLLMENT							
	7	OF NOS. 1 HEREON							
	8	APPROVED BY THE SECRETARY OF INTERIOR Mar 26 1904							
	9								
	10								
	11								
	12	ENROLLMENT							
	13	OF NOS. 2 and 3 HEREON APPROVED BY THE SECRETARY							
	14	OF INTERIOR Dec 12, 1902							
	15								
	16								
	17								

TRIBAL ENROLLMENT OF PARENTS

	Name of Father	Year	County	Name of Mother	Year	County
1	George Brown	1896	Non Citz	Mattie Brown	Dead	Non Citz
2	Josh Crowder	Dead	Jackson	Sibbie Crowder	"	Jackson
3	No 1			No 2		
4						
5						
6			No2 on 1896 roll as Frances Crowder			
7			No.3 Enrolled June 11th, 1900.			
8						
9			For child of Nos 1&2 see NB (Mar 3-1905) Card No 35.			
10						
11						
12						
13						
14						
15					#1 & 2	
16					Date of Application for Enrollment	5/9/99
17	P.O. Boswell I.T. 4/6/05					

4

Choctaw By Blood Enrollment Cards 1898-1914

RESIDENCE: Jackson COUNTY.
POST OFFICE: Mayhew, I.T.

Choctaw Nation

Choctaw Roll
(Not Including Freedmen)

CARD NO.
FIELD NO. 1505

Dawes' Roll No.	NAME	Relationship to Person	AGE	SEX	BLOOD	TRIBAL ENROLLMENT		
						Year	County	No.
4224	1 Bench, John 24	First Named	21	M	3/8	1896	Jackson	1511
NB 804	2 " James Clayton							
	3							
	4							
	5							
	6							
	7							
	8							
	9							
	10							
	11	ENROLLMENT						
	12	OF NOS. 1 HEREON APPROVED BY THE SECRETARY						
	13	OF INTERIOR DEC 12 1902						
	14							
	15							
	16							
	17							

TRIBAL ENROLLMENT OF PARENTS

Name of Father	Year	County	Name of Mother	Year	County
1 Christ Bench	Dead	Jackson	Nancy Bench	Dead	Jackson
2 No 1			Mary M Bench	Born	Mch 1-06
3					
4					
5	For child of No.1 see N.B. (Apr 26, 1906) No. 804				
6					
7					
8					
9					
10					
11					
12					
13					
14					
15					
16			Date of Application for Enrollment		5/9/99
17					

Choctaw By Blood Enrollment Cards 1898-1914

RESIDENCE: Kiamitia COUNTY. **Choctaw Nation** Choctaw Roll CARD NO.
POST OFFICE: Goodland, I.T. (Not Including Freedmen) FIELD NO. 1506

Dawes' Roll No.	NAME		Relationship to Person	AGE	SEX	BLOOD	TRIBAL ENROLLMENT		
							Year	County	No.
IW 895	1 Russell, William	33	First Named	30	M	I.W.	1896	Kiamitia	14975
4225	2 " Emma	32	Wife	29	F	1/4	1896	"	10846
4226	3 " Nettie	9	Dau	6	"	1/8	1896	"	10847
4227	4 " Etta	6	"	2	"	1/8			
4228	5 " Ether[sic]	1	"	6wks	"	1/8			
	6								
	7								
	8	ENROLLMENT OF NOS. 2 3 4 and 5 HEREON APPROVED BY THE SECRETARY OF INTERIOR DEC 12 1902							
	9								
	10								
	11	ENROLLMENT OF NOS. 1 HEREON APPROVED BY THE SECRETARY OF INTERIOR AUG 3 1904							
	12								
	13								
	14								
	15								
	16								
	17								

TRIBAL ENROLLMENT OF PARENTS

	Name of Father	Year	County	Name of Mother	Year	County
1	Arch Russell	1896	Non Citz	Jane Russell	Dead	Non Citz
2	James Usrey	1896	" "	Melinda Usrey	"	Kiamitia
3	No 1			No 2		
4	No 1			No 2		
5	No 1			No 2		
6						
7	No 1 on 1896 roll as Billy Russell.					
8						
9	Document presented purporting to be a copy of					
10	license and certificate of marriage, sworn by H.C. Bohanan and O.O. Gooding, 3rd day of					
11	September 1896. They say original was					
12	exhibited to them. Originals may have					
13	been sent to Dawes Commission in 1897.					
14	No.5 born Oct. 16, 1901: Enrolled Nov. 27, 1901.					
15					#1 to 4 inc	
16					Date of Application for Enrollment	5/9/99
17	P.O. Hugo, I.T. 12/4 '02					

6

Choctaw By Blood Enrollment Cards 1898-1914

RESIDENCE: Kiamitia	COUNTY.	**Choctaw Nation**			Choctaw Roll	CARD No.	
POST OFFICE: Goodland, I.T.					(Not Including Freedmen)	FIELD No. 1507	

Dawes' Roll No.		NAME		Relationship to Person	AGE	SEX	BLOOD	TRIBAL ENROLLMENT		
								Year	County	No.
4229	1	Spring, Willie	38	First Named	35	M	3/8	1896	Kiamitia	11486
I.W. 76	2	" Hattie	34	Wife	31	F	I.W.	1896	"	15050
4230	3	" Laura D	13	Dau	10	"	3/16	1896	"	11488
4231	4	" Granville L	11	Son	8	M	3/16	1896	"	11489
4232	5	" Nannie	9	Dau	6	F	3/16	1896	"	11490
4233	6	" Lillie M	7	"	4	"	3/16	1896	"	11491
4234	7	" William B	6	Son	2	M	3/16			
4235	8	" Carrie H.	3	Dau	1mo	F	3/16			
4236	9	" Baziel	2	Son	5mo	M	3/16			
4237	10	" Hazel Edna	1	dau	2mo	F	3/16			
	11	ENROLLMENT								
	12	OF NOS. 13456789and10 HEREON APPROVED BY THE SECRETARY								
	13	OF INTERIOR DEC 12 1902								
	14	ENROLLMENT								
	15	OF NOS. ~~~ 2 ~~~ HEREON APPROVED BY THE SECRETARY								
	16	OF INTERIOR JUN 13 1903								
	17									

TRIBAL ENROLLMENT OF PARENTS

	Name of Father	Year	County	Name of Mother	Year	County
1	William Spring	1896	Kiamitia	Jane Spring	Dead	Kiamitia
2	William Self	1896	Non Citz	Carrie Self	1896	Non Citz
3	No 1			No 2		
4	No 1			No 2		
5	No 1			No 2		
6	No 1			No 2		
7	No 1			No 2		
8	No 1			No 2		
9	No 1			No 2		
10	No.1			No.2		
11						
12	No3 on 1896 roll as Lauridella Spring					
13	No4 " 1896 " " Louis G. "					
14	No.9 Enrolled March 28, 1901					
15	No10 born Sept. 18, 1902: enrolled Dec. 5, 1902					
	For child of Nos. 1&2 see NB (March 3, 1903) #1076				Date of Application for Enrollment	#1 to 8 inc 5/9/99
16						
17	P.O. Hugo, I.T. 12/5 '02					

Choctaw By Blood Enrollment Cards 1898-1914

Dawes' Roll No.	NAME	Relationship to Person	AGE	SEX	BLOOD	TRIBAL ENROLLMENT		
						Year	County	No.
I.W. 1290	1 Purtle, Thomas 37	First Named	35	M	I.W.	1896	Kiamitia	14937
	2							
	3							
	4							
	5							
	6							
	7							
	8							
	9							
	10							
	11	ENROLLMENT						
	12	OF NOS. 1 HEREON APPROVED BY THE SECRETARY						
	13	OF INTERIOR Mar 14, 1905						
	14							
	15							
	16							
	17							

TRIBAL ENROLLMENT OF PARENTS

Name of Father	Year	County	Name of Mother	Year	County
1 Thos. Purtle	Dead	Non Citz	Nancy Purtle	1896	Non Citz
2					
3					
4					
5					
6	On 1896 roll as Thomas Purdle				
7	No. 1 formerly husband of Jane Purtle, 1893 Towson, No. 294				
8	and who died in 1894. Also formerly husband of				
9	Lucinda Nanomantube, Choctaw roll No 3167.				
10					
11					
12					
13					
14					
15					
16				Date of Application for Enrollment	5/9/99
17	P.O. Spencerville, I.T. 12/11 02				

P.O. Hugo, I.T. 1/4/04

8

RESIDENCE: Chickasaw Natn ~~COUNTY.~~
POST OFFICE: Silo, Panola Co., I.T.

Choctaw Nation

Choctaw Roll
(Not Including Freedmen)

CARD NO.
FIELD NO. 1509

Dawes' Roll No.	NAME		Relationship to Person	AGE	SEX	BLOOD	TRIBAL ENROLLMENT		
							Year	County	No.
4238	1 Odelle, Ada	29	First Named	26	F	1/2	1896	Kiamitia	9960
4239	2 " Pearl	11	Dau	8	"	1/4	1896	"	9961
4240	3 " Willie	5	Son	2	M	1/4			
14673	4 " Girtie	1	Dau	3½mo	F	1/4			
	5								
	6								
	7								
	8								
	9	ENROLLMENT							
	10	OF NOS. 1 2 and 3 HEREON APPROVED BY THE SECRETARY							
	11	OF INTERIOR DEC 12 1902							
	12								
	13	ENROLLMENT							
	14	OF NOS. 4 HEREON APPROVED BY THE SECRETARY							
	15	OF INTERIOR May 20 1903							
	16								
	17								

TRIBAL ENROLLMENT OF PARENTS

	Name of Father	Year	County	Name of Mother	Year	County
1	Joe Spring	Dead	Kiamitia	Lucretia Spring	Dead	Kiamitia
2	Henry Odelle	1896	Non Citz	No 1		
3	" "	1896	" "	No 1		
4	" "		" "	N⁰1		
5						
6						
7	No 1 on 1896 roll as Eda Odelle					
8	N⁰4 Born July 19, 1902; enrolled Nov. 8, 1902					
9	For child of No 1 see N.B (Apr 26 06) Card #613					
10						
11						
12						
13						
14						
15						
16				Date of Application for Enrollment		5/9/99
17						

9

Choctaw By Blood Enrollment Cards 1898-1914

RESIDENCE: Kiamitia	COUNTY.	**Choctaw Nation**	**Choctaw Roll** (Not Including Freedmen)	CARD NO.
POST OFFICE: Grant, I.T.				FIELD NO. 1510

Dawes' Roll No.	NAME	Relationship to Person	AGE	SEX	BLOOD	TRIBAL ENROLLMENT		
						Year	County	No.
4241	1 Huland, Isabelle 38	First Named	35	F	1/2	1896	Kiamitia	5776
4242	2 " Amanda 13	Dau	10	"	1/4	1896	"	5777
4243	3 " Mattie 6	"	3	"	1/4	1896	"	5778
	4							
	5							
	6	ENROLLMENT						
	7	OF NOS. 1 – 2 and 3 HEREON						
	8	APPROVED BY THE SECRETARY OF INTERIOR DEC 12 1902						
	9							
	10							
	11							
	12							
	13							
	14							
	15							
	16							
	17							

TRIBAL ENROLLMENT OF PARENTS

Name of Father	Year	County	Name of Mother	Year	County
1 Enoch Brashears	Dead	Kiamitia	Louisa Moore	Dead	Kiamitia
2 Mack Huland	"	Non Citz	No 1		
3 " "	"	" "	No 1		
4					
5					
6					
7		No1 on 1896 roll as Isabelle Holland			
8		No2 " 1896 " " Manda "			
9		No3 " 1896 " " Mattie "			
10					
11		No 1 is now the wife of Ambrose L. Rice, on Choctaw Card #1490			
12					
13				Date of Application for Enrollment.	
14					
15 P.O. Dibble I.T. 10/17/02				5/9/99	
16					
17					

Choctaw By Blood Enrollment Cards 1898-1914

RESIDENCE: Kiamitia   COUNTY.   **Choctaw Nation**   **Choctaw Roll**   CARD NO.
POST OFFICE: Goodland, I.T.   *(Not Including Freedmen)*   FIELD NO. 1511

Dawes' Roll No.	NAME		Relationship to Person	AGE	SEX	BLOOD	TRIBAL ENROLLMENT		
							Year	County	No.
4244	1 Oakes, George W	50	First Named	47	M	1/8	1896	Kiamitia	9937
4245	2 " Aurilla G	47	Wife	44	F	1/2	1896	"	9938
4246	3 " David F	19	Son	16	M	1/4	1896	"	9939
4247	4 Claxton, Arizona	17	Dau	14	F	1/4	1896	"	9940
4248	5 " Pearl B	15	"	12	"	1/4	1896	"	9941
I.W. 1603	6 " Elsie J		Wife of No 3	16	"	I W			
	7								
	8	ENROLLMENT							
	9	OF NOS. 1 2 3 4 and 5 HEREON APPROVED BY THE SECRETARY							
	10	OF INTERIOR DEC 12 1902							
	11								
	12	ENROLLMENT							
	13	OF NOS. ~~~6~~~ HEREON APPROVED BY THE SECRETARY							
	14	OF INTERIOR FEB 12 1907							
	15								
	16								
	17								

TRIBAL ENROLLMENT OF PARENTS

	Name of Father	Year	County	Name of Mother	Year	County
1	Thos. Oakes	Dead	Non Citz	Harriet Oakes	1896	Kiamitia
2	S.N. Fulsom	1896	Towson	Susan Fulsom	Dead	"
3	No 1			No 2		
4	No 1			No 2		
5	No 1			No 2		
6						
7						
8						
9						
10						
11	No1 on 1896 roll as Geo. W. Oakes					
12	No2 " 1896 " " Orilla G. "					
13	No.4 is now the wife of John M. Claxton on Choctaw card #D.612[?]					
14	No6 placed hereon under order of the Commissioner to the Five Civilized Tribes					
15	of Oct 23-1906, holding that application was made for her enrollment within #1to5 inc				Date of Application for Enrollment.	
16	the time provided by the Act of Congress approved April 26-1906					
	For children of Nos #&^ see NB (March 3,1905) #1126				5/9/99	
17	P.O. Hugo, I.T. 12/5/-'02					

Choctaw By Blood Enrollment Cards 1898-1914

RESIDENCE: **Kiamitia**   COUNTY.   **Choctaw Nation**   Choctaw Roll   CARD NO.
POST OFFICE: Goodland, I.T.   (Not Including Freedmen)   FIELD NO. 1512

Dawes' Roll No.	NAME	Relationship to Person	AGE	SEX	BLOOD	TRIBAL ENROLLMENT Year	County	No.
4249	1 Hart, Eastman H 46	First Named	43	M	3/4	1896	Kiamitia	5729
4250	2 " Lemon Jr ED PRIOR TO SEPTEMBER 25, 1902	Son	23	"	3/8	1896	"	5736
4251	3 " Pearl 13	Dau	10	F	3/8	1896	"	5731
4252	4 " Eastman Jr 11	Son	8	M	3/8	1896	"	5732
4253	5 " John M 9	"	6	"	3/8	1896	"	5734
4254	6 " Lula 8	Dau	5	F	3/8	1896	"	5733
4255	7 " Gertrude 7	"	4	"	3/8	1896	"	5735
I.W. 178	8 " Mattie	Wife	49	F	I.W.			14638
	9							
	10 ENROLLMENT OF NOS. 123456and7 HEREON APPROVED BY THE SECRETARY							
	11 OF INTERIOR DEC 12 1902							
	12 No2 died Nov. - 1899; proof of death filed Dec 8 1902							
	13 Nº8 transferred from Choctaw card #D.587. See							
	14 decision of March 26, 1903.							
	15 ENROLLMENT							
	16 OF NOS. ~~~ 8 ~~~ HEREON APPROVED BY THE SECRETARY							
	17 OF INTERIOR JUN 13 1903							

TRIBAL ENROLLMENT OF PARENTS

	Name of Father	Year	County	Name of Mother	Year	County
1	Lemon Hart	1896	Kiamitia	Sukey McCain	Dead	Kiamitia
2	No1			Mattie Hart	1896	Non-Citz
3	No1			" "	1896	" "
4	No1			" "	1896	" "
5	No1			" "	1896	" "
6	No1			" "	1896	" "
7	No1			" "	1896	" "
8	Chapman		non-citizen			
9						
10	No3 is now married to George Anderson a non citizen evidence of marriage filed Dec 6,1902					
11	No1 on 1896 roll as Eastman Hart					
12	No5 " 1896 " " Jno M. "					
13	Evidence as to marriage of parents of				1 to 7 inc	
14	above children must be supplied				Date of Application for Enrollment.	
15	Evidence of marriage filed July 7 1900					
16	Mattie Hart mother of above children on Choctaw card D.587				5/9/99	
17	For child of No3 see NB (Apr 26'06) Card #178					

No.2 died Nov. - 1899: Enrollment cancelled by Department July 8, 1904

12

Choctaw By Blood Enrollment Cards 1898-1914

RESIDENCE: Kiamitia COUNTY. **Choctaw Nation** **Choctaw Roll** CARD NO.
POST OFFICE: Goodland, I.T. *(Not Including Freedmen)* FIELD NO. 1513

Dawes' Roll No.	NAME	Relationship to Person	AGE	SEX	BLOOD	TRIBAL ENROLLMENT		
						Year	County	No.
4256 1 Roebuck, David B ²⁵		First Named	22	M	1/2	1896	Kiamitia	10816
2								
3								
4								
5								
6								
7	ENROLLMENT							
8	OF NOS. 1 HEREON APPROVED BY THE SECRETARY							
9	OF INTERIOR DEC 12 1902							
10								
11								
12								
13								
14								
15								
16								
17								

TRIBAL ENROLLMENT OF PARENTS

	Name of Father	Year	County	Name of Mother	Year	County
1	Dave Roebuck	Dead	Kiamitia	Melina Roebuck	1896	Kiamitia
2						
3						
4						
5						
6						
7						
8						
9						
10						
11						
12						
13						
14						
15						
16			Date of Application for Enrollment	5/9/99		
17						

Choctaw By Blood Enrollment Cards 1898-1914

RESIDENCE: Kiamitia   COUNTY. **Choctaw Nation**   **Choctaw Roll** (Not Including Freedmen) CARD NO.
POST OFFICE: Nelson, I.T.   FIELD NO. 1514

Dawes' Roll No.	NAME	Relationship to Person	AGE	SEX	BLOOD	TRIBAL ENROLLMENT Year	County	No.
4257	1 Frazier, Kizzie 48	First Named	45	F	Full	1896	Kiamitia	4252
	2							
	3							
	4							
	5	ENROLLMENT						
	6	OF NOS. 1 HEREON APPROVED BY THE SECRETARY						
	7	OF INTERIOR DEC 12 1902						
	8							
	9							
	10							
	11							
	12							
	13							
	14							
	15							
	16							
	17							

TRIBAL ENROLLMENT OF PARENTS

	Name of Father	Year	County	Name of Mother	Year	County
1	Elum Mackey	Dead	Blue	Mary Fulson[sic]	Dead	Blue
2						
3						
4						
5	No.1 "Died prior to September 25, 1901: not entitled to land or money."					
6	See copy of Indian Office letter of November 7, 1907. (I.T. 82863-1907.)					
7	Above notation cancelled by Dept. Authority of 12/15/13 (Dept. Letter 2546-13)					
8						
9						
10						
11						
12						
13						
14						
15						
16				DATE OF APPLICATION FOR ENROLLMENT	5/9/99	
17						

Choctaw By Blood Enrollment Cards 1898-1914

RESIDENCE: Kiamitia
POST OFFICE: Nelson, I.T.

COUNTY. **Choctaw Nation**

Choctaw Roll (Not Including Freedmen)

CARD NO.
FIELD NO. **1515**

Dawes' Roll No.	NAME	Relationship to Person	AGE	SEX	BLOOD	TRIBAL ENROLLMENT		
						Year	County	No.
4258	1 Hotinlobi, Liney ⁵³	First Named	50	F	Full	1893	Jackson	344
4259	2 Frazier, Siney ¹³	Dau	10	"	"	1903	"	346
	3							
	4							
	5							
	6							
	7	ENROLLMENT OF NOS. 1 and 2 HEREON						
	8	APPROVED BY THE SECRETARY OF INTERIOR Dec 12 1902						
	9							
	10							
	11							
	12							
	13							
	14							
	15							
	16							
	17							

TRIBAL ENROLLMENT OF PARENTS

	Name of Father	Year	County	Name of Mother	Year	County
1	Ho-tin-lobi	Dead	Red River	Pisa-ho-ke-tema	Dead	Jackson
2	Jackson Frazier	1896	Jackson	No 1		
3						
4						
5	No 1 on 1893 Pay roll Page 39, No 344, Jackson Co, as Liney Hotilabbie					
6	No 2 " 1893 " " " 39, " 346 " "					
7	No 1 on 1896 Roll as Lain Hotayubbi, Page 142, No 5814, Jackson Co.					
	No 2 " 1896 " " Sinie " " 142 " 5815 " "					
8	No 1 is now wife of Edmund Gardner, Choctaw Card #1431					
9						
10						
11						
12						
13						
14					Date of Application for Enrollment.	
15						
16					5/9/99	
17						

Choctaw By Blood Enrollment Cards 1898-1914

RESIDENCE: Kiamitia   COUNTY, **Choctaw Nation**   **Choctaw Roll**   CARD NO.
POST OFFICE: Goodland, I.T.   *(Not Including Freedmen)*   FIELD NO. **1516**

Dawes' Roll No.	NAME	Relationship to Person First Named	AGE	SEX	BLOOD	Year	County	No.
4260	1 Cooper, Moses ~~DIED PRIOR TO SEPTEMBER 25, 1902~~	First Named	36	M	Full	1896	Kiamitia	2688
4261	2 " Lucy ²³	Wife	20	F	"	1896	"	2689
4262	3 " Sampson ⁹	S.Son	6	M	"	1896	"	2690
4263	4 " Nelson ⁶	Son	3	"	"	1896	"	2691
4264	5 " Mary ⁴	Dau	1	F	"			
4265	6 " Ellen ~~DIED PRIOR TO SEPTEMBER 25, 1902~~	Dau	6mo	F	"			
	7							
	8							
	9							
	10							
	11	ENROLLMENT						
	12	OF NOS. 1 2 3 4 5 and 6 HEREON APPROVED BY THE SECRETARY						
	13	OF INTERIOR Dec 12 1902						
	14							
	15							
	16							
	17							

TRIBAL ENROLLMENT OF PARENTS

Name of Father	Year	County	Name of Mother	Year	County
1 ~~Alfred Cooper~~	~~Dead~~	~~Kiamitia~~	~~Betsey Cooper~~	~~Dead~~	~~Jackson~~
2 Michael Pitchlynn	1896	"	Miley Pitchlynn	"	Kiamitia
3 Morris Nelson	Dead	"	No 2		
4 No 1			No 2		
5 No 1			No 2		
6 ~~No 1~~			~~No 2~~		
7					
8					
9					
10	For child of No 2 see N.B (Apr. 26, 1906) Card No. 36				
11	No.6 Enrolled July 20, 1901				
12	No.2 is wife of Johnny James, Choctaw Card No. 1453				
13	~~No 1 Died Dec. – 1901, proof of death filed Dec. 5, 1902.~~ No 6 " in 1901: " " " " " 5, 1902.				
14	No.1 died Dec. – 1901: No 6 died - -, 1901: Enrollment cancelled by Department July 8, 1904				
15				Date of Application for Enrollment:	#1 to 5 inc
16					5/9/99
17					

16

RESIDENCE: Kiamitia
POST OFFICE: Goodland, I.T.
COUNTY: **Choctaw Nation**
Choctaw Roll (Not Including Freedmen)
CARD No.
FIELD No. **1517**

Dawes' Roll No.	NAME		Relationship to Person First Named	AGE	SEX	BLOOD	TRIBAL ENROLLMENT		
							Year	County	No.
4266	1 Nail, Joe	36	First Named	33	M	3/4	1896	Kiamitia	9735
I.W. 706	2 " Paralee	⟨33⟩	Wife	29	F	I.W.	1896	"	14903
4267	3 " Mary	11	Dau	8	"	3/8	1896	"	9736
4268	4 " Susan	8	"	5	"	3/8	1896	"	9737
4269	5 " Minnie	6	"	3	"	3/8	1896	"	9738
4270	6 " Charles C.	4	Son	1	M	3/8	ENROLLMENT OF NOS. ___ 2 ___ HEREON APPROVED BY THE SECRETARY OF INTERIOR May – 7 1904		
4271	7 " George G.	1	Son	1/2	M	3/8			
16114	8 Winship, Riley		S.Son	14	M	1/4			
N.B.130	9		Now See Decision of March 2 1904						
	10	ENROLLMENT OF NOS. 13456 and 7 HEREON	No1 on 1896 roll as Joel Nail						
	11	APPROVED BY THE SECRETARY	No2 " 1896 " " Permelia Nail						
	12	OF INTERIOR Dec 12 1902					See Pet. #W-114		
	13 No7 died Feb 6, 1901: proof of death						No.7 Enrolled Sept. 9, 1901		
	14 filed Dec 5, 1902.								
	15 Certified copy of bill of divorce between No2								
	16 and her former husband filed Jan'y [?], 1902.								
	17								

TRIBAL ENROLLMENT OF PARENTS

	Name of Father	Year	County	Name of Mother	Year	County
1	Morris Nail	Dead	Kiamitia	Sophia Holefield	Dead	Kiamitia
2	John Mullins	"	Non Citz	Mary Mullins	1896	Non Citz
3	No 1			No 2		
4	No 1			No 2		
5	No 1			No 2		
6	No 1			No 2		
7	No 1			No 2		
8	Simeon Winship (1177)			No.2		

For child of Nos 1&2 are NB (March 3, 1905) #121

9 No.7 died Feb 6, 1901: Enrollment cancelled by Department July 8, 1904
10 Nos 1&2 were married in 1890 or 1891 by Eastman Battiest, a
11 Choctaw Minister who gave no certificate of marriage. See
   evidence of Joe Nail and Wilson Thomas. Affidavits as to
12 marriage filed December 16. 1902.
13 No6 Affidavit of birth to be supplied. Rec'd May 11/99
14 For child of Nos 1&2 see NB *Apr 26 '06) #130

Date of Application for Enrollment.
#1 to 6 inc 5/9/99

15 [on back No.8 placed on this card July 17, 1906 under order of Commissioner to the Five
16 of page] Civilized Tribes of June 23, 1906 holding that application was made for his
17 enrollment within the time limited by the provisions of the Act of Congress
   approved July 1 1902

P.O. Nelson, I.T. 12/26, '02   over

Choctaw By Blood Enrollment Cards 1898-1914

RESIDENCE: **Kiamitia**   COUNTY.   **Choctaw Nation**   **Choctaw Roll**   CARD No.

POST OFFICE: **Goodland, I.T.**   *(Not Including Freedmen)*   FIELD No.   1518

Dawes' Roll No.		NAME		Relationship to Person First Named	AGE	SEX	BLOOD	TRIBAL ENROLLMENT		
								Year	County	No.
4272	1	Thompson, James	59	First Named	56	M	Full	1896	Kiamitia	12347
4273	2	" Eliza	40	Wife	37	F	"	1896	"	12348
4274	3	ED PRIOR TO SEPTEMBER 25, 1902 " Mary		Dau	7	"	"	1896	"	12349
4275	4	" Simon	8	Son	5	M	"	1896	"	12350
	5									
	6									
	7									
	8									
	9									
	10									
	11	ENROLLMENT								
	12	OF NOS. 1 2 3 and 4 HEREON APPROVED BY THE SECRETARY								
	13	OF INTERIOR DEC 12 1902								
	14									
	15									
	16									
	17									

TRIBAL ENROLLMENT OF PARENTS

	Name of Father	Year	County	Name of Mother	Year	County
1	Afa-mum-tubbe	Dead	Towson		Dead	Towson
2	An-cha-hubbee	"		Liney	"	Kiamitia
3	No 1			No 2		
4	No 1			No 2		
5						
6						
7						
8			N°3 died July 19, 1899, proof of death filed Nov. 14, 1902			
9			No.3 died July 13, 1899: Enrollment cancelled by Department July 8, 1904.			
10						
11						
12						
13						
14						
15				Date of Application for Enrollment.		
16				5/10/99		
17						

RESIDENCE: Kiamitia   COUNTY. **Choctaw Nation**   **Choctaw Roll**   CARD No.

POST OFFICE: Grant, I.T.   (Not Including Freedmen)   FIELD No.   1519

Dawes' Roll No.	NAME	Relationship to Person	AGE	SEX	BLOOD	TRIBAL ENROLLMENT		
						Year	County	No.
I.W. 77	1 Traylor, John E 29	First Named	26	M	I.W.	1896	Kiamitia	15109
4276	2 " Jincy 22	Wife	19	F	3/4	1896	Kiamitia	9398
4277	3 " Mandie M 4	Dau	5mo	"	3/8			
4278	4 " Willie Everett 1	Son	2mo	M	3/8			
	5							
	6							
	7	ENROLLMENT OF NOS. 2 3 and 4 HEREON APPROVED BY THE SECRETARY OF INTERIOR DEC 12 1902						
	8							
	9	ENROLLMENT OF NOS. 1 ～～～～ HEREON APPROVED BY THE SECRETARY OF INTERIOR JUN 13 1903						
	10							
	11							
	12							
	13							
	14							
	15							
	16							
	17							

TRIBAL ENROLLMENT OF PARENTS

	Name of Father	Year	County	Name of Mother	Year	County
1	Joe Traylor	Dead	Non Citz	Susan Traylor	1896	Non Citz
2	Sam McCann	1896	Kiamitia	Sallie McCann	1896	Kiamitia
3	No1			No2		
4	No1			No2		
5						
6	No2 on 1896 roll as Jincy McCann					
7						
8	No3 Affidavit of birth to be supplied. Recd May 10/99					
9						
10	No1 on 1896 roll as Jno. E. Traylor.					
11	No. 4 born Sept. 27 1901: Enrolled Nov. 27, 1901.					
12	For child of Nos 1&2, see N.B. (Apr. 26, 1906) Card No. 119.					
13						
14						
15				#1 to 3		
16				DATE OF APPLICATION FOR ENROLLMENT. 5/10/99		
17	P.O. Miah, I.T. 12/5 '02					

PO Sawyers IT 7/31/03

Choctaw By Blood Enrollment Cards 1898-1914

RESIDENCE: Kiamitia   COUNTY.   **Choctaw Nation**   **Choctaw Roll**   CARD No.
POST OFFICE: Frogville, I.T.   *(Not Including Freedmen)*   FIELD No.   1520

Dawes' Roll No.	NAME	Relationship to Person	AGE	SEX	BLOOD	TRIBAL ENROLLMENT		
						Year	County	No.
4279	1 Henderson, George W.	First Named	22	M	3/4	1896	Kiamitia	5781
DP	" Lillie	Wife	19	F	I.W.			
	3							
	4							
	5							
	6	ENROLLMENT						
	7	OF NOS. 1 HEREON APPROVED BY THE SECRETARY						
	8	OF INTERIOR DEC 12 1902						
	9							
	10							
	11							
	12							
	13							
	14							
	15	REFUSED. JAN 16 1907						
	16	No2 Evidence requested 3/29/04						
	17	RECORD FORWARDED DEPARTMENT.						

TRIBAL ENROLLMENT OF PARENTS

Name of Father	Year	County	Name of Mother	Year	County
1 Thos. E. Henderson	1896	Kiamitia	Annie Henderson	Dead	Kiamitia
2 Jesse Wilson	1896	Non Citz	Sarah Wilson	"	Non Citz
3					
4			ACTION APPROVED BY		
5			SECRETARY OF INTERIOR.		
6				FEB 27 1907	
7 No1 on 1896 roll as Geo. W. Henderson			NOTICE OF DEPARTMENTAL ACTION FORWARDED ATTORNEYS FOR CHOCTAW		
8			AND CHICKASAW NATIONS.	APR 3- 1907	
9					
10			NOTICE OF DEPARTMENTAL ACTION FORWARDED ATTORNEY FOR APPLICANT		
11				APR 3- 1907	
12			NOTICE OF DEPARTMENTAL ACTION MAILED APPLICANT.		
13				APR 3- 1907	
14					
15 P.O. Woodville I.T. 4/17/06				Date of Application for Enrollment.	
16 According to letter from Chick Land Office				5/10/99	
17 PO is still Frogville IT 4/9/05					

20

Choctaw By Blood Enrollment Cards 1898-1914

RESIDENCE: Kiamitia   COUNTY. **Choctaw Nation**   **Choctaw Roll** CARD NO.
POST OFFICE: Antlers, I.T.   *(Not Including Freedmen)* FIELD NO. **1521**

Dawes' Roll No.	NAME	Relationship to Person First Named	AGE	SEX	BLOOD	TRIBAL ENROLLMENT		
						Year	County	No.
4280	1 Winston, Charles K ⁶⁴	First Named	61	M	Full	1896	Kiamitia	13702
DEAD.	2 " Samantha	Wife	46	F	I.W.	1896	"	15181
	3							
	4							
	5 ENROLLMENT							
	6 OF NOS. 1 HEREON							
	APPROVED BY THE SECRETARY							
	7 OF INTERIOR DEC 12 1902							
	8							
	9 No. 2 HEREON DISMISSED UNDER							
	ORDER OF THE COMMISSION TO THE FIVE							
	10 CIVILIZED TRIBES OF MARCH 31, 1905.							
	11							
	12							
	13							
	14							
	15							
	16							
	17							

TRIBAL ENROLLMENT OF PARENTS

	Name of Father	Year	County	Name of Mother	Year	County
1	O-na-tubbee	Dead	Blue	Tush-pa-huna	Dead	Blue
2	J.N. Daniel	"	Non-Citz	Mary Daniel	1896	Non-Citz
3						
4						
5	No.1 DIED PRIOR TO SEPTEMBER 25, 1902, Not entitled to land or money. See Indian Office Letter July 27, 1907					(I.T. 64826-1907)
6	No1 on 1896 roll as C. K. Winston					
7						
8	No2 on 1896 roll as Samantha Winston					
9						
10	No2 died Dec – 1901; proof of death filed Dec 6, 1902.					
11						
12	No.1 is husband of No.2 on Choctaw Card No. 1183.					
13						
14					Date of Application for Enrollment.	
15						
16					5/10/99	
17	See Petition #W-197					

Choctaw By Blood Enrollment Cards 1898-1914

RESIDENCE: Kiamitia   COUNTY. **Choctaw Nation**   Choctaw Roll *(Not Including Freedmen)*   CARD NO.

POST OFFICE: Nelson, I.T.   FIELD NO. 1522

Dawes' Roll No.	NAME	Relationship to Person First Named	AGE	SEX	BLOOD	TRIBAL ENROLLMENT Year	County	No.
4281	1 Le Flore, Isaac 41	First Named	38	M	1/2	1896	Kiamitia	8107
14674	2 " Jefferson 1	Son	3wks	M	1/4			
I.W. 813	3 " Lizzie ㉔	Wife	24	F	I.W.			
4								
5								
6								
7	ENROLLMENT							
8	OF NOS. 1 HEREON APPROVED BY THE SECRETARY							
9	OF INTERIOR DEC 12 1902							
10								
11	ENROLLMENT							
12	OF NOS. 2 HEREON APPROVED BY THE SECRETARY							
13	OF INTERIOR MAY 20 1903							
14	ENROLLMENT							
15	OF NOS. 3 HEREON APPROVED BY THE SECRETARY							
16	OF INTERIOR MAY 21 1904							
17								

TRIBAL ENROLLMENT OF PARENTS

	Name of Father	Year	County	Name of Mother	Year	County
1	John LeFlore	Dead	Kiamitia	Jane LeFlore	Dead	Kiamitia
2	Nº1			Lizzie LeFlore		non citz
3	Petty	dead	noncitizen	Mary Wright		noncitizen
4						
5	No3 transferred from Choctaw card D943 April 16,1904. See decision of March 15,1904					
6						
7						
8						
9	Nº1 is husband of Lizzie LeFlore-non-citizen. Evidence of					
10	marriage filed Oct. 11, 1902. Now on file in 7D-943					
11	Nº2 Born Sept 22, 1902, enrolled Oct. 11, 1902 Wife of Nº1 is Lizzie LeFlore on Choctaw card #D943.					
12						
13						
14						
15					Date of Application for Enrollment.	
16					5/10/99	
17	P.O. Antlers I.T. 12/2/02					

Choctaw By Blood Enrollment Cards 1898-1914

RESIDENCE: Kiamitia   COUNTY. **Choctaw Nation**   **Choctaw Roll** CARD No.
POST OFFICE: Grant, I.T.   *(Not Including Freedmen)*   FIELD No. **1523**

Dawes' Roll No.	NAME	Relationship to Person	AGE	SEX	BLOOD	TRIBAL ENROLLMENT		
						Year	County	No.
4282	1 Williams, Israel ³²	First Named	29	M	Full	1896	Kiamitia	13776
4283	2 " Sealy ²⁹	Wife	26	F	"	1896	"	13777
4284	3 " Stephen ⁵	Son	6mo	M	"			
4286	4 Glover, Samuel ¹⁰	S Son	7	"	1/2	1896	Kiamitia	4837
4285	5 Williams, Pearley Myrtle ²	Dau	3mo	F	Full			
	6 12/8/1916 No.5 hereon is probably a duplicate of Choctaw Minor No. 899 Card #867							
	7							W.H.A
	8							
	9							
	10							
	11	ENROLLMENT						
	12	OF NOS. 1 2 3 4 and 5 HEREON APPROVED BY THE SECRETARY						
	13	OF INTERIOR Dec 12 1902						
	14							
	15							
	16							
	17							

TRIBAL ENROLLMENT OF PARENTS

	Name of Father	Year	County	Name of Mother	Year	County
1	Wᵐ Meashintubby	1896	Wade	Betsey Meashintubby	1896	Nashoba
2	Thos. Henderson	1896	Kiamitia	Annie Henderson	Dead	Kiamitia
3	No 1			No 2		
4	William Glover	1896	Non Citz	No 2		
5	No. 1			No. 2		
6						
7						
8	No2 on 1896 roll as Cealy Williams					
9	No4 " 1896 " Sam Glover					
10						
11	No3 Affidavit of birth to be supplied. Recd. May 17/99					
12	No.5 Enrolled March 5th, 1901. Born Dec 19, 1900 4/20/38-JOE					
13	For three children of Nos 1&2 see NB (Apr 26-06) Card #867					
14						
15				Date of Application for Enrollment.	For Nos 1 to 4 incl.	
16					5/10/99	
17						

Choctaw By Blood Enrollment Cards 1898-1914

RESIDENCE: **Kiamitia**   COUNTY. **Choctaw Nation**   **Choctaw Roll** CARD No.
POST OFFICE: Frogville, I.T.   *(Not Including Freedmen)* FIELD No. **1524**

Dawes' Roll No.	NAME	Relationship to Person	AGE	SEX	BLOOD	TRIBAL ENROLLMENT		
						Year	County	No.
4287	1 Henderson, Thomas E ⁶²	First Named	59	M	Full	1896	Kiamitia	5780
	2							
	3							
	4							
	5							
	6							
	7							
	8							
	9							
	10							
	11	ENROLLMENT						
	12	OF NOS. 1 HEREON APPROVED BY THE SECRETARY						
	13	OF INTERIOR Dec 12 1902						
	14							
	15							
	16							
	17							

TRIBAL ENROLLMENT OF PARENTS

	Name of Father	Year	County	Name of Mother	Year	County
1	Edwin Henderson		Died in Louisiana	Sally Henderson	Dead	Red River
2						
3						
4						
5						
6						
7						
8						
9						
10						
11						
12						
13						
14					Date of Application for Enrollment.	
15						
16					5/10/99	
17						

24

Choctaw By Blood Enrollment Cards 1898-1914

RESIDENCE: Kiamitia		COUNTY.	**Choctaw Nation**			**Choctaw Roll** *(Not Including Freedmen)*	CARD NO.	
POST OFFICE: Frogville, I.T.							FIELD NO.	1525

Dawes' Roll No.	NAME		Relationship to Person	AGE	SEX	BLOOD	TRIBAL ENROLLMENT		
							Year	County	No.
4288	1 Henderson, Lucy	39	First Named	36	F	Full	1893	Kiamitia	91
4289	2 Anukwiatubbee, Mattie	4	Dau	8	"	"	1893	"	92
	3								
	4								
	5								
	6	ENROLLMENT							
	7	OF NOS. 1 and 2 HEREON APPROVED BY THE SECRETARY							
	8	OF INTERIOR DEC 12 1902							
	9								
	10								
	11								
	12								
	13								
	14								
	15								
	16								
	17								

TRIBAL ENROLLMENT OF PARENTS

	Name of Father	Year	County	Name of Mother	Year	County
1	Thos. E. Henderson	1896	Kiamitia	Sillen Apak[???]tubbee	Dead	Kiamitia
2	Anukwiatubbee	Dead		No 1		
3						
4	No1 on 1893 Pay roll, Page 12, No 91, Kiamitia Co					
5	No2 " 1893 " " " 12 " 92 " " as Mattie Anukwatube					
6	No.1 also on 1896 Choctaw roll as Lucy Henderson, page 141, #5782.					
7	The discrepancy in ages is accounted for by mistake in copying					
8	from original record, the original roll of Kiamitia county being					
9	exhibited when this notation was made, and the ages correspond					
10	thereon Aug. 18, 1900					
11	No.2 also on 1896 Choctaw roll as Mattie Byington: page 28, #1100					
12						
13						
14						
15					Date of Application for Enrollment.	
16					5/10/99	
17						

25

Choctaw By Blood Enrollment Cards 1898-1914

RESIDENCE: Kiamitia   COUNTY. **Choctaw Nation**   **Choctaw Roll** (Not Including Freedmen)   CARD No.

POST OFFICE: Grant, I.T.   FIELD No. 1526

Dawes' Roll No.	NAME	Relationship to Person First Named	AGE	SEX	BLOOD	TRIBAL ENROLLMENT Year	County	No.
4290	1 Everidge, Joseph W ⁴⁸	First Named	45	M	3/8	1896	Kiamitia	3802
I.W.78	2 " Bettie ³⁰	Wife	27	F	I.W.	1896	"	14500
see 5356	3 " Joseph H	Son	22	M	3/8	1896	"	3811
4291	4 " Josie M ¹³	Dau	10	F	3/8	1896	"	3804
4292	5 " Governor J ¹¹	Son	8	M	3/8	1896	"	3801
4293	6 " Ophelia ⁸	Dau	5	F	3/16	1896	"	3805
4294	7 " Tommie ⁶	"	3	"	3/16	1896	"	3805
4295	8 " Lydia Gertrude ²	Dau	1mo	F	3/16			
4296	9 " Robbie ¹	Dau	2mo	F	3/16			
	10							
	11	ENROLLMENT				ENROLLMENT		
	12	OF NOS. 1 4 5 6 7 8 and 9 HEREON APPROVED BY THE SECRETARY				OF NOS. ~~~ 2 ~~~ HEREON APPROVED BY THE SECRETARY		
	13	OF INTERIOR DEC 12 1902				OF INTERIOR JUN 13 1903		
	14							

No 3 transferred to Choctaw card #5356

card, Dec. 8th, 1900.

TRIBAL ENROLLMENT OF PARENTS

	Name of Father	Year	County	Name of Mother	Year	County
1	J.W. Everidge	1896	Kiamitia	Sophie Everidge	Dead	Kiamitia
2	Robert Wilson	1896	Non Citz	Frances Wilson	1896	Non Citz
3	No 1			Susan Everidge	Dead	Towson
4	No 1			" "	"	"
5	No 1			" "	"	"
6	No 1			No 2		
7	No 1			No 2		
8	No 1			No 2		
9						
10						
11	No1 on 1896 roll as Joe Everidge					
12	No2 " 1896 " " Betty "					
13	No3 " 1896 " " Joe H. / No5 " 1896 " " Gov. J "					
14	No.8 Enrolled July 16, 1900	Born 6/5/00				
15					#1 to 7 inc	
16	No 9 Born May 31, 1902, enrolled July 29,			Date of Application for Enrollment	5/10/99	
17						

26

Choctaw By Blood Enrollment Cards 1898-1914

RESIDENCE: Kiamitia	COUNTY:	Choctaw Nation	Choctaw Roll	CARD No.
POST OFFICE: Grant, I.T.			(Not Including Freedmen)	FIELD No. 1527

Dawes' Roll No.		NAME	Relationship to Person First Named	AGE	SEX	BLOOD	TRIBAL ENROLLMENT		
							Year	County	No.
DEAD.	1	Everidge, Joel W		70	M	1/4	1896	Kiamitia	3799
4297	2	" Susan L 31	Dau	28	F	3/8	1896	"	3800
	3								
	4								
	5	ENROLLMENT							
	6	OF NOS. 2 HEREON APPROVED BY THE SECRETARY							
	7	OF INTERIOR DEC 12 1902							
	8								
	9								
	10								
	11	No. 1 HEREON DISMISSED UNDER							
	12	ORDER OF THE COMMISSION TO THE FIVE							
	13	CIVILIZED TRIBES OF MARCH 31, 1905.							
	14								
	15								
	16								
	17								

Judge Everedge Dead.

A Paris dispatch says: Judge J. W. Everedge of the Supreme Court of the Choctaw Nation, died yesterday evening at his home a Grant of heart trouble, aged 75 years. Deceased migrated with the Choctaws from Mississippi as a little boy when they ceded their lands. His father was a white man. The deceased was one of the most prominent men in the Nation and has been judge of the Supreme court ever since 1878.

TRIBAL ENROLLMENT OF PARENTS

	Name of Father	Year	County	Name of Mother	Year	County
1	Thos Everidge	Dead	Non Citz	Eve Everidge	Dead	Kiamitia
2	No 1			Sophie Everidge	"	"
3						
4						
5						
6						
7						
8						
9						
10						
11	No1 on 1896 roll as J.W. Everidge.					
12						
13	No.1 died May 5, 1901, proof of death filed Dec. 8, 1902					
14						
15						
16				Date of Application for Enrollment 5/10/99		
17						

Choctaw By Blood Enrollment Cards 1898-1914

RESIDENCE: Kiamitia   COUNTY. **Choctaw Nation**   **Choctaw Roll** (Not Including Freedmen)   CARD No.

POST OFFICE: Goodland I.T.   FIELD No. **1528**

Dawes' Roll No.	NAME		Relationship to Person First Named	AGE	SEX	BLOOD	TRIBAL ENROLLMENT		
							Year	County	No.
4298	1 Spring, Lula M	12	First Named	9	F	1/4	1896	Kiamitia	11493
	2								
	3								
	4								
	5								
	6								
	7								
	8								
	9								
	10								
	11								
	12								
	13								
	14								
	15								
	16								
	17								

> ENROLLMENT
> OF NOS. 1 HEREON
> APPROVED BY THE SECRETARY
> OF INTERIOR Dec 12 1902

TRIBAL ENROLLMENT OF PARENTS

	Name of Father	Year	County	Name of Mother	Year	County
1	Braz. Spring	Dead	Kiamitia	Nannie Spring	Dead	Non Citz
2						
3						
4						
5						
6						
7						
8						
9		On 1896 roll as Lula Spring. She is now living with				
10		William Self, her grandfather, Mother was a white				
11		woman. See testimony of Siney Miller as to marriage				
12						
13						
14						
15						
16				Date of Application for Enrollment	5/10/99	
17						

28

Choctaw By Blood Enrollment Cards 1898-1914

RESIDENCE: Kiamitia   COUNTY. **Choctaw Nation**   **Choctaw Roll** (*Not Including Freedmen*)   CARD NO.

POST OFFICE: Grant, I.T.   FIELD NO. 1529

Dawes' Roll No.	NAME	Relationship to Person First Named	AGE	SEX	BLOOD	TRIBAL ENROLLMENT Year	County	No.
4299	1 Roberts, Daniel 32	29	M	Full	1896	Kiamitia	10819
4300	2 ~~ED PRIOR TO SEPTEMBER 25, 1902~~ Sophia	Wife	23	F	"	1896	"	10820
4301	3 " Eliza 6	Dau	2	"	"			
	4							
	5							
	6							
	7							
	8							
	9							
	10							
	11	ENROLLMENT						
	12	OF NOS. 1 2 and 3 HEREON APPROVED BY THE SECRETARY						
	13	OF INTERIOR DEC 12 1902						
	14							
	15							
	16							
	17							

TRIBAL ENROLLMENT OF PARENTS

	Name of Father	Year	County	Name of Mother	Year	County
1	Layman Robert[sic]	1896	Jackson	Tillie Bond	Dead	Towson
2	~~Sam Hayes~~	~~Dead~~	~~Kiamitia~~	~~Mary Hayes~~	"	~~Kiamitia~~
3	No 1			No 2		
4						
5						
6		No.1 is Husband of Mandy Anderson, Choctaw Card No 357				
7		No2 died Oct, 1899; proof of death filed Dec 5, 1902				
8		~~No. 2 died Oct. 1899; Enrollment cancelled by Department July 8, 1904~~				
9		For child of No 1 see N.B. (Apr. 26, 1906) Card No. 88				
10						
11						
12						
13						
14				Date of Application for Enrollment.		
15						
16				5/10/99		
17						

Choctaw By Blood Enrollment Cards 1898-1914

RESIDENCE: Kiamitia
POST OFFICE: Grant, I.T.

COUNTY. **Choctaw Nation**

Choctaw Roll
(Not Including Freedmen)

CARD NO.
FIELD NO. 1530

Dawes' Roll No.		NAME		Relationship to Person First Named	AGE	SEX	BLOOD	TRIBAL ENROLLMENT		
								Year	County	No.
4302	1	Roberson, Lymon	43	First Named	40	M	Full	1896	Kiamitia	10828
4303	2	" Sophia	43	Wife	40	F	"	1896	"	10829
4304	3	" Tobias	24	Son	21	M	"	1896	"	10830
4305	4	" Anrilla	16	Dau	13	F	"	1896	"	10831
	5									
	6									
	7									
	8									
	9									
	10									
	11	ENROLLMENT								
	12	OF NOS. 1 2 3 and 4 HEREON APPROVED BY THE SECRETARY								
	13	OF INTERIOR DEC 12 1902								
	14									
	15									
	16									
	17									

TRIBAL ENROLLMENT OF PARENTS

	Name of Father	Year	County	Name of Mother	Year	County
1	John Roberson	Dead	Kiamitia	Betsey Hayes	Dead	Kiamitia
2	Chas McGee	"	Towson	Winnie McGee	"	Towson
3	No 1			No 2		
4	No 1			No 2		
5						
6						
7						
8			No 2 on 1896 roll as Sophie Roberson			
9			No 4 " 1896 " " Anella "			
10						
11						
12						
13						
14						
15						
16				Date of Application for Enrollment	5/10/99	
17						

RESIDENCE: Kiamitia	COUNTY.	Choctaw Nation	Choctaw Roll	CARD No.
POST OFFICE: Frogville, I.T.			(Not Including Freedmen)	FIELD No. **1531**

Dawes' Roll No.	NAME		Relationship to Person First Named	AGE	SEX	BLOOD	TRIBAL ENROLLMENT		
							Year	County	No.
4306	1 Durant, Rias	43	First Named	40	M	Full	1896	Kiamitia	3456
4307	2 " Hannah	31	Wife	28	F	"	1896	"	3457
4308	3 " George	15	Son	12	M	"	1896	"	3458
43..	4 " Sarah	13	Dau	10	F	"	1896	"	3459
	5								
	6								
	7								
	8								
	9	ENROLLMENT OF NOS 1 2 3 and 4 HEREON APPROVED BY THE SECRETARY OF INTERIOR DEC 12 1902							
	10								
	11								
	12								
	13								
	14								
	15								
	16								
	17								

TRIBAL ENROLLMENT OF PARENTS

	Name of Father	Year	County	Name of Mother	Year	County
1	Roberson Durant	Dead	Towson	Mary Bohanan	Dead	Nashoba
2	Chufate-ubbee	"	Kiamitia	Beckie Chufateubbee	"	Kiamitia
3	No 1			No 2		
4	No 1			No 2		
5						
6			No 1 on 1896 roll as Rivas Durant.			
7						
8						
9						
10						
11						
12						
13						
14						
15						
16				Date of Application for Enrollment	5/10/99	
17						

Choctaw By Blood Enrollment Cards 1898-1914

RESIDENCE: Kiamitia   COUNTY. **Choctaw Nation**   **Choctaw Roll**   CARD NO.
POST OFFICE: Antlers, I.T.   9/8/05   *(Not Including Freedmen)*   FIELD NO.   **1532**

1525 NAME		Relationship to Person First Named	AGE	SEX	BLOOD	TRIBAL ENROLLMENT		
						Year	County	No.
1 Murphy, Edna	33	First Named	30	F	I.W	1896	Kiamitia	14825
2								
3								
4								
5								
6								
7								
8								
9								
10								
11								
12								
13								
14								
15								
16								
17								

GRANTED
NOV 11 1905

ENROLLMENT
OF NOS. ~~~1~~~ HEREON
APPROVED BY THE SECRETARY
OF INTERIOR MAR 14 1906

TRIBAL ENROLLMENT OF PARENTS

	Name of Father	Year	County	Name of Mother	Year	County
1	J. T. Brumett	Dead	Non Citz	Melissa Brumett	1896	Non Citz
2						
3						
4						
5			No 1 was formerly wife of James Murphy, No. 753 1885 Census Roll			
6			and also 1893 Pay Roll Kiamitia County			
7						
8						
9			On 1896 roll as Eddie Murphy			
10						
11						
12			Notify L. P Davenport Atty Antlers I.T.			
13						
14					Date of Application	
15					for Enrollment.	
16	P O Hamden I.T.				5/10/99	
17	P O Hugo I.T. 8/2/04		Antlers 9/8/05			

Choctaw By Blood Enrollment Cards 1898-1914

RESIDENCE: Kiamitia
POST OFFICE: Grant, I.T.

COUNTY. **Choctaw Nation**

Choctaw Roll
(Not Including Freedmen)

CARD NO.
FIELD NO. 1533

Dawes' Roll No.	NAME		Relationship to Person	AGE	SEX	BLOOD	TRIBAL ENROLLMENT		
							Year	County	No.
4310	1 Tonitubbi, Sam	52	First Named	49	M	Full	1896	Kiamitia	12357
4311	2 " Elsie	61	Wife	58	F	"	1896	"	12358
15404	3 Wood, Minnie	6	Ward	2 1/2	"	1/2			
	4								
	5								
	6								
	7	ENROLLMENT OF NOS. 1 and 2 HEREON APPROVED BY THE SECRETARY OF INTERIOR DEC 12 1902							
	8								
	9								
	10								
	11	ENROLLMENT OF NOS. ~~ 3 ~~ HEREON APPROVED BY THE SECRETARY OF INTERIOR MAY 9 1904							
	12								
	13								
	14								
	15								
	16								
	17								

TRIBAL ENROLLMENT OF PARENTS

	Name of Father	Year	County	Name of Mother	Year	County
1	Tonitubbi	Dead	Kiamitia		Dead	Kiamitia
2	Fitch-a-p-tubbee	"	Towson	Hoh-ta-la	"	Towson
3	John Woods	1896	Non Citz	Sissie Anukevia tubbee	"	Kiamitia
4						
5						
6		Mother of No 3 on 1893 Kiamitia as Alice Flinn				
7		Mother of No 3 Sissy Arowatubbi on 1896 Choctaw roll No 459.				
8		Above notation is error				
9		More testimony required				
10		Nº3 Proof of birth filed Jany 13, 1904.				
11						
12						
13						
14					Date of Application for Enrollment	
15						
16					5/10/99	
17						

33

Choctaw By Blood Enrollment Cards 1898-1914

RESIDENCE: Kiamitia   COUNTY. **Choctaw Nation**   **Choctaw Roll**   CARD NO.

POST OFFICE: Grant, I.T.   *(Not Including Freedmen)*   FIELD NO.   1534

Dawes' Roll No.	NAME	Relationship to Person First Named	AGE	SEX	BLOOD	TRIBAL ENROLLMENT Year	County	No.
4312	1 Speaker, Millie ⁴⁶	First Named	43	F	Full	1896	Kiamitia	11494
	2							
	3							
	4							
	5	ENROLLMENT						
	6	OF NOS. 1 HEREON APPROVED BY THE SECRETARY						
	7	OF INTERIOR DEC 12 1902						
	8							
	9							
	10							
	11							
	12							
	13							
	14							
	15							
	16							
	17							

TRIBAL ENROLLMENT OF PARENTS

	Name of Father	Year	County	Name of Mother	Year	County
1	John Roberson	Dead	Kiamitia	Betsey Roberson	Dead	Kiamitia
2						
3						
4						
5						
6						
7						
8						
9						
10						
11						
12						
13						
14					Date of Application for Enrollment.	
15						
16					5/10/99	
17	P.O. Hugo, I.T. 9/14/07					

Choctaw By Blood Enrollment Cards 1898-1914

RESIDENCE: Kiamitia   COUNTY. **Choctaw Nation**   **Choctaw Roll** *(Not Including Freedmen)* CARD NO.

POST OFFICE: Antlers, I.T.   FIELD NO. 1535

Dawes' Roll No.	NAME	Relationship to Person	AGE	SEX	BLOOD	TRIBAL ENROLLMENT		
						Year	County	No.
4313	1 Watkins, Jonas 43	First Named	40	M	Full	1896	Jacks Fork	14135
4314	2 " Sina 37	Wife	34	F	"	1896	" "	14136
	3							
	4							
	5	ENROLLMENT						
	6	OF NOS. 1 and 2 HEREON						
	7	APPROVED BY THE SECRETARY OF INTERIOR DEC 12 1902						
	8							
	9							
	10							
	11							
	12							
	13							
	14							
	15							
	16							
	17							

TRIBAL ENROLLMENT OF PARENTS

Name of Father	Year	County	Name of Mother	Year	County
1 E-losh-tubbee	Dead	Kiamitia	Bessie	Dead	Jacks Fork
2 Tom Harris	"	Towson		"	Towson
3					
4					
5					
6					
7				.	
8					
9					
10					
11					
12					
13					
14				Date of Application for Enrollment.	
15				5/10/99	
16					
17					

Choctaw By Blood Enrollment Cards 1898-1914

RESIDENCE: Kiamitia   COUNTY. **Choctaw Nation**   **Choctaw Roll** *(Not Including Freedmen)*   CARD NO.

POST OFFICE: Grant, I.T.   FIELD NO. **1536**

Dawes' Roll No.	NAME	Relationship to Person First Named	AGE	SEX	BLOOD	TRIBAL ENROLLMENT		
						Year	County	No.
DEAD. 1	Cobb, James	Named	20	M	Full	1896	Kiamitia	2684
2								
3								
4	No. 1 HEREON DISMISSED UNDER							
5	ORDER OF THE COMMISSION TO THE FIVE							
6	CIVILIZED TRIBES OF MARCH 31, 1905							
7								
8								
9								
10								
11								
12								
13								
14								
15								
16								
17								

TRIBAL ENROLLMENT OF PARENTS

	Name of Father	Year	County	Name of Mother	Year	County
1	Simon Cobb	Dead	Towson	Sibbie Cobb	Dead	Towson
2						
3						
4						
5						
6	On 1896 roll as Jim Cobb					
7						
8	Nº1 Died in July 1899, proof of death filed Oct. 29, 1902					
9						
10						
11						
12						
13						
14						
15						
16					Date of Application for Enrollment	5/10/99
17						

Choctaw By Blood Enrollment Cards 1898-1914

RESIDENCE: Kiamitia
POST OFFICE: Grant, I.T.

COUNTY. **Choctaw Nation**

Choctaw Roll
(Not Including Freedmen)

CARD NO.
FIELD NO. 1537

Dawes' Roll No.	NAME	Relationship to Person First Named	AGE	SEX	BLOOD	TRIBAL ENROLLMENT		
						Year	County	No.
4315	1 Roberts, Moses ²⁹	First Named	26	M	Full	1896	Kiamitia	10826
	2							
	3							
	4							
	5							
	6							
	7	ENROLLMENT						
	8	OF NOS. 1 HEREON APPROVED BY THE SECRETARY						
	9	OF INTERIOR DEC 12 1902						
	10							
	11							
	12							
	13							
	14							
	15							
	16							
	17							

TRIBAL ENROLLMENT OF PARENTS

	Name of Father	Year	County	Name of Mother	Year	County
1	Gibson Roberts	Dead	Kiamitia	Siney Roberts	Dead	Kiamitia
2						
3						
4						
5						
6						
7						
8						
9						
10						
11						
12						
13						
14						
15						
16				Date of Application for Enrollment	5/10/99	
17						

Choctaw By Blood Enrollment Cards 1898-1914

RESIDENCE: Kiamitia   COUNTY. **Choctaw Nation**   **Choctaw Roll**   CARD NO.
POST OFFICE: Goodland, I.T   *(Not Including Freedmen)*   FIELD NO.   1538

Dawes' Roll No.	NAME	Relationship to Person First Named	AGE	SEX	BLOOD	TRIBAL ENROLLMENT		
						Year	County	No.
4316	1 Pitchlynn, Michael ³³	First Named	30	M	Full	1896	Kiamitia	10438
	2							
	3							
	4							
	5	ENROLLMENT						
	6	OF NOS. I HEREON APPROVED BY THE SECRETARY						
	7	OF INTERIOR DEC 12 1902						
	8							
	9							
	10							
	11							
	12							
	13							
	14							
	15							
	16							
	17							

TRIBAL ENROLLMENT OF PARENTS

Name of Father	Year	County	Name of Mother	Year	County
1 Pa-la-chee	Dead	Kiamitia		Dead	Kiamitia
2					
3					
4	No.1 died on or about May 10, 1902: Enrollment cancelled by				
5	Secretary of Interior, October 5, 1905 (I.T.D. [illegible]				
6					
7	March 19, 1909 Department requests report				
8	April 2 1909 Report to Department				
9	June 14 1909 Department held that case is not analogous to the Goldsby case and declined to take any action looking to enroll-				
10	ment of No.1 hereon.				
11					
12					
13					
14					
15					
16				Date of Application for Enrollment	5/10/99
17					

Choctaw By Blood Enrollment Cards 1898-1914

RESIDENCE: Kiamitia   COUNTY. **Choctaw Nation**   **Choctaw Roll**   CARD NO.
POST OFFICE: Goodland, I.T.   *(Not Including Freedmen)*   FIELD NO.   1539

Dawes' Roll No.	NAME		Relationship to Person	AGE	SEX	BLOOD	TRIBAL ENROLLMENT		
							Year	County	No.
4317	Jefferson, Anna	25	First Named	22	F	1/4	1896	Chick. Dist	7387
4318	" Malinda	6	Dau	3	"	1/8			
4319	Joseph F	DIED PRIOR TO SEPTEMBER 25, 1902	Son	8mo	M	1/8			
4									
5									
6									
7	ENROLLMENT								
8	OF NOS. 1 2 and 3 HEREON APPROVED BY THE SECRETARY								
9	OF INTERIOR DEC 12 1902								
10									
11									
12									
13									
14									
15									
16									
17									

TRIBAL ENROLLMENT OF PARENTS

	Name of Father	Year	County	Name of Mother	Year	County
1	Josh Crowder	Dead	Non Citz	Sibbie Crowder	Dead	Jackson
2	Joe Jefferson	1896	Chick Roll	No 1		
3	" "	1896	" "	No 1		
4						
5						
6						
7						
8						
9	No1 on 1893 Pay roll, Page 16, No 147, Jackson County, as					
10	Anna Carroll. Should not this refer to No 146 Annie Crowder?					
11						
12	No1 on 1896 roll as Jimmie Jefferson					
13						
14	Husband of No1 on Chickasaw Card No 1419					
15	No3 died March 21, 1900; proof of death filed Dec 12, 1902					
16	No.1 is under indictment for murder.					
17	No 3 died March 21, 1900; Enrollment cancelled by Department July 8, 1904					

Date of Application for Enrollment.

5/10/99

39

Choctaw By Blood Enrollment Cards 1898-1914

RESIDENCE: Kiamitia
POST OFFICE: Grant, I.T

COUNTY. **Choctaw Nation**

Choctaw Roll
(Not Including Freedmen)

CARD NO.
FIELD NO. **1540**

Dawes' Roll No.	NAME		Relationship to Person	AGE	SEX	BLOOD	TRIBAL ENROLLMENT		
							Year	County	No.
I.W. **79**	1 Ervin, Eddie E.	39	First Named	36	M	I.W.	1896	Kiamitia	14501
4320	2 " Rudy	27	Wife	24	F	1/2	1896	"	3807
4321	3 " Lizzie	10	Dau	7	"	1/4	1896	"	3808
4322	4 " Willie M	7	"	4	"	1/4	1896	"	3809
4323	5 " David	5	Son	2	M	1/4			
4324	6 " Louie	2	"	2mo	M	1/4			
4325	7 " Florence	1	Dau	1mo	F	1/4			
	8								
	9								
	10								
	11	ENROLLMENT							
	12	OF NOS. 23456and7 HEREON APPROVED BY THE SECRETARY							
	13	OF INTERIOR DEC 12 1902							
	14	ENROLLMENT OF NOS. 1 ~~~~~~ HEREON							
	15	APPROVED BY THE SECRETARY OF INTERIOR JUN 13 1903							
	16								
	17								

TRIBAL ENROLLMENT OF PARENTS

	Name of Father	Year	County	Name of Mother	Year	County
1	William Ervin	Dead	Non Citz	Elizabeth Ervin	1896	Non Citz
2	Dave Roebuck	"	Kiamitia	Melina Roebuck	1896	Kiamitia
3	No 1			No 2		
4	No 1			No 2		
5	No 1			No 2		
6	No 1			No 2		
7	Nº1			Nº2		
8						
9	No2 on 1896 roll as Ruddy Ervin					
10	No4 " 1896 " " Cory E. "					
11						
12	No5 Affidavit of birth to be supplied. Recd May 17/99					
13	Nº7 Born April 8, 1902: enrolled May 14, 1902					
14	Evidence of marriage of Nos 1 and 2 filed Dec 9, 1902				#1 to 5 inc	
	For child of Nos 1&2 see N.B. (Apr. 26, 1906) Card No. 84				Date of Application for Enrollment.	
15						
16					5/10/99	
17	P.O. Rudy[sic] I.T. 5/7/06				No6 enrolled Nov 1/99	

Choctaw By Blood Enrollment Cards 1898-1914

RESIDENCE: Kiamitia   COUNTY. **Choctaw Nation**   **Choctaw Roll** CARD No.
POST OFFICE: Grant, I.T.   *(Not Including Freedmen)*   FIELD No. **1541**

Dawes' Roll No.	NAME	Relationship to Person	AGE	SEX	BLOOD	TRIBAL ENROLLMENT		
						Year	County	No.
4326	1 Ervin, Viola ^19	First Named	16	F	3/4	1896	Kiamitia	3798
	2							
	3							
	4							
	5							
	6							
	7							
	8							
	9							
	10							
	11							
	12							
	13							
	14							
	15							
	16							
	17							

ENROLLMENT
OF NOS. 1 HEREON
APPROVED BY THE SECRETARY
OF INTERIOR Dec. 12, 1902

TRIBAL ENROLLMENT OF PARENTS

	Name of Father	Year	County	Name of Mother	Year	County
1	Columbus Ervin	1896	Kiamitia	Malaney Hayes	Dead	Towson
2						
3						
4	For child of No 1 see N.B. (Apr. 26, 1906) Card No. 131.					
5						
6						
7						
8						
9						
10						
11						
12						
13						
14						
15						
16				Date of Application for Enrollment	5/10/96[sic]	
17						

Choctaw By Blood Enrollment Cards 1898-1914

RESIDENCE: **Kiamitia**	COUNTY.				**Choctaw Roll** (Not Including Freedmen)	CARD NO.	
POST OFFICE: **Goodland, I.T.**	**Choctaw Nation**					FIELD NO.	**1542**

Dawes' Roll No.	NAME	Relationship to Person First Named	AGE	SEX	BLOOD	TRIBAL ENROLLMENT		
						Year	County	No.
DP 1/28/07	1 Law, James H.		24	M	I.W			
4327	2 " Dora L 22	Wife	19	F	1/16	1896	Kiamitia	9969
	3							
	4							
	5 ENROLLMENT							
	6 OF NOS. 2 HEREON APPROVED BY THE SECRETARY							
	7 OF INTERIOR DEC 12 1902							
	8 No 1	FEB 6 1907						
	9 REFUSED							
	10 COPY OF DECISION FORWARDED							
	11 APPLICANT FEB 6 1907							
	12 COPY OF DECISION FORWARDED ATTORNEYS FOR CHOCTAW AND							
	13 CHICKASAW NATIONS. FEB 6 1907							
	RECORD FORWARDED DEPARTMENT							
	15							
	16 FEB 6 1907							
	17							

TRIBAL ENROLLMENT OF PARENTS						
Name of Father	Year	County	Name of Mother	Year	County	
1 G. A. Law	1896	Non Citz	Lieucretia S. Law	Dead	Non Citz	
2 J. E. Oakes	1896	Kiamitia	Josephine Oakes	1896	" "	
3						
4		Evidence of marriage of parents of No2 exhibited. Attached to Card No 1543				
5						
6		No2 on 1896 roll as Cora Oakes.				
7			ACTION APPROVED BY MAR 4 1907			
8			SECRETARY OF INTERIOR.			
9						
10			NOTICE OF DEPARTMENTAL ACTION FORWARDED ATTORNEYS FOR CHOCTAW			
11			AND CHICKASAW NATIONS. APR 13 1907			
12			NOTICE OF DEPARTMENTAL			
13			ACTION MAILED APPLICANT. APR 13 1907			
14						
15			Date of Application for Enrollment.			
16			5/10/99			
17 P.O. Hugo I.T. 2/06						

42

RESIDENCE: Kiamitia   COUNTY. **Choctaw Nation**   **Choctaw Roll** CARD No.

POST OFFICE: Goodland, I.T.   *(Not Including Freedmen)*   FIELD No. 1543

Dawes' Roll No.	NAME	Relationship to Person First Named	AGE	SEX	BLOOD	TRIBAL ENROLLMENT Year	County	No.
4328	1 Oakes, Joel 43	First Named	40	M	1/8	1896	Kiamitia	9968
I.W. 80	2 " Josephine E 40	Wife	37	F	I.W.	1896	"	14912
4329	3 McBride Florence V 21	Dau	18	"	1/16	1896	"	9970
4330	4 Oakes Lizzie 19	"	16	"	1/16	1896	"	9971
4331	5 " Bertie 17	Son	14	M	1/16	1896	"	9972
4332	6 " Effie 14	Dau	11	F	1/16	1896	"	9974
4333	7 " Sarah E 12	"	9	"	1/16	1896	"	9974
I.W. 637	8 McBride, Thomas L 31	Hus of No 3	31	M	I.W			
	9							
	10 ENROLLMENT OF NOS. 13456and7 HEREON APPROVED BY THE SECRETARY							
	11 OF INTERIOR DEC 12 1902							
	12 ENROLLMENT							
	13 OF NOS. ~~ 2 ~~ HEREON APPROVED BY THE SECRETARY							
	14 OF INTERIOR JUN 13 1903							
	15 ENROLLMENT							
	16 OF NOS. 8 HEREON APPROVED BY THE SECRETARY							
	17 OF INTERIOR MAR 26 1904							

TRIBAL ENROLLMENT OF PARENTS

	Name of Father	Year	County	Name of Mother	Year	County
1	Thos. W. Oakes	Dead	Non Citz	Harriet Oakes	1896	Kiamitia
2	John L Cronk	1896	" "	Emiline Cronk	Dead	Non Citz
3	No 1			No 2		
4	No 1			No 2		
5	No 1			No 2		
6	No 1			No 2		
7	No 1			No 2		
8	Thomas McBride	Dead	noncitizen	Mary McBride		noncitizen
9						
10	No2 on 1896 roll as Josephine Oakes					
11	No3 " 1896 " Virgie "					
12	No5 " 1896 " Bertha "					
13	No7 " 1896 " Eva "					
	No.3 is now the wife of Thomas L McBride on Choctaw Card #D 635, June 17, 1901.					
14	No8 transferred from Choctaw card D 635 January 23 1904,					
15	See decision of January 6, 1904.			Date of Application for Enrollment.		
16				5/10/99		
17	P.O. Hugo, I.T. 12/3 '02					

Choctaw By Blood Enrollment Cards 1898-1914

RESIDENCE: Kiamitia   COUNTY.   **Choctaw Nation**   **Choctaw Roll** *(Not Including Freedmen)*   CARD No.
POST OFFICE: Goodland, I.T.   FIELD No. 1544

Dawes' Roll No.	NAME	Relationship to Person First Named	AGE	SEX	BLOOD	TRIBAL ENROLLMENT Year	County	No.
4334	1 Oakes, Elizabeth 57	First Named	54	F	1/8	1893	Kiamitia	566
	2							
	3							
	4							
	5	ENROLLMENT						
	6	OF NOS. 1 HEREON APPROVED BY THE SECRETARY						
	7	OF INTERIOR DEC 12 1902						
	8							
	9							
	10							
	11							
	12							
	13							
	14							
	15							
	16							
	17							

TRIBAL ENROLLMENT OF PARENTS

Name of Father	Year	County	Name of Mother	Year	County
1 Thomas Oakes	Dead	Non Citz	Harriet Oakes	1896	Kiamitia
2					
3					
4					
5	On 1893 Pay roll, Page 69, No 566, Kiamitia County				
6					
7					
8					
9					
10					
11					
12					
13					
14					
15					
16			Date of Application for Enrollment 5/10/99		
17					

44

Choctaw By Blood Enrollment Cards 1898-1914

RESIDENCE: Kiamitia   COUNTY. **Choctaw Nation**   **Choctaw Roll**   CARD NO.

POST OFFICE: Grant, I.T   *(Not Including Freedmen)*   FIELD NO.   1545

Dawes' Roll No.	NAME	Relationship to Person	AGE	SEX	BLOOD	TRIBAL ENROLLMENT		
						Year	County	No.
4335	1 Russell, James ^48	First Named	45	M	1/2	1896	Kiamitia	10827
	2							
	3							
	4							
	5							
	6							
	7	ENROLLMENT						
	8	OF NOS. 1 HEREON APPROVED BY THE SECRETARY						
	9	OF INTERIOR DEC 12 1902						
	10							
	11							
	12							
	13							
	14							
	15							
	16							
	17							

TRIBAL ENROLLMENT OF PARENTS

	Name of Father	Year	County	Name of Mother	Year	County
1	John Russell	Dead	Non Citz	Sallie Russell	Dead	Kiamitia
2						
3						
4						
5						
6						
7						
8						
9						
10						
11						
12						
13						
14						
15						
16				Date of Application for Enrollment	5/10/99	
17						

Choctaw By Blood Enrollment Cards 1898-1914

RESIDENCE: Kiamitia
POST OFFICE: Grant, I.T.

COUNTY. **Choctaw Nation**

Choctaw Roll (Not Including Freedmen)

CARD NO.
FIELD NO. **1546**

Dawes' Roll No.		NAME		Relationship to Person First Named	AGE	SEX	BLOOD	TRIBAL ENROLLMENT		
								Year	County	No.
I.W. **14**	1	Raulston, Robert M	51	First Named	48	M	I.W	1896	Kiamitia	14977
4336	2	" Arabella W	38	Wife	35	F	1/2	1896	"	10838
4337	3	" Martin V	16	Son	12	M	1/4	1896	"	10839
4338	4	" Nora D	14	Dau	11	F	1/4	1896	"	10840
4339	5	" Anna L	12	"	9	"	1/4	1896	"	10841
4340	6	" John F	9	Son	6	M	1/4	1896	"	10842
4341	7	" Sophia	6	Dau	3	F	1/4	1896	"	10843
4342	8	" Robert E.	2	Son	7mo	M	1/4			
	9									
	10	ENROLLMENT OF NOS. 234567and8 HEREON APPROVED BY THE SECRETARY OF INTERIOR DEC 12 1902								
	11									
	12									
	13	ENROLLMENT OF NOS. ~~~ 1 ~~~ HEREON APPROVED BY THE SECRETARY OF INTERIOR JUN 13 1903								
	14									
	15									
	16									
	17									

TRIBAL ENROLLMENT OF PARENTS

	Name of Father	Year	County	Name of Mother	Year	County
1	Smith Raulston	Dead	Non Citz	Emma Raulston	Dead	Non Citz
2	Joel Everidge	1896	Kiamitia	Sophie Everidge	"	Kiamitia
3	No 1			No 2		
4	No 1			No 2		
5	No 1			No 2		
6	No 1			No 2		
7	No 1			No 2		
8	No 1			No 2		
9						
10	No1 on 1896 roll as Robt. M. Ralston					
11	No2 " 1896 " " Arabella "					
12	No3 " 1896 " " Martha B. "					
	No4 " 1896 " " Nora D "					
13	No5 " 1896 " " Anna L "					
14	No6 " 1896 " " Jno. F. "					
15	No7 " 1896 " " Sophia "					
16	No8 Enrolled February 21, 1901					
	Evidence of marriage of Nos 1-2 filed Dec. 15, 1902			Date of Application for Enrollment 5/10/99		
17	P.O. Frogville, I.T. 12/2/ '02					

Choctaw By Blood Enrollment Cards 1898-1914

RESIDENCE: **Kiamitia**　COUNTY.　**Choctaw Nation**　**Choctaw Roll** *(Not Including Freedmen)*　CARD NO.

POST OFFICE: **Goodland, I.T.**　FIELD NO. **1547**

Dawes' Roll No.	NAME	Relationship to Person First Named	AGE	SEX	BLOOD	TRIBAL ENROLLMENT		
						Year	County	No.
4343	1 Pitchlynn, Betsy *DIED PRIOR TO SEPTEMBER 25, 1902*		88	F	Full	1896	Kiamitia	10435
	2							
	3							
	4							
	5							
	6							
	7							
	8							
	9							
	10							
	11	ENROLLMENT OF NOS. 1 HEREON APPROVED BY THE SECRETARY OF INTERIOR DEC 12 1902						
	12							
	13							
	14							
	15							
	16							
	17							

TRIBAL ENROLLMENT OF PARENTS

	Name of Father	Year	County	Name of Mother	Year	County
1	Ah-fa-ma-tubbee		Dead in Mississippi	Ah-to-ba-huna		Dead in Mississippi
2						
3						
4						
5			On 1896 roll as Mrs. Betsy Pitchlynn			
6						
7			No1 died January 30, 1901; proof of death filed Dec 5, 1902			
8			No.1 died Jan 30 1901: Enrollment cancelled by Department July 8, 1904			
9						
10						
11						
12						
13						
14						
15						
16				Date of Application for Enrollment	5/10/99	
17						

47

Choctaw By Blood Enrollment Cards 1898-1914

RESIDENCE: Kiamitia   COUNTY. **Choctaw Nation**   **Choctaw Roll**   CARD No.
POST OFFICE: Goodland, I.T   *(Not Including Freedmen)*   FIELD No.   1548

Dawes' Roll No.	NAME		Relationship to Person First Named	AGE	SEX	BLOOD	TRIBAL ENROLLMENT		
							Year	County	No.
4344	1 Bacon, Silas	40	First Named	37	M	Full	1896	Kiamitia	1432
4345	2 " Eliza	43	Wife	40	F	"	1896	"	1433
4346	3 McCann, Ben	13	Ward	10	M	1/2	1896	Blue	9424
	4								
	5								
	6	ENROLLMENT							
	7	OF NOS. 1 2 and 3 HEREON APPROVED BY THE SECRETARY							
	8	OF INTERIOR DEC 12 1902							
	9								
	10								
	11								
	12								
	13								
	14								
	15								
	16								
	17								

TRIBAL ENROLLMENT OF PARENTS

	Name of Father	Year	County	Name of Mother	Year	County
1	Loman Bacon	Dead	Blue	Caroline Bacon	Dead	Kiamitia
2	Thos Koneubbee	"	Kiamitia	Amy	"	"
3				Molsey McCann	"	Blue
4						
5	Father of No.3 is supposed to be a white man, name unknown.					
6						
7	No2 on 1896 roll as Elias Bacon					
8						
9						
10						
11						
12						
13						
14						
15						
16				DATE OF APPLICATION FOR ENROLLMENT. 5/10/99		
17						

Choctaw By Blood Enrollment Cards 1898-1914

RESIDENCE: Kiamitia	COUNTY.					
POST OFFICE: Goodland, I.T.	Choctaw Nation		Choctaw Roll (Not Including Freedmen)	CARD NO. FIELD NO. 1549		

Dawes' Roll No.	NAME	Relationship to Person First Named	AGE	SEX	BLOOD	TRIBAL ENROLLMENT		
						Year	County	No.
4347	1 Pistokeha, Carrie DIED PRIOR TO SEPTEMBER 25, 1902	First Named	27	F	3/4	1896	Kiamitia	5744
4348	2 Bohanan, Minnie 10	Dau	7	"	5/8	1896	"	1426
4349	3 " , Dave 7	Son	4	M	5/8	1896	"	1427
	4							
	5							
	6							
	7							
	8							
	9							
	10							
	11 ENROLLMENT							
	12 OF NOS. 1 2 and 3 HEREON APPROVED BY THE SECRETARY							
	13 OF INTERIOR Dec. 12, 1902							
	14							
	15							
	16							
	17							

TRIBAL ENROLLMENT OF PARENTS

	Name of Father	Year	County	Name of Mother	Year	County
1	Edmund Homma	Dead	Kiamitia	Sillen Homma	Dead	Kiamitia
2	John Bohanan	"	"	No 1		
3	" "	"	"	No 1		
4						
5						
6	No.1 on 1896 roll as Caroline Homma					
7	No.1 died Feb 6, 1901: Proof of death filed Dec. 15, 1902					
8	No.1 died Feb 6, 1901: Enrollment cancelled by Department July 8, 1904					
9						
10						
11						
12						
13						
14						
15						
16				Date of Application for Enrollment	5/10/99	
17						

49

Choctaw By Blood Enrollment Cards 1898-1914

RESIDENCE: Kiamitia   COUNTY. **Choctaw Nation**   **Choctaw Roll** CARD NO.
POST OFFICE: Goodland, I.T.   *(Not Including Freedmen)* FIELD NO. **1550**

Dawes' Roll No.	NAME		Relationship to Person First Named	AGE	SEX	BLOOD	TRIBAL ENROLLMENT		
							Year	County	No.
4350	1 Roebuck, Edward	29	Named	26	M	1/2	1896	Kiamitia	10814
4351	2 " Betsy	26	Wife	23	F	Full	1896	"	1425
4352	3 " Percy L.	4	Son	5mo	M	3/4			
4353	4 " Henry	1	Son	4mo	M	3/4			
	5								
	6								
	7								
	8								
	9								
	10								
	11	ENROLLMENT							
	12	OF NOS. 1 2 3 and 4 HEREON APPROVED BY THE SECRETARY							
	13	OF INTERIOR Dec. 12, 1902							
	14								
	15								
	16								
	17								

TRIBAL ENROLLMENT OF PARENTS

	Name of Father	Year	County	Name of Mother	Year	County
1	Dave Roebuck	Dead	Kiamitia	Melina Roebuck	1896	Kiamitia
2	Anthony Bohanan	1896	"	Lizzie Bohanan	1896	"
3	No 1			No 2		
4	No 1			No 2		
5						
6	No2 on 1896 roll as Betsy Bohanan					
7	No4 born March 10-1902: Enrolled July 17-1902					
8	For child of Nos 1&2 see N.B.(Apr 26, 1906) Card No. 180.					
	" " " " " " " (March 3,1905) " " 1127.					
9						
10						
11						
12						
13						
14						
15					Date of Application for Enrollment.	
16					5/10/99	
17						

Choctaw By Blood Enrollment Cards 1898-1914

RESIDENCE: Kiamitia   COUNTY. **Choctaw Nation**   **Choctaw Roll** *(Not Including Freedmen)*   CARD NO. / FIELD NO. **1551**

POST OFFICE: Antlers, I.T.

Dawes' Roll No.	NAME	Relationship to Person	AGE	SEX	BLOOD	TRIBAL ENROLLMENT		
						Year	County	No.
	1 Wilson, Alice M ²⁴	First Named	21	F	3/8	1896	Kiamitia	12342
	2 Hynson, Perry ¹⁷	Bro	14	M	3/8	1896	"	5761
	3 Wilson, Fannie Florence ²	Dau	2	F	3/16			
	4							
	5							
	6							
	7	ENROLLMENT OF NOS. 1 and 2 HEREON						
	8	APPROVED BY THE SECRETARY						
	9	OF INTERIOR Dec 12, 1902						
	10							
	11	ENROLLMENT OF NOS. 3 HEREON						
	12	APPROVED BY THE SECRETARY						
	13	OF INTERIOR May 20, 1903						
	14							
	15							
	16							
	17							

TRIBAL ENROLLMENT OF PARENTS

	Name of Father	Year	County	Name of Mother		Year	County
1	Noland Hynson	1896	Intermarried	Minnie Hynson		Dead	Kiamitia
2	" "	1896	"	"	"	"	"
3	D.C. Wilson			No.1			
4							
5							
6			No2 on 1896 roll as Perry Hyson				
7							
8			Father of above people on card No. 2153 5807				
9			No1 is now the wife of D.C. Wilson, Feby, 15, 1901				
10			No.3 Enrolled Dec 11, 1902				
11							
12							
13							
14			For child of No.1 see NB (Mar 3-1905) Card #62.				
15							
16						Date of Application for Enrollment	5/10/99
17	P.O. Hugo I.T. 12/2 '02						

P.O. Ravia I.T. 4/20/05

Choctaw By Blood Enrollment Cards 1898-1914

RESIDENCE: Tobucksy
POST OFFICE: McAlester, I.T.

COUNTY. **Choctaw Nation**

Choctaw Roll
(Not Including Freedmen)

CARD NO.
FIELD NO. **1552**

Dawes' Roll No.	NAME	Relationship to Person	AGE	SEX	BLOOD	TRIBAL ENROLLMENT		
						Year	County	No.
I.W. 1099	1 Marcum, Joshua	First Named	27	M	I.W.	1896	Tobucksy	14812
	2							
	3							
	4							
	5							
	6	ENROLLMENT						
	7	OF NOS. ~~ 1 ~~ HEREON APPROVED BY THE SECRETARY						
	8	OF INTERIOR Nov. 16, 1904						
	9							
	10							
	11							
	12							
	13							
	14							
	15							
	16							
	17							

TRIBAL ENROLLMENT OF PARENTS

	Name of Father	Year	County	Name of Mother	Year	County
1	Randolph Marcum	Dead	Non Citz	Eliz. Marcum	Dead	Non Citz
2						
3						
4						
5						
6	For child of No.1 see NB (Apr. 26 '06) #1148					
7						
8						
9						
10						
11						
12						
13						
14						
15						
16					Date of Application for Enrollment	5/10/99
17	P.O. Juanita I.T. 12/18 02					

Choctaw By Blood Enrollment Cards 1898-1914

RESIDENCE: Kiamitia COUNTY. **Choctaw Nation** **Choctaw Roll** CARD NO.
POST OFFICE: Nelson, I.T. *(Not Including Freedmen)* FIELD NO. 1553

Dawes' Roll No.	NAME	Relationship to Person First Named	AGE	SEX	BLOOD	TRIBAL ENROLLMENT Year	County	No.
4356	1 Frazier, Kelly 40		37	M	Full	1896	Kiamitia	4249
4357	2 " Ellen 38	Wife	35	F	"	1896	Jacks Fork	12500
4358	3 Colbert, Mary DIED PRIOR TO SEPTEMBER 25, 1902	S. Dau	6	"	"	1896	" "	12501
	4							
	5							
	6							
	7							
	8							
	9							
	10							
	11	ENROLLMENT OF NOS. 1 2 and 3 HEREON						
	12	APPROVED BY THE SECRETARY						
	13	OF INTERIOR DEC 12 1902						
	14							
	15							
	16							
	17							

TRIBAL ENROLLMENT OF PARENTS

	Name of Father	Year	County	Name of Mother	Year	County
1	Sexton Frazier	Dead	Kiamitia	Sho-te-tun-na	Dead	Kiamitia
2	Sam Samuel			Betsy Samuel	"	"
3	Allison Colbert	1896	Atoka	No 2		
4						
5						
6						
7			No2 on 1896 roll as Ellen Thompson			
8			No3 " 1896 " " Mary "			
9			No.3 died May 5 1902: Enrolled July 8, 1904			
10						
11						
12						
13						
14				Date of Application for Enrollment.		
15						
16				5/10/99		
17						

53

Choctaw By Blood Enrollment Cards 1898-1914

RESIDENCE: Jackson COUNTY. **Choctaw Nation** Choctaw Roll CARD No.
POST OFFICE: Mayhew, I.T. (Not Including Freedmen) FIELD NO. 1554

Dawes' Roll No.	NAME	Relationship to Person First Named	AGE	SEX	BLOOD	TRIBAL ENROLLMENT		
						Year	County	No.
4359	1 Wade, Daniel F. 46	First Named	43	M	Full	1896	Jackson	13792
4360	2 " Malinda 51	Wife	48	F	3/4	1896	"	13793
4361	3 " Emerson 13	Son	10	M	7/8	1896	"	13794
4362	4 Battiest, William 19	S. Son	16	"	5/8	1896	"	1465
	5							
	6							
	7							
	8							
	9							
	10							
	11	ENROLLMENT						
	12	OF NOS. 1 2 3 and 4 HEREON APPROVED BY THE SECRETARY						
	13	OF INTERIOR DEC 12 1902						
	14							
	15							
	16							
	17							

TRIBAL ENROLLMENT OF PARENTS

Name of Father	Year	County	Name of Mother	Year	County
1 Jerry Wade	Dead	Jackson	Vicey Wade	1896	Jackson
2 William James	"	Towson	Phoebe James	Dead	Towson
3 No 1			No 2		
4 John Battiest	Dead	Kiamitia	No 2		
5					
6					
7					
8 No1 on 1896 roll as D. F. Wade					
9					
10					
11					
12					
13					
14					
15					
16			Date of Application for Enrollment		5/10/99
17					

Choctaw By Blood Enrollment Cards 1898-1914

RESIDENCE: Jackson COUNTY. **Choctaw Nation** **Choctaw Roll** CARD NO.
POST OFFICE: Mayhew, I.T. *(Not Including Freedmen)* FIELD NO. **1555**

Dawes' Roll No.	NAME	Relationship to Person First Named	AGE	SEX	BLOOD	TRIBAL ENROLLMENT		
						Year	County	No.
4363	1 Wade, Vicey 81		78	F	Full	1896	Jackson	13795
*4364	2 Anotubbee, Simon 22	Ward	19	M	"	1896	"	376
	3							
	4							
	5							
	6	ENROLLMENT						
	7	OF NOS. 1 and 2 HEREON APPROVED BY THE SECRETARY						
	8	OF INTERIOR Dec. 12, 1902						
	9							
	10							
	11							
	12							
	13							
	14							
	15							
	16							
	17							

TRIBAL ENROLLMENT OF PARENTS

	Name of Father	Year	County	Name of Mother	Year	County
1	Ben Battiest		Dead in Mississippi			Dead in Mississippi
2	Thos. Anotubbee		Cedar	Susan Anotubbee	"	Cedar
3						
4						
5						
6			No2 on 1896 roll as Simon Anotayabbi.			
7			Nos 1 and 2 said to be dead.			
8						
9			*"Died prior to Sept. 25, 1902: not entitled to land or money"			
10			(See Indian Office letter of Aug. 22, 1911, No. 1369-1911)			
11						
12						
13						
14					Date of Application for Enrollment.	
15						
16					5/10/99	
17						

55

RESIDENCE: Kiamitia   COUNTY: **Choctaw Nation**   **Choctaw Roll** (Not Including Freedmen)   CARD No.
POST OFFICE: Grant, I.T.   FIELD No. 1556

Dawes' Roll No.	NAME	Relationship to Person First Named	AGE	SEX	BLOOD	TRIBAL ENROLLMENT		
						Year	County	No.
4365	1 Everidge, Robert T. 45	First Named	42	M	3/8	1896	Kiamitia	3767
I.W. 81	2 " Lula 35	Wife	32	F	I.W.			
4366	3 " Edward M 11	Son	8	M	3/16	1896	"	3768
4367	4 " Clara W. 9	Dau	6	F	3/16	1896	"	3769
4368	5 DIED PRIOR TO SEPTEMBER 25, 1902 Thomas H	Son	4	M	3/16	1896	"	3770
4369	6 " David M.H. 5	"	1½	"	3/16			
4370	7 " Effie 3	Dau	3½mo	F	3/16			
4371	8 " Eva Laura 1	Dau	6wks	F	3/16			
	9							
	10	ENROLLMENT OF NOS. 134567and8 HEREON APPROVED BY THE SECRETARY OF INTERIOR DEC 12 1902						
	11							
	12							
	13	ENROLLMENT OF NOS. 2 HEREON APPROVED BY THE SECRETARY OF INTERIOR JUN 13 1903						
	14							
	15							
	16							
	17							

TRIBAL ENROLLMENT OF PARENTS

	Name of Father	Year	County	Name of Mother	Year	County
1	J.W. Everidge	1896	Kiamitia	Sophie Everidge	Dead	Kiamitia
2	Thos. Hulen	1896	Non Citz	Angeline Hulen	1896	Non Citz
3	No 1			No 2		
4	No 1			No 2		
5	No 1			No 2		
6	No 1			No 2		
7	No 1			No 2		
8	No.1			No.2		
9	No1 on 1896 roll as Rob. T. Everidge					
10	No3 " 1896 " " Ed M "					
11	No5 " 1896 " " Thos. H. " No.8 Enrolled July 30, 1901					
12	For child of Nos 1&2 see N.B. (Apr.26,1906) Card No113.					
13	No.5 died May 9, 1902; proof of death filed Dec 6, 1902					
14	No.5 died May 9, 1902. Enrollment cancelled by Department July 8, 1904					
15	For child of Nos1&2 see NB (March 3 1905) card No743				No7 enrolled Dec 19/99
16						Date of Application for Enrollment. 5/10/99
17						→ 1 to 6 inc

Choctaw By Blood Enrollment Cards 1898-1914

RESIDENCE: Kiamitia   COUNTY. **Choctaw Nation**   **Choctaw Roll** CARD NO.
POST OFFICE: Frogville, I.T.   *(Not Including Freedmen)* FIELD NO. 1557

Dawes' Roll No.	NAME	Relationship to Person First Named	AGE	SEX	BLOOD	TRIBAL ENROLLMENT		
						Year	County	No.
4372	1 Crittenden, Johnny ²⁴	First Named	21	M	1/2	1893	Towson	138
	2							
	3							
	4							
	5							
	6							
	7							
	8							
	9							
	10							
	11	ENROLLMENT						
	12	OF NOS. 1 HEREON APPROVED BY THE SECRETARY						
	13	OF INTERIOR DEC 12 1902						
	14							
	15							
	16							
	17							

TRIBAL ENROLLMENT OF PARENTS

Name of Father	Year	County	Name of Mother	Year	County
1 Jack Crittenden	1896	Non Citz	Sissy Crittenden	1896	Kiamitia
2					
3					
4 On 1893 Pay roll as Johny Garland, Page 15, No 138 Towson Co.					
5					
6 No.1 is husband of Mattie Crittenden and father of the children on					
7 Chickasaw freedman Card #854. See affidavits and evidence of marriage					
8 filed with that case, July 23, 1901.					
9					
10 For child of No 1 see NB (Apr 26-06) Card #670					
11					
12					
13					
14					
15				Date of Application for Enrollment	5/10/99
16					
17					

Choctaw By Blood Enrollment Cards 1898-1914

RESIDENCE: Kiamitia   COUNTY. **Choctaw**

POST OFFICE: Grant, I.T.   *(Not including Freedmen)*

Dawes' Roll No.	NAME	Relationship to Person First Named	AGE	SEX	BLOOD	TRIBAL ENROLLMENT Year	County	No.
4373	1 Hayes, Forbis 37	First Named	34	M	Full	1896	Kiamitia	5747
4374	2 " Millie 44	Wife	41	F	"	1896	"	5748
4375	3 " John 11	Son	8	M	"	1896	"	5749
4376	4 " Wilson (DIED PRIOR TO SEPTEMBER 25, 1902)	"	2	"	"			
	5							
	6							
	7							
	8							
	9							
	10							
	11	ENROLLMENT						
	12	OF NOS. 1 2 3 and 4 HEREON APPROVED BY THE SECRETARY						
	13	OF INTERIOR DEC 12 1902						
	14							
	15							
	16							
	17							

TRIBAL ENROLLMENT OF PARENTS

	Name of Father	Year	County	Name of Mother	Year	County
1	Sam Hayes	Dead	Kiamitia	Mary Hayes	Dead	Kiamitia
2	John Temus	"	"	Rhoda Temus	"	Jackson
3	No 1			No 2		
4	No 1			No 2		
5						
6			No4 Affidavit of birth to be supplied. Recd May 10/99			
7						
8			No4 died Aug. 4, 1899; proof of death filed Dec 5, 1902			
9			No.4 died Aug 4, 1899; Enrollment cancelled by Department July 8, 1904			
10						
11						
12						
13						
14						
15						
16					Date of Application for Enrollment	5/10/99
17						

RESIDENCE: Kiamitia   COUNTY: **Choctaw Nation**   **Choctaw Roll** (Not Including Freedmen)   CARD NO.   FIELD NO. 1559

POST OFFICE: Nelson, I.T.

Dawes' Roll No.	NAME	Relationship to Person First Named	AGE	SEX	BLOOD	TRIBAL ENROLLMENT Year	County	No.
4377	1 Roebuck, Ben 43	First Named	40	M	1/2	1896	Kiamitia	10853
I.W. 707	2 " Nancy A. 44	Wife	42	F	I.W.	1896	"	14976
4378	3 " Edward 17	Son	14	M	1/4	1896	"	10854
4379	4 " Oscar 15	"	12	"	1/4	1896	"	10855
4380	5 " Oliver 15	"	12	"	1/4	1896	"	10856
4381	6 " Elmira 12	Dau	9	F	1/4	1896	"	10857
4382	7 " Isabelle 9	"	6	"	1/4	1896	"	10858
4383	8 " Ettie 7	"	4	"	1/4	1896	"	10859
4384	9 " Ulyssus 6	Son	3	M	1/4			
4385	10 " Susan 4	Dau	3mo	F	1/4			
4386	11 " Clarissy M 1	Dau	4mo	F	1/4			
	12							
	13	ENROLLMENT OF NOS. 1345678910and11 HEREON APPROVED BY THE SECRETARY						
	14	OF INTERIOR DEC 12 1902						
	15							
	16							
	17							

TRIBAL ENROLLMENT OF PARENTS

	Name of Father	Year	County	Name of Mother	Year	County
1	Ephriam[sic] Roebuck	Dead	Kiamitia	Clarissa Walker	1896	Kiamitia
2	Jas Taylor	"	Non Citz	Sally Taylor	Dead	Non Citz
3	No 1			No 2		
4	No 1			No 2		
5	No 1			No 2		
6	No 1			No 2		
7	No 1			No 2		
8	No 1			No 2		
9	No 1			No 2		
10	No 1			No 2		
11	No 1			No 2		
12	No2 See Decision of March 2 '04			ENROLLMENT OF NOS. ~~~ 2 ~~~ HEREON		
13	No3 on 1896 roll as Ed Roebuck			APPROVED BY THE SECRETARY		
14	No6 " 1896 " " Almira "			OF INTERIOR MAY -7 1904		#1 to 10 inc
15				Date of Application for Enrollment.		
16	Nos 9-10 Affidavits of birth to be supplied Recd May 17			5/10/99		
17	No11 born Aug.6,1901: Enrolled Dec 3, 1901.					

Choctaw By Blood Enrollment Cards 1898-1914

RESIDENCE: Kiamitia   COUNTY. **Choctaw Nation** **Choctaw Roll** CARD No.
POST OFFICE: Goodland, I.T.   *(Not Including Freedmen)* FIELD No. **1560**

Dawes' Roll No.	NAME	Relationship to Person First Named	AGE	SEX	BLOOD	TRIBAL ENROLLMENT Year	County	No.
4387	1 Thompson, James E. 61	First Named	58	M	Full	1896	Kiamitia	12351
4388	2 " Elizabeth 43	Wife	40	F	"	1896	"	12352
4389	3 Patterson, Thomas 18	Ward	15	M	"	1896	"	12353
	4							
	5							
	6							
	7							
	8							
	9							
	10							
	11	ENROLLMENT						
	12	OF NOS. 1 – 2 and 3 HEREON APPROVED BY THE SECRETARY						
	13	OF INTERIOR Dec. 12, 1902						
	14							
	15							
	16							
	17							

TRIBAL ENROLLMENT OF PARENTS

	Name of Father	Year	County	Name of Mother	Year	County
1		Died	in Mississippi	E-la-che-huna	Dead	Kiamitia
2	Ho-ma-by	Dead	Kiamitia	Shum-ma	"	"
3	Jefferson Hosa	"	"	Elizabeth Chafa	"	"
4						
5						
6	No3 on 1896 roll as Thomas Thompson					
7	No3 also on Choctaw Card #1679 cancelled Sept. 10, 1902.					
8						
9						
10						
11						
12						
13						
14						
15						
16					Date of Application for Enrollment	5/10/99
17	P.O. Hugo, I.T. 12/2 02					

60

Choctaw By Blood Enrollment Cards 1898-1914

RESIDENCE: Kiamitia	COUNTY.					Choctaw Roll		CARD NO.	
POST OFFICE: Frogville, I.T.	**Choctaw Nation**					(Not Including Freedmen)		FIELD NO.	**1561**

Dawes' Roll No.	NAME	Relationship to Person First Named	AGE	SEX	BLOOD	TRIBAL ENROLLMENT		
						Year	County	No.
4390	1 Crittenden, Sissa 48	First Named	45	F	Full	1893	Towson	136
4391	2 " , Isabelle 20	Dau	17	"	1/2	1893	"	139
4392	3 " , Carrie 15	"	12	"	1/2	1893	"	140
4393	4 " , Herold 9	Son	6	M	1/2	1893	"	142
4394	5 " , Annie 6	Dau	2	F	1/2			
4395	6 " , Mary 8	G. Dau	4	"	1/2			
	7							
	8							
	9							
	10							
	11 ENROLLMENT							
	12 OF NOS. 12345and6 HEREON APPROVED BY THE SECRETARY							
	13 OF INTERIOR Dec. 12, 1902.							
	14							
	15							
	16							
	17							

TRIBAL ENROLLMENT OF PARENTS

Name of Father	Year	County	Name of Mother	Year	County
1 Israel Garland	Dead	Towson	Isabelle Garland	Dead	Towson
2 Jack Crittenden	1896	Non Citz	No 1		
3 " "	1896	" "	No 1		
4 " "	1896	" "	No 1		
5 " "	1896	" "	No 1		
6 Dick Harkins	Dead	Towson	Frances Crittenden	Dead	Towson
7					
8 No 1 on 1893 Pay roll Page 15, No. 136, Towson Co., as Sissa Garland					
9 No.2 " 1893 " " " 15, " 139 " " " Isabelle "					
10 No.3 " 1893 " " " 15, " 140 " " " Carrie "					
No.4 " 1893 " " " 15, " 142 " " " Herald "					
11 No.3 is now the wife of Joe Willis on Chickasaw Freedman Card #1211 Evidence of					
12 Marriage filed Dec. 5, 1902.					
13					
14				Date of Application for Enrollment:	
15					
16				5/10/99	
17					

Choctaw By Blood Enrollment Cards 1898-1914

RESIDENCE: Kiamitia   COUNTY. **Choctaw Nation**   **Choctaw Roll** (*Not Including Freedmen*)   CARD NO.

POST OFFICE: Nelson, I.T.   FIELD NO. **1562**

Dawes' Roll No.	NAME	Relationship to Person First Named	AGE	SEX	BLOOD	TRIBAL ENROLLMENT Year	County	No.
DEAD	1 Smallwood, William DEAD		80	M	1/4	1896	Kiamitia	11518
4396	2 " , Narcissa 61	Wife	58	F	1/4	1896	"	11519
4397	3 Murray, Rebecca 44	Dau	41	"	1/4	1896	"	11520
4398	4 Smallwood, Mary 23	G. Dau	20	"	3/8	1896	"	11521
4399	5 " ,William Jr 20	G. Son	17	M	3/8	1896	"	11522
4400	6 " , Martha 17	G. Dau	14	F	3/8	1896	"	11523
	7							
	8							
	9	ENROLLMENT OF NOS. 2 3 4 5 and 6 HEREON APPROVED BY THE SECRETARY OF INTERIOR Dec. 12, 1902						
	10							
	11							
	12							
	13	No. 1 hereon dismissed under order of						
	14	the Commission to the Five Civilized						
	15	Tribes of March 31, 1905.						
	16							
	17							

TRIBAL ENROLLMENT OF PARENTS

	Name of Father	Year	County	Name of Mother	Year	County
1	Elisha Smallwood	Dead	Non Citz	Mary Smallwood	Dead	Kiamitia
2	Miles Barefield	Dead	" "	Sophia Barefild[sic]	"	"
3	No 1			Mary Smallwood	"	"
4	Martin Smallwood	Dead	Kiamitia	Catherine Smallwood	"	"
5	" "	"	"	" "	"	"
6	" "	"	"	" "	"	"
7						
8	No5 on 1896 roll as Wm Smallwood					
9	No3 is now the wife of Frank Murray on Choctaw Card #3352.					
10	a white man, who was formerly married to Sallie Murray listed on that card. See letter filed herewith. Jan. 14, 1902.					
11	No1 Died Jany, 1902: Proof of death filed Apr 2- 1902.					
12						
13						
14					Date of Application for Enrollment.	
15						
16					5/10/99	
17						

Choctaw By Blood Enrollment Cards 1898-1914

RESIDENCE: Jackson
POST OFFICE: Mayhew, I.T.

COUNTY. **Choctaw Nation** (Not Including Freedmen)

Choctaw Roll

CARD NO. FIELD NO. **1563**

Dawes' Roll No.	NAME	Relationship to Person First Named	AGE	SEX	BLOOD	TRIBAL ENROLLMENT Year	TRIBAL ENROLLMENT County	TRIBAL ENROLLMENT No.
4401	1 Bacon, Alfred [DIED PRIOR TO SEPTEMBER 25, 1902]		42	M	Full	1896	Jackson	1523
4402	2 " , Eliza	41 Wife	38	F	"	1896	"	1524
4403	3 " , Mary	21 Dau	18	"	"	1896	"	1526
4404	4 Jones , Lena	23 S. Dau	20	"	"	1896	"	7134
4405	5 " , Isaac	21 S. Son	18	M	"	1896	"	7139
4406	6 " , David	16 "	13	"	"	1896	"	7135
4407	7 " , Jane [DIED PRIOR TO SEPTEMBER 25, 1902]	G. Dau	15mo	F	"			
14677	8 Durant, Fannie	2 Dau of No 3	2½	F	"			
	9	ENROLLMENT						
	10	OF NOS. 123456 and 7 HEREON APPROVED BY THE SECRETARY						
	11	OF INTERIOR Dec 12, 1902						
	12	No1 died March 6, 1902: Proof of						
	13	death filed Dec. 8, 1902.						
	14	No7 died May 20, 1902: Proof of death filed Dec. 8, 1902.						
	15	ENROLLMENT						
	16	OF NOS. 8 HEREON APPROVED BY THE SECRETARY						
	17	OF INTERIOR May 20, 1903.						

TRIBAL ENROLLMENT OF PARENTS

Name of Father	Year	County	Name of Mother	Year	County
1 Ismon Bacon	Dead	Red River	Nancy Bacon	Dead	Red River
2 Mitchell LeFlore	"	Towson	Mahale Jones	1896	" "
3 No 1			Isabelle Bacon	Dead	Jackson
4 Gibson Jones	Dead	Jackson	No 2		
5 " "	"	"	No 2		
6 " "	"	"	No 2		
7 Joseph Jones	1896	Kiamitia	No 3		
8 Sammie Durant		Choctaw	No 3		
9 No1 died March 6,1901: No7 died May 20,1902: Enrollment cancelled by Department July 8, 1904					
10 No8 born June 10, 1900: enrolled Dec 6, 1902					
11 No7 Affidavit of birh to be supplied. Recd May 17/99					
12 No4 on 1896 roll as Lonie Jones For child of No6 see NB (March 3, 1905) #1052					
13 No5 in Pen. For child of No3 see NB (Apr 26-06) Card #640 #678 #4 Enrollment #7174 Page 177 erroneous. See to this					
14 No4 tribal enrollment should be #7134. See Choctaw card #3855. Tribal enrollment #7174 belongs					
15 evidently to Marcus A. Jones on Choctaw Card #3855. See pages 175-177 of 1896 Choctaw Census roll.					
16				Date of Application for Enrollment. 5/10/99	
17					

63

Choctaw By Blood Enrollment Cards 1898-1914

RESIDENCE: Jackson COUNTY. **Choctaw Nation** Choctaw Roll
POST OFFICE: Mayhew, I.T. *(Not Including Freedmen)*

Dawes' Roll No.		NAME		Relationship to Person First Named	AGE	SEX	BLOOD	TRIBAL ENROLLMENT		
								Year	County	No.
4408	1	LeFlore, Phelin		First Named	45	M	1/4	1896	Jackson	8122
4409	2	" Sophia	41	Wife	38	F	1/4	1896	"	8123
See 5342	3	" Allen		Son	19	M	1/4	1896	"	8124
4410	4	" Isaac	20	"	17	"	1/4	1896	"	8125
4411	5	" Susan	15	Dau	12	F	1/4	1896	"	8126
4412	6	" Eliza		"	10	"	1/4	1896	"	8127
4413	7	" Hattie	11	"	8	"	1/4	1896	"	8128
4414	8	" Jesse	9	Son	6	M	1/4	1896	"	8129
4415	9	" Frank	7	"	4	"	1/4	1896	"	8130
4416	10	" Carrie	6	Dau	3	F	1/4	1896	"	8131
4417	11	" Ada	5	"	16mo	"	1/4			
See 1522	12	" Jefferson		Gr Son	3wks	M	1/8			
	13	N⁰5 is wife of Hampton Goins Choctaw card #3571. 12/1/02								
	14	N⁰6 Died June 6,1900, proof of death filed Dec. 24, 1902								
	15	ENROLLMENT OF NOS.1 2 4 5 6 7 8 9 10 and 11 HEREON APPROVED BY THE SECRETARY			No.3 transferred to Choctaw card #5342						
	16	OF INTERIOR DEC 12 1902			N⁰12 transferred to Choctaw card #1522						
	17	For child of No5 see NB(Apr 26-06) Card No 630									
		N⁰1 died Oct 20,1900, proof of death filed Dec. 24,1902.									

TRIBAL ENROLLMENT OF PARENTS

	Name of Father	Year	County	Name of Mother	Year	County
1	Mitchell LeFlore	Dead	Towson	Mahaley Jones	1896	Red River
2	Cornelius Jones	"	Red River	Pollie Jones	Dead	" "
3	No 1			No 2		
4	No 1			No 2		
5	No 1			No 2		
6	No 1			No 2		
7	No 1			No 2		
8	No 1			No 2		
9	No 1			No 2		
10	No 1			No 2		
11	No 1			No 2		
12	N⁰4			Lizzie LeFlore		non-citizen
13	N⁰4 is now the husband of Lizzie LeFlore non-citizen. Evidence of marriage filed Oct. 11, 1902					
14	No6 on 1896 roll as Lizzie LeFlore					#1 to 11 inc
15	N⁰12 Born Sept. 22, 1902, enrolled Oct. 11, 1902				Date of Application for Enrollment.	
16	No11 Affidavit of birth to be supplied. Recd June 1/99				5/10/99	
17	The above mentioned notation as to No4 is an error. Should have been on Choctaw card #1522					

No.1 died Oct.20,1900: No.6 died June6,1900: Enrollment cancelled by Department July 8, 1904.

64

Choctaw By Blood Enrollment Cards 1898-1914

RESIDENCE: Kiamitia
POST OFFICE: Grant, I.T.

COUNTY. **Choctaw Nation**

Choctaw Roll CARD NO.
(Not Including Freedmen) FIELD NO. **1565**

Dawes' Roll No.	NAME	Relationship to Person	AGE	SEX	BLOOD	TRIBAL ENROLLMENT		
						Year	County	No.
4418	1 Speaker, Martin ²⁵	First Named	22	M	Full	1896	Kiamitia	11495
4419	2 " Sophia ²³	Wife	20	F	"	1893	"	453
	3							
	4							
	5	ENROLLMENT						
	6	OF NOS. 1 and 2 HEREON APPROVED BY THE SECRETARY						
	7	OF INTERIOR Dec. 12, 1902						
	8							
	9							
	10							
	11							
	12							
	13							
	14							
	15							
	16							
	17							

TRIBAL ENROLLMENT OF PARENTS

	Name of Father	Year	County	Name of Mother	Year	County
1	Tom Speaker	Dead	Kiamitia	Milly Speaker	1896	Kiamitia
2	Charles Billy	"	"	Betsey Billy	Dead	"
3						
4						
5						
6	No.2 on 1893 Pay roll as Sophia Billy, Page 56, No 453, Kiamitia Co.					
7	No.2 also on 1896 Choctaw roll as Sophie Miley achubbe, page 218, #8727					
8						
9						
10						
11						
12						
13						
14					Date of Application for Enrollment.	
15						
16					5/10/99	
17						

Choctaw By Blood Enrollment Cards 1898-1914

RESIDENCE: **Kiamitia**　COUNTY.　**Choctaw Nation**　**Choctaw Roll**　CARD NO.
POST OFFICE:　**Grant, I.T.**　*(Not Including Freedmen)*　FIELD NO. **1566**

Dawes' Roll No.	NAME		Relationship to Person First Named	AGE	SEX	BLOOD	TRIBAL ENROLLMENT		
							Year	County	No.
4420	1 Nelson, Isaac	28	First Named	25	M	Full	1896	Kiamitia	9743
4421	2 " Emma	38	Wife	35	F	"	1896	"	9744
4422	3 " Georgie A.	12	Dau	9	"	"	1896	"	9745
4423	4 " Allington T	9	Son	6	M	"	1896	"	9746
4424	5 " Leo B.	7	"	4	"	"	1896	"	9747
4425	6 " Grace M	6	Dau	3	F	"	1896	"	9748
4426	7 " Patsy	4	"	5mo	"	"			
4427	8 " Annie	19	Ward	16	"	"	1896	Kiamitia	9749
4428	9 " Cole E.	1	Son	2mo	M	"			
	10								
	11	ENROLLMENT							
	12	OF NOS. 1 2 3 4 5 6 7 8 and 9 HEREON APPROVED BY THE SECRETARY							
	13	OF INTERIOR Dec. 12, 1902							
	14								
	15								
	16								
	17								

TRIBAL ENROLLMENT OF PARENTS

	Name of Father	Year	County	Name of Mother	Year	County
1	Coleman Nelson	Dead	Jacks Fork	Rhoda Nelson	1896	Jacks Fork
2	Ellis Choate	1896	Kiamitia	Patsey Choate	1896	Kiamitia
3	No 1			No 2		
4	No 1			No 2		
5	No 1			No 2		
6	No 1			No 2		
7	No 1			No 2		
8	Eastman Isaac	Dead	Kiamitia	Molsey Murphy	1896	Towson
9	No 1			No 2		
10						
11						
12	No 3 on 1896 roll as Geo. A. Nelson					
13	No 4 " 1896 " " Linton T. "					
14	No 9 born Feby. 1, 1902; enrolled March 28, 1902					
15	For child of Nos 1&2 see N.B. (March 3, 1905) #1073			#1 to 8 inc		
16				Date of Application for Enrollment. 5/10/99		
17						

Choctaw By Blood Enrollment Cards 1898-1914

RESIDENCE: Kiamitia	COUNTY.	**Choctaw Nation**		**Choctaw Roll** *(Not Including Freedmen)*	CARD NO.	
POST OFFICE: Grant, I.T.					FIELD NO.	**1567**

Dawes' Roll No.	NAME		Relationship to Person First Named	AGE	SEX	BLOOD	TRIBAL ENROLLMENT		
							Year	County	No.
4429	1 Nelson, Gabriel	52	First Named	49	M	Full	1896	Kiamitia	9757
4430	2 " Mary	DIED PRIOR TO SEPTEMBER 25, 1935	Wife	32	F	"	1896	"	9758
4431	3 " Willy	21	Son	18	M	"	1896	"	9759
4432	4 " Wilson	17	"	14	"	"	1896	"	9760
4433	5 Homer, Laura	19	S Dau	16	F	"	1896	"	790
	6								
	7								
	8								
	9								
	10								
	11	ENROLLMENT OF NOS. 1 2 3 4 and 5 HEREON							
	12	APPROVED BY THE SECRETARY							
	13	OF INTERIOR Dec. 12, 1902							
	14								
	15								
	16								
	17								

TRIBAL ENROLLMENT OF PARENTS

	Name of Father	Year	County	Name of Mother	Year	County
1	Cole Nelson	Dead	Jacks Fork	Rhoda Nelson	1896	Jacks Fork
2	Enoch Brashears	"	Kiamitia	Louisa Brashears	Dead	Kiamitia
3	No 1			Nancy Nelson	"	Jacks Fork
4	No 1			" "	"	" "
5	James Homer	Dead	Kiamitia	Mary Nelson	1896	Kiamitia
6						
7	No5 on 1893 Pay roll Page 95, No 790, Kiamitia Co					
8	No.5 on 1896 Choctaw as Louisa Homma, page 141, #5779.					
9	No 2 Died May 1, 1901. Proof of death filed Oct. 27, 1902					
10	No.1 is husband of Susan Gibson					
11	No.5 gone to Chickasaw Nation.					
12	No.2 died - - 1901, Enrollment cancelled by Department Sept. 16, 1904.					
13						
14					Date of Application for Enrollment.	
15						
16	PO. Antlers, I.T.				5/10/99	
17						

67

Choctaw By Blood Enrollment Cards 1898-1914

POST OFFICE: Olain, I.T.   1506   1508

Dawes' Roll No.	NAME		Relationship to Person First Named	AGE	SEX	BLOOD	TRIBAL ENROLLMENT		
							Year	County	No.
4434	1 Kaneubbe, Moses	41	First Named	38	M	Full	1896	Kiamitia	7612
4435	2 " Betsy	28	Wife	25	F	"	1896	"	7613
4436	3 " Hampton	10	Son	7	M	"	1896	"	7614
4437	4 " Thomas	6	"	3	"	"	1896	"	7615
14678	5 " Eliza	4	Dau	1	F	"			
	6								
	7	ENROLLMENT							
	8	OF NOS. 1 2 3 and 4 HEREON							
	9	APPROVED BY THE SECRETARY OF INTERIOR DEC 12 1902							
	10								
	11	ENROLLMENT							
	12	OF NOS. 5 HEREON							
	13	APPROVED BY THE SECRETARY OF INTERIOR MAY 20 1903							
	14								
	15								
	16								
	17								

TRIBAL ENROLLMENT OF PARENTS

	Name of Father	Year	County	Name of Mother	Year	County
1	Thos. Kaneubbe	Dead	Kiamitia	Emma Kaneubbe	Dead	Kiamitia
2	Lymon Robison	1896	"	Eliz. Hotema	"	"
3	No 1			No 2		
4	No 1			No 2		
5	No 1			No 2		
6						
7						
8	No 5 born Aug 1, 1901; Enrolled Nov. 24, 1902					
9	For child of Nos 1&2 see NB (March 3, 1905) #1186					
10						
11						
12						
13						
14						
15						
16					Date of Application for Enrollment.	5/10/99
17	P.O. [Illegible] I.T. 11/24/02					

#1 to

RESIDENCE:	Jackson	COUNTY,	**Choctaw Nation**				Choctaw Roll		CARD NO.	
POST OFFICE:	Mayhew, I.T.						*(Not Including Freedmen)*		FIELD NO.	1569

Dawes' Roll No.	NAME	Relationship to Person First Named	AGE	SEX	BLOOD	TRIBAL ENROLLMENT		
						Year	County	No.
14679	1 Thomas, Susan 38	First Named	35	F	Full	1896	Jackson	367
14680	2 LeFlore, Jackie	Son	1	M	"			
14681	3 Thomas, Isom Perry 1	Son	1	M	1/2			
4								
5								
6								
7	ENROLLMENT OF NOS. 1 2 and 3 HEREON							
8	APPROVED BY THE SECRETARY OF INTERIOR May 20, 1903							
9								
10								
11								
12								
13								
14								
15								
16								
17								

TRIBAL ENROLLMENT OF PARENTS

	Name of Father	Year	County	Name of Mother	Year	County
1	John Allen	Dead	Jackson	Siney Allen	Dead	Jackson
2	Allen LeFlore	1896	"	No 1		
3	Wilson Thomas		Claim Choctaw	No 1		
4						
5						
6						
7	No 1 is now the wife of Wilson Thomas, evidence of marriage					
8	filed Oct. 24, 1902 No 3 Born Oct. 25, 1901, enrolled Oct. 24, 1902					
9	No.2 died – –, 1901; Enrollment cancelled by Department July 8, 1904.					
10	For child of No 1 see N.B. (March 3, 1905) #1089					
11						
12						
13						
14					#1 & 2	
15					Date of Application for Enrollment.	
16					5/10/99	
17	P.O. Soper I.T. 4/17/05					

69

Choctaw By Blood Enrollment Cards 1898-1914

RESIDENCE: Jackson   COUNTY.   **Choctaw Nation**   *(Not Including Freedmen)*   FIELD NO. 1570
POST OFFICE: Crowder, I.T.

Dawes' Roll No.	NAME		Relationship to Person First Named	AGE	SEX	BLOOD	TRIBAL ENROLLMENT		
							Year	County	No.
15405	1	Crowder, George 27	First Named	24	M	1/4	1896	Jackson	2750
	2								
	3								
	4								
	5								
	6								
	7								
	8								
	9								
	10								
	11								
	12								
	13								
	14								
	15								
	16								
	17								

ENROLLMENT
OF NOS. ~~~ 1 ~~~ HEREON
APPROVED BY THE SECRETARY
OF INTERIOR MAY 9 1904

TRIBAL ENROLLMENT OF PARENTS

	Name of Father	Year	County	Name of Mother	Year	Co
1	Thos. C. Crowder	1896	Jackson	Flora Crowder	Dead	Cher
2						
3						
4	Brother of Bolden Crowder Card #1501 Fallis[sic] Card #1456					
5						
6	Mother, a Cherokee, died about twenty years ago					
7	Has never claimed rights in the Cherokee Nation					
8	See if on Cherokee Rolls. No					
9	No1 on 1885 Choctaw Census Roll, Kiamitia Co, No 584.					
10	No1 never applied as a Cherokee nor is his name					
11	on any Cherokee roll: see letter of Cherokee					
12	Land Office of December 12, 1903.					
13	For child of No1 see N.B. (Apr. 26, 1906) Card No.8					
14						
15						
16						
17						

Date of Application for Enrollment.   5/10/99

Choctaw By Blood Enrollment Cards 1898-1914

RESIDENCE: Kiamitia   COUNTY. **Choctaw Nation**   **Choctaw Roll**   CARD No.
POST OFFICE: Goodland, I.T.   *(Not Including Freedmen)*   FIELD No. 1571

Dawes' Roll No.	NAME		Relationship to Person First Named	AGE	SEX	BLOOD	TRIBAL ENROLLMENT		
							Year	County	No.
4438	1 Folsom, Sim	42	First Named	39	M	Full	1896	Kiamitia	4232
4439	2 " Joe	13	Son	10	"	"	1896	"	4233
4440	3 " Frank	8	"	5	"	"	1896	"	4234
	4								
	5								
	6	ENROLLMENT							
	7	OF NOS. 1 – 2 and 3 HEREON APPROVED BY THE SECRETARY							
	8	OF INTERIOR DEC 2 1902							
	9								
	10								
	11								
	12								
	13								
	14								
	15								
	16								
	17								

TRIBAL ENROLLMENT OF PARENTS

	Name of Father	Year	County	Name of Mother	Year	County
1	Lee Folsom	Dead	Kiamitia	Siney Folsom	Dead	Kiamitia
2	No 1			Susan Folsom	"	"
3	No 1			" "	"	"
4						
5						
6	No 1 is now Husband of Lena Watkins, Choc. Card #1773					
7	No3 adopted by Sarah Nohio on Choc Card #1597					
8	For child of No.1 see NB (March 3 1905) #1080					
9						
10						
11						
12						
13						
14						
15						
16					Date of Application for Enrollment	5/10/99
17						

71

Choctaw By Blood Enrollment Cards 1898-1914

RESIDENCE: Kiamitia   COUNTY. **Choctaw Nation**   **Choctaw Roll**   CARD NO.
POST OFFICE: Grant, I.T.   *(Not Including Freedmen)*   FIELD NO. **1572**

Dawes' Roll No.	NAME		Relationship to Person First Named	AGE	SEX	BLOOD	TRIBAL ENROLLMENT		
							Year	County	No.
4441	₁ Wesley, Ben	48	First Named	45	M	Full	1896	Kiamitia	13740
4442	₂ " Viney	50	Wife	47	F	"	1896	"	13741
	3								
	4								
	5								
	6								
	7								
	8								
	9								
	10								
	11	ENROLLMENT OF NOS. 1 and 2 HEREON							
	12	APPROVED BY THE SECRETARY							
	13	OF INTERIOR DEC 12 1902							
	14								
	15								
	16								
	17								

TRIBAL ENROLLMENT OF PARENTS

	Name of Father	Year	County	Name of Mother	Year	County
₁	Fe-cho-po-tubbee	Dead	Cedar	No-wa-ho-ya	Dead	Kiamitia
₂	Ah-che-le-tubbee	"	Kiamitia	Pollie	"	"
3						
4						
5						
6						
7						
8						
9						
10						
11						
12						
13						
14						
15				Date of Application for Enrollment.		
16				5/10/99		
17						

72

Choctaw By Blood Enrollment Cards 1898-1914

RESIDENCE: Kiamitia	COUNTY.	**Choctaw Nation**	Choctaw Roll	CARD NO.	
POST OFFICE: Goodland, I.T.			(Not Including Freedmen)	FIELD NO. 1573	

Dawes' Roll No.	NAME	Relationship to Person First Named	AGE	SEX	BLOOD	TRIBAL ENROLLMENT Year	County	No.
4443	1 Colbert, Nick 30	First Named	27	M	1/8	1896	Kiamitia	2687
	2							
	3							
	4							
	5	ENROLLMENT						
	6	OF NOS. 1 HEREON APPROVED BY THE SECRETARY						
	7	OF INTERIOR DEC 12 1902						
	8							
	9							
	10							
	11							
	12							
	13							
	14							
	15							
	16							
	17							

TRIBAL ENROLLMENT OF PARENTS

	Name of Father	Year	County	Name of Mother	Year	County
1	Dave Colbert	1896	Colored man	Lucinda Maytubbee	Dead	Kiamitia
2						
3						
4						
5						
6						
7						
8						
9						
10						
11						
12						
13						
14						
15					Date of Application for Enrollment 5/10/99	
16						
17	P.O. Nelson, I.T. 12/2 '02					

73

Choctaw By Blood Enrollment Cards 1898-1914

Choctaw Nation

Choctaw Roll (*Not Including Freedmen*)

CARD NO. FIELD NO. 1574

Dawes' Roll No.		NAME	Relationship to Person First Named	AGE	SEX	BLOOD	TRIBAL ENROLLMENT		
							Year	County	No.
4444	1	Elachetubbi, Loman		58	M	Full	1896	Kiamitia	6301
4445	2	" Liney 55	Wife	52	F	"	1896	"	6302
4446	3	" Simelly 16	Ward	13	"	"	1896	"	6305
	4								
	5								
	6								
	7								
	8								
	9								
	10								
	11	ENROLLMENT							
	12	OF NOS. 1 – 2 and 3 HEREON APPROVED BY THE SECRETARY							
	13	OF INTERIOR DEC 12 1902							
	14								
	15								
	16								
	17								

DIED PRIOR TO SEPTEMBER 25, 1902

TRIBAL ENROLLMENT OF PARENTS

	Name of Father	Year	County	Name of Mother	Year	County
1	Elachetubbi	Dead	Blue	Ta-na-pe-hoya	Dead	Kiamitia
2	Chuk-mo-by	"		Ho-te-a-to-na	"	"
3	Lamon Chukmoby	"	Kiamitia	Francey	"	"
4						
5						
6		No1 on 1896 roll as Loman Ilachetubbi				
7		No2 " 1896 " " Lena "				
8		No3 " 1896 " " Simelly "				
9		No1 died March 17, 1901: proof of death filed Dec 8, 1902.				
10		No.2 is now the wife of Franceway Battiest, Choc Card #1918.				
11		No.1 died March 17, 1901: Enrollment cancelled by Department Sept 16 1904				
12						
13						
14						
15				Date of Application for Enrollment.		
16				5/10/99		
17						

Choctaw By Blood Enrollment Cards 1898-1914

RESIDENCE: Jackson   COUNTY. **Choctaw Nation**   **Choctaw Roll** (Not Including Freedmen)   CARD NO.

POST OFFICE: Crowder, I.T.   FIELD NO. 5

Dawes' Roll No.	NAME	Relationship to Person First Named	AGE	SEX	BLOOD	Year	County	
4447	1 Crowder, Eli ²⁵	First Named	22	M	1/2	1893	Jackson	112
	2							
	3							
	4							
	5							
	6							
	7							
	8							
	9							
	10							
	11							
	12							
	13							
	14							
	15							
	16							
	17							

ENROLLMENT
OF NOS. 1 HEREON
APPROVED BY THE SECRETARY
OF INTERIOR DEC 12 1902

TRIBAL ENROLLMENT OF PARENTS

Name of Father	Year	County	Name of Mother	Year	County
1 Josh Crowder	Dead	Jackson	Sibbie Crowder	Dead	Jackson
2					
3					
4	On 1893 Pay roll, Page 13, No 112 Jackson Co				
5	For children of No.1 see NB (March 3, 1905) #1437				
6					
7					
8					
9					
10					
11					
12					
13					
14					
15					
16			Date of Application for Enrollment	5/10/99	
17					

Choctaw By Blood Enrollment Cards 1898-1914

RESIDENCE: Kiamitia   COUNTY. **Choctaw Nation**   **Choctaw Roll** *(Not Including Freedmen)*   CARD NO.
POST OFFICE: Goodland, I.T.   FIELD NO. 1576

Dawes' Roll No.	NAME	Relationship to Person First Named	AGE	SEX	BLOOD	TRIBAL ENROLLMENT		
						Year	County	No.
4448	1 Wilson, Daniel 41	Named	38	M	Full	1896	Kiamitia	13707
4449	2 " Susan 43	Wife	40	F	"	1896	"	13708
4450	3 Billy, Johnson 17	S. Son	14	M	"	1896	"	1416
4451	4 Homma, Joe 20	Ward	17	"	"	1896	"	5786
4452	5 " Nancy 17	"	14	F	"	1896	"	5787
4453	6 Edwards, Benjamin 12	"	9	M	"	1896	"	3766
	7							
	8							
	9							
	10							
	11							
	12							
	13							
	14							
	15							
	16							
	17							

ENROLLMENT
OF NOS. 12345and6 HEREON
APPROVED BY THE SECRETARY
OF INTERIOR DEC 12 1902

TRIBAL ENROLLMENT OF PARENTS

	Name of Father	Year	County	Name of Mother	Year	County
1	Ka-nun-tubbee	Dead	Kiamitia	Amy	Dead	Kiamitia
2	Cohn-sey	"	Towson	Seamey	"	Towson
3	Alexon Billy	"	Cedar	No 2		
4	Impson Homma	"	Kiamitia	Sophia Homma	Dead	Kiamitia
5	" "	"	"	" "	"	"
6	Edwards	"	Towson	Sarah Edwards	"	Towson
7						
8						
9						
10						
11						
12						
13						
14						
15						
16					Date of Application for Enrollment May	
17	P.O. Hugo, I.T. 12/31/02					

Choctaw By Blood Enrollment Cards 1898-1914

RESIDENCE: Kiamitia   COUNTY. **Choctaw Nation**   **Choctaw Roll**   CARD NO.
POST OFFICE: Goodland, I.T.   *(Not Including Freedmen)*   FIELD NO.   1577

Dawes' Roll No.	NAME	Relationship to Person First Named	AGE	SEX	BLOOD	TRIBAL ENROLLMENT		
						Year	County	No.
4454 1	Mihyachubbee, Joseph	45	45	M	Full	1896	Kiamitia	8725
4455 2	~~ED PRIOR TO SEPTEMBER 25, 1940~~ " Sillen	Wife	37	F	"	1896	"	8726
4456 3	" Lizzie 2	Dau	3mo	F	"			
4								
5								
6								
7								
8								
9								
10								
11	ENROLLMENT							
12	OF NOS. 1 2 and 3 HEREON APPROVED BY THE SECRETARY							
13	OF INTERIOR DEC 12 1902							
14								
15								
16								
17								

TRIBAL ENROLLMENT OF PARENTS

	Name of Father	Year	County	Name of Mother	Year	County
1	Mihyachubbie	Dead	Kiamitia	Patsey	Dead	Kiamitia
2	~~Billy Batubbee~~	"	"	~~Ellen Batubbee~~	"	"
3	No.1			No.2		
4						
5			No2 on 1896 roll as Ellen Mihyachubbee			
6						
7			No3 Enrolled January 2 1901			
8						
9			No2 Died Oct. 1901; proof of Death filed Dec 5, 1902.			
10			~~No. 2 died died Oct. 1901; Enrollment cancelled by Department July 8, 1904~~			
11						
12						
13						
14					Date of Application for Enrollment.	
15						
16					5/10/99	
17						

Choctaw By Blood Enrollment Cards 1898-1914

RESIDENCE: **Kiamitia**
POST OFFICE: **Grant, I.T.**

COUNTY. **Choctaw Nation**

Choctaw Roll
(Not Including Freedmen)

CARD NO.
FIELD NO. **1578**

Dawes' Roll No.	NAME	Relationship to Person	AGE	SEX	BLOOD	TRIBAL ENROLLMENT Year	County	No.
4457	1 Wood, Amanda R. ²⁶	First Named	23	F	1/2	1896	Kiamitia	13772
4458	2 " Edgar ¹¹	S Son	7	M	1/4	1895	"	13773
4459	3 " George H. ⁷	Son	3	"	1/4	1895	"	13774
4460	4 " Thomas L ⁶	"	2	"	1/4			
4461	5 " Robert Dewey ³	"	6mo	"	1/4			
I.W. 179	6 " John W.	husband	36	M	I.W.			
	7							
	8 ENROLLMENT							
	9 OF NOS. 1 2 3 4 and 5 HEREON APPROVED BY THE SECRETARY							
	10 OF INTERIOR Dec. 12, 1902							
	11							
	12							
	13							
	14 ENROLLMENT							
	15 OF NOS. ~~ 6 ~~ HEREON APPROVED BY THE SECRETARY							
	16 OF INTERIOR Jun 13, 1903							
	17							

TRIBAL ENROLLMENT OF PARENTS

	Name of Father	Year	County	Name of Mother	Year	County
1	Enoch Brashears	Dead	Kiamitia	Louisa Brashears	Dead	Kiamitia
2	John W. Wood	1896	Intermarried	Jane Wood	"	"
3	" " "	1896	"	No 1		
4	" " "	1896	"	No 1		
5	" " "	1896	"	No 1		
6	William Wood	1896	non citizen	Nannie Wood	1896	non citizen
7						
8	No 3 on 1896 roll as Geo. H. Woods					
9	Surname on 1896 roll as "Woods"					
10						
11	Husband of No 1 John W. Wood on Card No. D.154.					
12	No2 on 1896 Choctaw roll as William Woods, page 361, #13773					
13	Full name of No.2 is William Edgar Woods					
14	No6 transferred from Choctaw Card #D154, see decision of May 1, 1903					
15	For child of No6 see N.B. (March 3,1905) #1091		No5 enrolled 6/5/1900		#1 to 4 inc	
16					Date of Application for Enrollment.	
17					5/10/99	

78

RESIDENCE: Kiamitia	COUNTY.	**Choctaw Nation**	**Choctaw Roll**	CARD NO.	
POST OFFICE: Grant, I.T.			(Not Including Freedmen)	FIELD NO. **1579**	

Dawes' Roll No.	NAME		Relationship to Person First Named	AGE	SEX	BLOOD	TRIBAL ENROLLMENT		
							Year	County	No.
4462	1 Bohanan, Harmon J	32	First Named	29	M	1/4	1896	Kiamitia	1454
DEAD	2 " Julia A		Wife	27	F	I.W.	1896	"	14319
4463	3 " James	14	Son	11	M	1/8	1896	"	1455
4464	4 " Lilie	6	Dau	3	F	1/8	1896	"	1456
I.W. 814	5 " Lula	20	Wife	20	F	I.W.			
	6								
	7	ENROLLMENT							
	8	OF NOS. 1 – 3 and 4 HEREON APPROVED BY THE SECRETARY							
	9	OF INTERIOR Dec 12, 1902							
	10								
	11	No. 2 Hereon dismissed under order of							
	12	the Commission to the Five Civilized Tribes of March 31, 1905.							
	13								
	14								
	15	ENROLLMENT OF NOS. 5 HEREON							
	16	APPROVED BY THE SECRETARY OF INTERIOR May 21, 1904							
	17								

TRIBAL ENROLLMENT OF PARENTS

	Name of Father	Year	County	Name of Mother	Year	County
1	Joshua Bohanan	Dead	Kiamitia	Eliz Bohanan	Dead	Non Citz
2	William Wood	"	Non Citz	Nannie Wood	1896	" "
3	No 1			No 2		
4	No 1			No 2		
5	Fate Grubbs		non citizen	Dolt Wages	Dead	non citizen
6						
7	No1 on 1896 roll as Hermon J. Bohanan.					
8						
9	No certificate of marriage of parents of No 1, but see					
10	testimony of Capt. Peter Maytubby.					
11	No 2 is dead. Died Sept. 12, 1901, proof of death filed April 9, 1902					
12	No1 is now the husband of Lula Bohanan a non-citizen certificate of marriage filed No5 transferred from Choctaw card D 939 April 15, 1904 see decision of March 15, 1904					
13						
14	For child of Nos 1&5 see N.B. (Apr 26 06) #163.				#1 to 4	
15	" " " " " " " (March 3,1905) #1188				Date of Application for Enrollment.	
16	P.O. Hugo I.T. 4/20/05				5/10/99	
17	Clear Creek, I.T.					

March 24, 1902

P.O. Valiant I.T. 11/28 02

Choctaw By Blood Enrollment Cards 1898-1914

RESIDENCE: Kiamitia   COUNTY. **Choctaw Nation**   **Choctaw Roll** *(Not Including Freedmen)*   CARD NO.

POST OFFICE: Goodland, I.T.   FIELD NO. 1580

Dawes' Roll No.	NAME	Relationship to Person First Named	AGE	SEX	BLOOD	TRIBAL ENROLLMENT		
						Year	County	No.
4465	1 Pisachubbe, Eunice 52	Named	49	F	Full	1896	Kiamitia	10432
4466	2 " William H. 19	Son	16	M	"	1896	"	5759
4467	3 " Robert 14	"	11	"	"	1896	"	10433
4468	4 " Edward 20	Ward	17	"	"	1896	"	10434
	5							
	6							
	7							
	8	ENROLLMENT						
	9	OF NOS. 1 2 3 and 4 HEREON APPROVED BY THE SECRETARY						
	10	OF INTERIOR DEC 12 1902						
	11							
	12							
	13							
	14							
	15							
	16							
	17							

TRIBAL ENROLLMENT OF PARENTS

	Name of Father	Year	County	Name of Mother	Year	County
1	Jackson Gardner	Dead	Blue	Viney Gardner	Dead	Blue
2	Joseph Pisachubbe	"	Kiamitia	No 1		
3	" "	"	"	No 1		
4	Simpson Pisachubbe	"	Jackson	Sallie Pisachubbe	Dead	Jackson
5						
6						
7		No2 on 1896 roll as William Harrison				
8		No.4 is Husband of Frances Byington, Choctaw Card 956				
9		For child of No2 see NB (Apr 26 '06) Card No 1203				
10		~~* Duplicate enrollment of No. 4466 not entitled to land or money~~				
11		~~under this number. "See Indian Office of Sept. 2, 1911~~ [remainder illegible]				
12						
13						
14						
15						
16				Date of Application for Enrollment	May 10/99	
17						

RESIDENCE: Kiamitia COUNTY. **Choctaw Nation** Choctaw Roll CARD NO.
POST OFFICE: Nelson, I.T. (Not Including Freedmen) FIELD NO. **1581**

Dawes' Roll No.	NAME		Relationship to Person First Named	AGE	SEX	BLOOD	TRIBAL ENROLLMENT		
							Year	County	No.
4469	1 Nelson, Silvey	43	First Named	40	F	Full	1896	Kiamitia	9761
4470	2 " Simon	17	Son	14	M	"	1896	"	9762
4471	3 " George	13	"	10	"	"	1896	"	9763
4472	4 " Elsie	11	Dau	8	F	"	1896	"	9764
4473	5 Edwards, Josephine		"	3	"	"	1896	"	3810
	6								
	7								
	8								
	9								
	10								
	11								
	12								
	13								
	14								
	15								
	16								
	17								

DIED PRIOR TO SEPTEMBER 25, 1902

ENROLLMENT
OF NOS. 1 2 3 4 and 5 THEREON
APPROVED BY THE SECRETARY
OF INTERIOR Dec. 12, 1902

TRIBAL ENROLLMENT OF PARENTS

	Name of Father	Year	County	Name of Mother	Year	County
1	Jackson Frazier	Dead	Jackson	Sarah Frazier	Dead	Jackson
2	Alfred Nelson	"	Kiamitia	No 1		
3	" "	"	"	No 1		
4	" "	"	"	No 1		
5	Ben Edwards		Sans Bois	No 1		
6						
7						
8						
9						
10						
11						
12			No 5 on 1896 roll as Josephine Edward			
13						
14			No 5 died July 10, 1899, proof of death filed Dec. 5, 1902			
15			No 5 died July 10, 1899; Enrollment cancelled by Department July 8, 1904.			
16					May 10/99	
17						

Choctaw By Blood Enrollment Cards 1898-1914

iamitia   COUNTY. **Choctaw Nation**   **Choctaw Roll**   CARD No.
Antlers, I.T.   *(Not Including Freedmen)*   FIELD No. 1582

Dawes' Roll No.	NAME		Relationship to Person First Named	AGE	SEX	BLOOD	TRIBAL ENROLLMENT		
							Year	County	No.
4474	1 Davis, Jefferson	59		56	M	Full	1896	Jacks Fork	3635
4475	2 " Susan	50	Wife	47	F	"	1896	" "	3636
4476	3 " Sissy	20	Dau	17	"	"	1896	" "	3634
	4								
	5								
	6								
	7								
	8								
	9								
	10								
	11	ENROLLMENT							
	12	OF NOS. 1 – 2 and 3 HEREON APPROVED BY THE SECRETARY							
	13	OF INTERIOR DEC 12 1902							
	14								
	15								
	16								
	17								

TRIBAL ENROLLMENT OF PARENTS

	Name of Father	Year	County	Name of Mother	Year	
1	George Davis	Dead	Kiamitia	Alo-ma-chi-hoya	Dead	
2	John Balatubbee	"	Cedar	Hol-ba-to-na	"	
3	No 1			Cillin Davis	"	
4						
5						
6	For child of No 3 see NB (Apr 26-06) Card #837					
7						
8						
9						
10						
11						
12						
13						
14				Date of Application for Enrollment.		
15				May 10 99		
16						
17	P.O. Hamden I.T 12/3/02					

RESIDENCE: Kiamitia   COUNTY. **Choctaw Nation**   **Choctaw Roll**   CARD NO.
POST OFFICE: Grant, I.T.   *(Not Including Freedmen)*   FIELD NO. 1583

Dawes' Roll No.	NAME	Relationship to Person First Named	AGE	SEX	BLOOD	TRIBAL ENROLLMENT Year	County	No.
4477	1 Abels, Henrietta E ²⁷	First Named	24	F	1/4	1896	Kiamitia	343
4478	2 " Margaret F ⁶	Dau	3	"	1/8	1896	"	344
4479	3 " Edward M ⁴	Son	8mo	M	1/8			
4480	4 " Lucile Belvin ²	Dau	6mo	F	1/8			
	5							
	6							
	7							
	8							
	9							
	10							
	11	ENROLLMENT OF NOS. 1 2 3 and 4 HEREON						
	12	APPROVED BY THE SECRETARY						
	13	OF INTERIOR DEC 12 1902						
	14							
	15							
	16							
	17							

TRIBAL ENROLLMENT OF PARENTS

	Name of Father	Year	County	Name of Mother	Year	County
1	Charles Oakes	1896	Kiamitia	Judith Oakes	Dead	Kiamitia
2	J. D. Abels	1896	Non Citz	No 1		
3	" "	1896	" "	No 1		
4	" "	1896	" "	No.1		
5						
6						
7			No1 on 1896 roll as Henrietta A. Abel			
8			No2 " 1896 " " Margaret "			
9			No4 Enrolled May 17, 1901			
10						
11						
12						
13						
14					Date of Application for Enrollment.	
15						
16					Date of Application for Enrollment. 5/10/99	
17						

Choctaw By Blood Enrollment Cards 1898-1914

RESIDENCE: Kiamitia   COUNTY. **Choctaw Nation**   **Choctaw Roll**   CARD No.

POST OFFICE: Goodland, I.T.   (Not Including Freedmen)   FIELD No. 1584

Dawes' Roll No.	NAME	Relationship to Person First Named	AGE	SEX	BLOOD	TRIBAL ENROLLMENT Year	County	No.
4481	1 McCann, Sam 44	First Named	41	M	Full	1896	Kiamitia	9396
4482	2 " Sallie 38	Wife	35	F	"	1896	"	9397
4483	3 " Wallace 9	Son	6	M	"	1896	"	9399
4484	4 " Willie 17	Ward	14	"	"	1896	"	9400
	5							
	6							
	7							
	8							
	9							
	10							
	11	ENROLLMENT						
	12	OF NOS. 1 2 3 and 4 HEREON APPROVED BY THE SECRETARY						
	13	OF INTERIOR DEC 12 1902						
	14							
	15							
	16							
	17							

TRIBAL ENROLLMENT OF PARENTS

	Name of Father	Year	County	Name of Mother	Year	County
1	Wallace McCann	Dead	Kiamitia	Martha McCann	Dead	Red River
2	Nicholas Battiest	"	Red River		"	" " "
3	No 1			No 2		
4		Dead			Dead	
5						
6						
7	Parents of No 4 died when he was an infant Names unknown					
8						
9						
10						
11						
12						
13						
14					Date of Application for Enrollment.	
15						
16					5/10/99	
17						

Choctaw By Blood Enrollment Cards 1898-1914

RESIDENCE: Kiamitia   COUNTY. **Choctaw Nation**   **Choctaw Roll**   CARD No.
POST OFFICE: Hampton, I.T.   *(Not Including Freedmen)*   FIELD No. **1585**

Dawes' Roll No.	NAME	Relationship to Person First Named	AGE	SEX	BLOOD	TRIBAL ENROLLMENT Year	County	No.
4485	1 Fulsom, Ellis 22	First Named	19	M	Full	1896	Kiamitia	4253
4486	2 Anchahubbi, David 17	Bro	14	"	"	1896	"	357
4487	3 " Aaron 14	"	11	"	"	1896	"	358
4488	4 " Sampson 8	"	5	"	"	1896	"	359
	5							
	6							
	7 ENROLLMENT							
	8 OF NOS. 1 2 3 and 4 HEREON APPROVED BY THE SECRETARY							
	9 OF INTERIOR Dec. 12, 1902							
	10							
	11							
	12							
	13							
	14							
	15							
	16							
	17							

TRIBAL ENROLLMENT OF PARENTS

	Name of Father	Year	County	Name of Mother	Year	County
1	Jacob Fulsom	Dead		Isabelle Fulsom	Dead	Kiamitia
2	Louis Anchahubbi	"	Kiamitia	" "	"	"
3	" "	"	"	" "	"	"
4	" "	"	"	" "	"	"
5						
6						
7						
8						
9						
10						
11						
12						
13						
14						
15						
16				Date of Application for Enrollment		
17				5/10/99		

Choctaw By Blood Enrollment Cards 1898-1914

RESIDENCE: Kiamitia   COUNTY. **Choctaw Nation**   **Choctaw Roll** *(Not Including Freedmen)*   CARD NO.
POST OFFICE: Grant, I.T.   FIELD NO. **1586**

Dawes' Roll No.	NAME	Relationship to Person First Named	AGE	SEX	BLOOD	TRIBAL ENROLLMENT		
						Year	County	No.
4489	1 Jacob, Elias 38	First Named	35	M	Full	1896	Kiamitia	7073
4490	2 " Cordelia 37	Wife	34	F	"	1896	"	7074
4491	3 Spring, Mollie 19	Dau	16	"	"	1896	"	7075
4492	4 Jacob, Margaret 14	"	11	"	"	1896	"	7076
4493	5 " Joseph 13	Son	10	M	"	1896	"	7077
4494	6 " Roxie 5	Dau	1	F	"			
4495	7 ~~DIED PRIOR TO SEPTEMBER 25, 1902~~ Fannie	~~Dau~~	~~3mo~~	F	"			
4496	8 Spring, Joshuaway 1	Grandson	2mo	M	7/8			
4497	9 ~~DIED PRIOR TO SEPTEMBER 25, 1902~~ Jacob, Josephine	~~Dau~~	~~2mo~~	F	Full			
	10							
	11							
	12	ENROLLMENT OF NOS. 12345678and9 HEREON						
	13	APPROVED BY THE SECRETARY						
	14	OF INTERIOR DEC 12 1902						
	15							
	16							
	17							

TRIBAL ENROLLMENT OF PARENTS

	Name of Father	Year	County	Name of Mother	Year	County
1	John Jacob	Dead	Kiamitia	Fannie Jacob	Dead	Kiamitia
2	Washington Nelson	"	"	Martha Nelson	"	"
3	No 1			No 2		
4	No 1			No 2		
5	No 1			No 2		
6	No 1			No 2		
7	~~No 1~~			~~No 2~~		
8	Eli Spring	1896	Kiamitia	No.3		
9	~~No. 1~~			~~No. 2~~		
10						
11			No2 on 1896 roll as Cordella Jacob			
12	~~No.7 died -- 1900: No.9 died April - 1901: Enrollment cancelled by Department July 8, 1904~~					
13			No.7 Enrolled June 23d, 1900			
14			No.3 is now the wife of Eli Spring on Choctaw card #1399, Dec. 12, 1901		#1 to 6	
15			No.8 born Oct. 2d, 1901: Enrolled Dec. 12, 1901.		Date of Application for Enrollment	
16			No.9 born Oct. 20, 1901: Enrolled Dec. 27, 1901. No 7 died in 1900; proof of death filed Dec 6, 1902.		5/11/99	
17			No 9 " April,1907; " " " " " "			

For child of No.4 see NB(March 3,1905) #1091.
   "   "   " No 3 "   " 86 "   "   " #1194

Choctaw By Blood Enrollment Cards 1898-1914

Dawes' Roll No.	NAME	Relationship to Person First Named	AGE	SEX	BLOOD	TRIBAL ENROLLMENT		
						Year	County	No.
4498	1 Christie, Sim 35	First Named	32	M	Full	1896	Kiamitia	2716
4499	2 " Lottie 36	Wife	33	F	"	1896	"	13779
4500	3 Williams, Emma 19	S. Dau	16	"	"	1896	"	13780
4501	4 " Maxey 14	S. Son	11	M	"	1896	"	13781
14682	5 Christie, Catharine 1	Dau of No 3	4mo	F	"			
	6							
	7							
	8							
	9							
	10							
	11							
	12							
	13							
	14							
	15							
	16							
	17							

ENROLLMENT
OF NOS. 1 2 3 and 4 HEREON
APPROVED BY THE SECRETARY
OF INTERIOR DEC 12 1902

ENROLLMENT
OF NOS. 5 HEREON
APPROVED BY THE SECRETARY
OF INTERIOR MAY 29 1903

TRIBAL ENROLLMENT OF PARENTS

Name of Father	Year	County	Name of Mother	Year	County
1 Louis Christie	Dead	Kiamitia	Levina Christie	Dead	Kiamitia
2 Joseph	"	"	Lainey	"	"
3 Tommie Williams	"	"	No 2		
4 " "	"	"	No 2		
5 Sim Christie			No 3		
6					
7 No 2 on 1896 roll as Lottie Williams					
8 No.2 also on 1896 Choctaw roll as Mollie Christie; page 65; #2717					
9 No5 born August 1, 1902: enrolled Dec. 9, 1902					
For child of Nos 1&2 see N B (Apr 26-06) Card #836					
10 " " " Nos 1&3 " " " " " "					
11					
12					
13					
14					
15				#1 to 4	
16			Date of Application for Enrollment.		5/11/99
17 P.O. Hugo, I.T.					

Choctaw By Blood Enrollment Cards 1898-1914

Dawes' Roll No.	NAME		Relationship to Person	AGE	SEX	BLOOD	TRIBAL ENROLLMENT		
							Year	County	No.
4502	1 Oakes, Charles D	61	First Named	58	M	1/8	1896	Kiamitia	9978
I.W. 82	2 " Margaret A	35	Wife	32	F	I.W.	1896	"	14913
4503	3 " Christopher	18	Son	15	M	1/4	1896	"	9980
4504	4 " Annie M	16	Dau	13	F	1/4	1896	"	9962
4505	5 " William W	12	Son	9	M	1/16	1896	"	9981
4506	6 " Henry F	10	"	7	"	1/16	1896	"	9982
4507	7 " Levana F	8	Dau	5	F	1/16	1896	"	9983
4508	8 " Laura B	6	"	3	"	1/16	1896	"	9989
4509	9 " Hamet	2	Dau	1mo	F	1/16			
4510	10 " Albert O.	1	Son	5mo	M	1/16			
	11								
	12	ENROLLMENT							
	13	OF NOS. 13456789 and 10 HEREON APPROVED BY THE SECRETARY							
	14	OF INTERIOR DEC 12 1902							
	15	ENROLLMENT OF NOS. ~~~ 2 ~~~ HEREON APPROVED BY THE SECRETARY							
	16	OF INTERIOR JUN 13 1903							
	17								

TRIBAL ENROLLMENT OF PARENTS

	Name of Father	Year	County	Name of Mother	Year	County
1	Thos. W. Oakes	Dead	Non Citz	Harriet N. Oakes	1896	Kiamitia
2	W. C. Bucanan	1896	" "	Ellen Bucanan	1896	Non Citz
3	No 1			Judia Oakes	Dead	Kiamitia
4	No 1			" "	"	"
5	No 1			No 2		
6	No 1			No 2		
7	No 1			No 2		
8	No 1			No 2		
9	No.1			No.2		
10	Nº1			Nº2		
11	No1 on 1896 roll as Chas. D. Oakes					
12	No2 " 1896 " " Margaret "					
13	No4 " 1896 " " Annie " No5 " 1896 " " Wm W. "			For child of Nos 1&2 see NB (March 3,1905) #1079[?]		
14	No6 " 1896 " " Henry "					
15	No7 " 1896 " " Savanna "					#1 to 8 inc
16	No.9 Enrolled Aug. 6th, 1900. Nº10 Born Dec. 12, 1901. enrolled May 19, 1902.				Date of Application for Enrollment.	5/11/99
17						

Choctaw By Blood Enrollment Cards 1898-1914

RESIDENCE: Kiamitia   COUNTY. **Choctaw Nation**   **Choctaw Roll**   CARD NO.
POST OFFICE: Nelson, I.T.   *(Not Including Freedmen)*   FIELD NO. **1589**

Dawes' Roll No.	NAME	Relationship to Person First Named	AGE	SEX	BLOOD	TRIBAL ENROLLMENT Year	TRIBAL ENROLLMENT County	TRIBAL ENROLLMENT No.
4511	1 Harrison, Sim ⁵⁴	First Named	51	M	3/4	1896	Kiamitia	5765
4512	2 Sinie DIED PRIOR TO SEPTEMBER 25, 1945	Wife	42	F	1/4	1896	"	5766
4513	3 " James H. ¹³	Son	10	M	1/2	1896	"	5770
	4							
	5							
	6							
	7							
	8	ENROLLMENT						
	9	OF NOS. 1 2 and 3 HEREON APPROVED BY THE SECRETARY						
	10	OF INTERIOR Dec. 12, 1902						
	11							
	12							
	13							
	14							
	15							
	16							
	17							

TRIBAL ENROLLMENT OF PARENTS

	Name of Father	Year	County	Name of Mother	Year	County
1	Henry Harrison	Dead	Kiamitia	Bettie Harrison	Dead	Kiamitia
2	Wᵐ Smallwood	1896	"	Sis Smallwood	1896	"
3	No 1			No 2		
4						
5						
6			No 3 on 1896 roll as Jimmie Harrison			
7						
8			No 2 died January 25, 1902: proof of death filed Dec. 5, 1902			
9			No.2 died Jan. 25, 1902: Enrollment cancelled by Department July 8, 1904.			
10						
11						
12						
13						
14					Date of Application for Enrollment.	
15						
16					5/11/99	
17	P.O. Hugo, I.T. 3/2/03					

Choctaw By Blood Enrollment Cards 1898-1914

RESIDENCE: Kiamitia   COUNTY. **Choctaw Nation**   **Choctaw Roll**   CARD NO.
POST OFFICE: Grant, I.T.   *(Not Including Freedmen)*   FIELD NO. 1590

Dawes' Roll No.	NAME	Relationship to Person First Named	AGE	SEX	BLOOD	TRIBAL ENROLLMENT Year	TRIBAL ENROLLMENT County	TRIBAL ENROLLMENT No.
4514	1 Oakes, George W. ²²	First Named	19	M	1/4	1896	Kiamitia	9974
I.W. 993	2 " Rosa E. ²²	Wife	19	F	I.W.	1896	"	14917
4515	3 " Beulah B. ⁵	Dau	16mo	"	1/8			
	4							
	5							
	6							
	7	ENROLLMENT OF NOS. 1 and 3 HEREON						
	8	APPROVED BY THE SECRETARY						
	9	OF INTERIOR Dec. 12, 1902						
	10							
	11	Take no further action relative to enrollment of No2						
	12	Protest of Attys for Choctaw and Cherokee Nations						
	13			Jan 23 04				
	14	ENROLLMENT OF NOS. ~2~ HEREON						
	15	APPROVED BY THE SECRETARY OF INTERIOR Oct. 21, 1904						
	16							
	17							

TRIBAL ENROLLMENT OF PARENTS

	Name of Father	Year	County	Name of Mother	Year	County
1	Chas D. Oakes	1896	Kiamitia	Judie Oakes	Dead	Kiamitia
2	W. C. Bucanan	1896	Non Citz	Ellen Bucanan	1896	Non Citz
3	No 1			No 2		
4						
5						
6	No 1 on 1896 roll as Geo. W. Oakes					
7	No 2 " 1896 " " Rosa "					
8	For child of Nos 1&2 see N.B. (March 3, 1905) #1149					
9	Decision signed by Com before Protest was received retd to jacket Feb. 17 '04					
10						
11						
12						
13						
14					Date of Application for Enrollment.	
15						
16					5/11/99	
17	P.O. Hamden I.T. 4/17/05					

Choctaw By Blood Enrollment Cards 1898-1914

RESIDENCE: Kiamitia   COUNTY. **Choctaw Nation**   **Choctaw Roll**   CARD NO.
POST OFFICE: Grant, I.T.   *(Not Including Freedmen)*   FIELD NO. 1591

Dawes' Roll No.	NAME		Relationship to Person	AGE	SEX	BLOOD	TRIBAL ENROLLMENT		
							Year	County	No.
4516	1 Oakes, John E	30	First Named	27	M	1/4	1896	Kiamitia	9984
I.W. 83	2 " Annie	30	Wife	27	F	I.W.	1896	"	14914
4517	3 " Thomas C	12	Son	9	M	1/8	1896	"	9985
4518	4 " Susan M	9	Dau	6	F	1/8	1896	"	9986
4519	5 " Nora M	6	"	3	"	1/8	1896	"	9987
4520	6 " Emma M	4	"	5mo	"	1/8			
	7								
	8								
	9								
	10								
	11	ENROLLMENT							
	12	OF NOS. 1 3 4 5 and 6 HEREON APPROVED BY THE SECRETARY							
	13	OF INTERIOR DEC 12 1902							
	14	ENROLLMENT OF NOS. 2 ~~~~ HEREON							
	15	APPROVED BY THE SECRETARY OF INTERIOR JUN 13 1903							
	16								
	17								

TRIBAL ENROLLMENT OF PARENTS

	Name of Father	Year	County	Name of Mother	Year	County
1	Chas. D. Oakes	1896	Kiamitia	Judie Oakes	Dead	Kiamitia
2	J. R. Reynolds	Dead	Non Citz	Sarah Reynolds	"	Non Citz
3	No 1			No 2		
4	No 1			No 2		
5	No 1			No 2		
6	No 1			No 2		
7						
8		No 1 on 1896 roll as John Oakes				
9		No 3 " 1896 " " Thos W. "				
10		No 4 " 1896 " " Susan "				
11						
12						
13						
14					Date of Application for Enrollment.	
15					5/11/99	
16						
17						

Choctaw By Blood Enrollment Cards 1898-1914

RESIDENCE: Kiamitia COUNTY. **Choctaw Nation** Choctaw Roll *(Not Including Freedmen)* CARD NO. FIELD NO. 1592

FICE: Grant, I.T.

NAME	Relationship to Person First Named	AGE	SEX	BLOOD	TRIBAL ENROLLMENT		
					Year	County	No.
1 Willis, Reuben 27	First Named	24	M	Full	1896	Kiamitia	13752
2							
3							
4							
5							
6							
7	ENROLLMENT						
8	OF NOS. 1 HEREON APPROVED BY THE SECRETARY						
9	OF INTERIOR DEC 12 1902						
10							
11							
12							
13							
14							
15							
16							
17							

TRIBAL ENROLLMENT OF PARENTS

Name of Father	Year	County	Name of Mother	Year	County
1 Eden Willis	Dead	Towson	Siney Willis	Dead	Towson
2					
3					
4					
5					
6	No.1 lives with No.1 on Choc. Card #1576				
7					
8					
9					
10					
11					
12					
13					
14					
15					
16				5/11/99	
17					

Choctaw By Blood Enrollment Cards 1898-1914

RESIDENCE: Kiamitia   COUNTY. **Choctaw Nation**   **Choctaw Roll**   CARD NO.

POST OFFICE: Grant, I.T.   *(Not Including Freedmen)*   FIELD NO. 1593

Dawes' Roll No.	NAME	Relationship to Person First Named	AGE	SEX	BLOOD	TRIBAL ENROLLMENT		
						Year	County	No.
4522	1 Wood, Ellis ⁴⁸	First Named	45	M	Full	1896	Kiamitia	13704
I.W.**815**	2 LeFlore, Carrie ⁶⁹	Wife	66	F	I.W.	1896	"	14769
4523	3 Wood, Edgar ⑩	Son	7	M	Full	1896	"	13705
	4							
	5	ENROLLMENT						
	6	OF NOS. 1 and 3 HEREON						
	7	APPROVED BY THE SECRETARY OF INTERIOR DEC 12 1902						
	8							
	9	ENROLLMENT						
	10	OF NOS. 2 HEREON						
	11	APPROVED BY THE SECRETARY OF INTERIOR MAY 21 1904						
	12							
	13							
	14							
	15							
	16							
	17							

TRIBAL ENROLLMENT OF PARENTS

Name of Father	Year	County	Name of Mother	Year	County
1 Sam Wood	Dead	Kiamitia	Ela-ho-tu-naq	Dead	Kiamitia
2 Chas. G Gooding	"	Non Citz	Esther Gooding	"	Non Citz
3 No 1			Agnes Wood	"	Kiamitia
4					
5					
6					
7					
8					
9					
10	No 1 on 1896 roll as Ellis Woods				
11	No 2 " 1896 " " Carrie LeFlore				
12	No 3 " 1896 " " Edgar Woods				
13					
14	Parents of No 2 could not be ascertained				
15	No.2 was divorced from No. 1, Aug. 20th, 1900 and given				Date of Application for Enrollment.
16	her name prior to said marriage, Carrie LeFlore: see bill of divorce filed this date Dec. 6, 1900				5/11/99
17	Evidence of marriage of No.2 and Basil L. LeFlore filed Jany. 21ˢᵗ, 1901.				

Choctaw By Blood Enrollment Cards 1898-1914

RESIDENCE:	Kiamitia	COUNTY.	Choctaw Nation	Choctaw Roll	CARD No.	
POST OFFICE:	Hampton, I.T.			(Not Including Freedmen)	FIELD No.	1594

Dawes' Roll No.	NAME (Hamden)		Relationship to Person First Named	AGE	SEX	BLOOD	TRIBAL ENROLLMENT		
							Year	County	No.
4524	1 Loman, Clay	49	First Named	46	M	Full	1896	Kiamitia	8091
4525	2 " Sillen	46	Wife	43	F	"	1896	"	8092
4526	3 Wilken	14	Son	11	M	"	1896	"	8093
4527	4 Nelson, Joe	26	S. Son	23	"	"	1896	"	9753
	5								
	6								
	7	ENROLLMENT							
	8	OF NOS. 1 2 3 and 4 HEREON APPROVED BY THE SECRETARY							
	9	OF INTERIOR Dec. 12, 1902							
	10								
	11								
	12								
	13								
	14								
	15								
	16								
	17								

TRIBAL ENROLLMENT OF PARENTS

	Name of Father	Year	County	Name of Mother	Year	County
1	James Loman	Dead	Cedar	Mary Thomas	Dead	Jacks Fork
2	Thompson Collin	"	Skullyville	Miley Gibson	"	Kiamitia
3	No 1			No 2		
4	Gabriel Nelson	1896	Kiamitia	No 2		
5						
6						
7			No2 on 1896 roll as Sarah Loman			
8			No3 " 1896 " Ben "			
9						
10						
11						
12						
13						
14						
15						
16				Date of Application for Enrollment		5/11/99
17	P.O. No.3 Antlers I.T. 2/15/07					

Choctaw By Blood Enrollment Cards 1898-1914

RESIDENCE: Wade   COUNTY.   **Choctaw Nation**   **Choctaw Roll** *(Not Including Freedmen)*   CARD NO.

POST OFFICE: Goodland, I.T.   FIELD NO. 1595

Dawes' Roll No.	NAME	Relationship to Person First Named	AGE	SEX	BLOOD	TRIBAL ENROLLMENT		
						Year	County	No.
4528	1 Wade, Julia 23	First Named	20	F	1/4	1896	Wade	13111
4529	2 " , Alberta 3	Dau	1 1/2	F	1/8			
12	3 Charley, Nellie							
	4							
	5							
	6							
	7							
	8							
	9							
	10							
	11	ENROLLMENT						
	12	OF NOS. 1 and 2 HEREON APPROVED BY THE SECRETARY						
	13	OF INTERIOR DEC 12 1902						
	14							
	15							
	16							
	17							

TRIBAL ENROLLMENT OF PARENTS

	Name of Father	Year	County	Name of Mother	Year	County
1	Gilbert Wade	Dead	Wade	Lydia Wade	Dead	Sugar Loaf
2	Unknown			No. 1		
3	Lard Charley			No. 1		Born Nov. 24 – 05
4						
5			On 1896 roll as Julia A. Wade			
6			No.2 Enrolled February 12, 1901			
7			For child of No.1, see N.B. (Apr. 26, 1906) Card No. 12.			
8						
9			No. 2 Died prior to September 25, 1902; not entitled to land or money.			
10			See Indian Office Letter April 20, 1908. (I.T. 19828 – 1908)			
11						
12						
13						
14						
15						
16				Date of Application for Enrollment		5/11/99
17						

Choctaw By Blood Enrollment Cards 1898-1914

RESIDENCE: Kiamitia   COUNTY.   **Choctaw Nation**   **Choctaw Roll**   CARD No.

POST OFFICE: Goodland, I.T.   *(Not Including Freedmen)*   FIELD No.   1596

Dawes' Roll No.		NAME	Relationship to Person First Named	AGE	SEX	BLOOD	TRIBAL ENROLLMENT		
							Year	County	No.
14027	1	Thomas, Lucinda		54	F	Full	1896	Kiamitia	12355
	2								
	3								
	4								
	5								
	6								
	7								
	8								
	9								
	10								
	11								
	12								
	13								
	14								
	15								
	16								
	17								

DIED PRIOR TO SEPTEMBER 25, 1902

ENROLLMENT OF NOS. ~ 1 ~ HEREON APPROVED BY THE SECRETARY OF INTERIOR   OCT 15 1903

TRIBAL ENROLLMENT OF PARENTS

	Name of Father	Year	County	Name of Mother	Year	County
1	Henry Martin	Dead	Kiamitia	Koneotuna	Dead	Kiamitia
2						
3						
4						
5						
6	No 1 died before Sept 25, 1902: Enrollment cancelled by Department May 2, 1906					
7						
8						
9						
10						
11						
12						
13						
14						
15						
16					Date of Application for Enrollment	5/11/99
17						

1893 Kiamitia   Page 112 - No 908

Choctaw By Blood Enrollment Cards 1898-1914

RESIDENCE: Kiamitia
POST OFFICE: Goodland, I.T.

COUNTY. **Choctaw Nation**

Choctaw Roll *(Not Including Freedmen)*

CARD NO.
FIELD NO. 1597

Dawes' Roll No.	NAME		Relationship to Person First Named	AGE	SEX	BLOOD	TRIBAL ENROLLMENT		
							Year	County	No.
4530	1 Nohio, Thompson	70	First Named	67	M	Full	1896	Kiamitia	9739
4531	2 " Sarah	53	Wife	50	F	"	1896	"	9740
4532	3 " Harrison	21	Son	18	M	"	1896	"	9741
	4								
	5								
	6								
	7	ENROLLMENT							
	8	OF NOS. 1 – 2 and 3 HEREON APPROVED BY THE SECRETARY							
	9	OF INTERIOR DEC 12 1902							
	10								
	11								
	12								
	13								
	14								
	15								
	16								
	17								

TRIBAL ENROLLMENT OF PARENTS

	Name of Father	Year	County	Name of Mother	Year	County
1	No-hi-o	Dead	Towson	Rachel Nihio	Dead	Towson
2	Num-pul-le	"	Jackson		"	Jackson
3	No 1			No 2		
4						
5						
6						
7						
8						
9						
10						
11						
12			No 3 is Husband of No 3 on Choctaw Card #1747			
13						
14						
15					Date of Application for Enrollment	5/11/99
16						
17	P.O. Hugo, I.T. 12/3, '02					

Choctaw By Blood Enrollment Cards 1898-1914

RESIDENCE: Kiamitia   COUNTY. **Choctaw Nation**   **Choctaw Roll**   CARD NO.
POST OFFICE: Goodland, I.T   (Not Including Freedmen)   FIELD NO. 1598

Dawes' Roll No.	NAME	Relationship to Person First Named	AGE	SEX	BLOOD	TRIBAL ENROLLMENT		
						Year	County	No.
4533	1 Lawachubbee, Saffie		69	F	Full	1896	Kiamitia	8081
	2							
	3							
	4							
	5							
	6							
	7							
	8							
	9							
	10							
	11							
	12							
	13							
	14							
	15							
	16							
	17							

ENROLLMENT
OF NOS. 1 HEREON
APPROVED BY THE SECRETARY
OF INTERIOR DEC 12 1902

TRIBAL ENROLLMENT OF PARENTS

	Name of Father	Year	County	Name of Mother	Year	County
1	Po-li-cha	Dead	in Mississippi	To-pu-na	Dead	in Mississippi
2						
3						
4						
5						
6						
7						
8	No 1 died in 1900; Enrollment cancelled by Department May 2, 1906					
9						
10						
11						
12						
13						
14						
15						
16					Date of Application for Enrollment	5/11/99
17						

Choctaw By Blood Enrollment Cards 1898-1914

RESIDENCE: Kiamitia   COUNTY. **Choctaw Nation**   **Choctaw Roll** (Not Including Freedmen)   CARD NO.

POST OFFICE: Antlers, I.T.   FIELD NO. **1599**

Dawes' Roll No.	NAME	Relationship to Person	AGE	SEX	BLOOD	TRIBAL ENROLLMENT Year	County	No.
4534	1 Billy, John 27	First Named	24	M	Full	1896	Kiamitia	1443
4535	2 " Louisiana 30	Wife	27	F	"	1893	Cedar	145
15976	3 " Josiah 1	Son	1	M	"			
	4							
	5							
	6							
	7	ENROLLMENT						
	8	OF NOS. 1 and 2 HEREON APPROVED BY THE SECRETARY						
	9	OF INTERIOR Dec 12 1902						
	10							
	11							
	12							
	13							
	14	ENROLLMENT						
	15	OF NOS. ~~~ 3 ~~~ HEREON APPROVED BY THE SECRETARY						
	16	OF INTERIOR Jun 16 1906						
	17							

TRIBAL ENROLLMENT OF PARENTS

	Name of Father	Year	County	Name of Mother	Year	County
1	Billy	Dead	Kiamitia	Ellen Billy	Dead	Kiamitia
2	Louis Edward	"	Towson	Sallie Edward	"	Towson
3	No 1			No 2		
4						
5	No2 on 1893 Pay roll as Louisana Edward, Page 13, No 145, Cedar Co					
6						
7						
8						
9	No3 born Aug 7, 1901. Proof of birth filed March 14, 1906					
10	Proof of birth of No.3 to be supplied No proof Aug 4 04					
11	No3 [sic] Granted Apr 24 1906					
12						
13						
14						
15					No 3 enrolled Dec 24, 1902.	
16				Date of Application for Enrollment	5/11/99	
17						

99

Choctaw By Blood Enrollment Cards 1898-1914

RESIDENCE: Kiamitia   COUNTY. **Choctaw Nation**   **Choctaw Roll** CARD NO.
POST OFFICE: Antlers, I.T.   (Not Including Freedmen)   FIELD NO. 1600

Dawes' Roll No.	NAME		Relationship to Person	AGE	SEX	BLOOD	TRIBAL ENROLLMENT		
							Year	County	No.
4536	1 Billy, Isabelle	29	First Named	26	F	Full	1896	Kiamitia	1444
4537	2 " Jimanna	19	Sister	16	"	"	1896	"	1445
	3								
	4								
	5								
	6								
	7								
	8								
	9								
	10								
	11	ENROLLMENT							
	12	OF NOS. 1 and 2 HEREON APPROVED BY THE SECRETARY							
	13	OF INTERIOR DEC 12 1902							
	14								
	15								
	16								
	17								

TRIBAL ENROLLMENT OF PARENTS

	Name of Father	Year	County	Name of Mother	Year	County
1	Billy	Dead	Kiamitia	Ellen Billy	Dead	Kiamitia
2	"	"	"	" "	"	"
3						
4						
5						
6						
7						
8						
9						
10						
11						
12						
13						
14						
15						
16				Date of Application for Enrollment		5/11/99
17						

Choctaw By Blood Enrollment Cards 1898-1914

RESIDENCE: Kiamitia COUNTY. **Choctaw Nation** **Choctaw Roll** CARD NO.
POST OFFICE: Goodland, I.T. *(Not Including Freedmen)* FIELD NO. **1601**

Dawes' Roll No.	NAME	Relationship to Person	AGE	SEX	BLOOD	TRIBAL ENROLLMENT		
						Year	County	No.
I.W. 1391	1 Harris, Cyrus L 34	First Named	31	M	I.W.	1896	Kiamitia	14640
	2							
	3							
	4							
	5							
	6							
	7							
	8							
	9							
	10							
	11	ENROLLMENT OF NOS. 1 HEREON APPROVED BY THE SECRETARY OF INTERIOR Mar 14 1905						
	12							
	13							
	14							
	15							
	16							
	17							

TRIBAL ENROLLMENT OF PARENTS

	Name of Father	Year	County	Name of Mother	Year	County
1	Robert C. Harris	Dead	Non Citz	Sopha Harris	Dead	Non Citz
2						
3						
4						
5						
6		No.1 formerly husband of Mary J Harris (nee Oakes)				
7		1893 Kiamitia, No. 552, and who died Feb. 6, 1896.				
8		For children of No 1 see N B (Apr 26 '06) #1115				
9						
10						
11						
12						
13						
14						
15					Date of Application for Enrollment.	
16	P.O. Soper I.T. 2/22/05				5/11/99	
17	P.O. Atlas I.T 12/29/04					

101

Choctaw By Blood Enrollment Cards 1898-1914

RESIDENCE: Kiamitia	COUNTY. **Choctaw Nation**	**Choctaw Roll** (Not Including Freedmen)	CARD NO.
POST OFFICE: Grant, I.T.			FIELD NO. 1602

Dawes' Roll No.	NAME	Relationship to Person	AGE	SEX	BLOOD	TRIBAL ENROLLMENT		
						Year	County	No.
4538	1 Hayes, Sam ²⁹	First Named	26	M	Full	1896	Kiamitia	5750
	2							
	3							
	4							
	5							
	6							
	7							
	8							
	9							
	10							
	11	ENROLLMENT						
	12	OF NOS. 1 HEREON APPROVED BY THE SECRETARY						
	13	OF INTERIOR DEC 12 1902						
	14							
	15							
	16							
	17							

TRIBAL ENROLLMENT OF PARENTS

	Name of Father	Year	County	Name of Mother	Year	County
1	Sam Hayes	Dead	Kiamitia	Mary Hayes	Dead	Kiamitia
2						
3						
4						
5						
6						
7						
8						
9						
10						
11						
12						
13						
14						
15						
16				Date of Application for Enrollment 5/11/99		
17						

Choctaw By Blood Enrollment Cards 1898-1914

RESIDENCE: Kiamitia	COUNTY.							
POST OFFICE: Goodland, I.T	**Choctaw Nation**				**Choctaw Roll** *(Not Including Freedmen)*	CARD NO. FIELD NO. 1603		

Dawes' Roll No.	NAME	Relationship to Person First Named	AGE	SEX	BLOOD	TRIBAL ENROLLMENT		
						Year	County	No.
4539	1 Oklabbi, Davis 65	First Named	62	M	Full	1896	Kiamitia	9956
4540	2 " Lena 13	Dau	10	F	1/2	1896	"	9957
4541	3 " Listic 6	"	3	"	1/2	1896	"	9958
	4							
	5							
	6							
	7							
	8							
	9							
	10							
	11	ENROLLMENT OF NOS. 1 – 2 and 3 HEREON						
	12	APPROVED BY THE SECRETARY						
	13	OF INTERIOR DEC 12 1902						
	14							
	15							
	16							
	17							

TRIBAL ENROLLMENT OF PARENTS

	Name of Father	Year	County	Name of Mother	Year	County
1	Oklabbi	Dead	Kiamitia		Dead	Kiamitia
2	No 1			Sissy Oklabbi	1896	Cherokee
3	No 1			" "	1896	"
4						
5						
6	Mother of Nos 2-3, a Cherokee. See testimony of No1					
7	as to marriage. ⟨ Not on Cherokee Rolls of 1894 or 1896. ⟩					
8	No.3 is not dead. See letter from No.1 filed April 2, 1901					
9						
10						
11						
12						
13						
14					Date of Application for Enrollment.	
15						
16					5/11/99	
17						

103

Choctaw By Blood Enrollment Cards 1898-1914

RESIDENCE: Kiamitia   COUNTY. **Choctaw Nation**   **Choctaw Roll**   CARD No.
POST OFFICE: Grant, I.T.   *(Not Including Freedmen)*   FIELD No.   1604

Dawes' Roll No.	NAME	Relationship to Person First Named	AGE	SEX	BLOOD	TRIBAL ENROLLMENT		
						Year	County	No.
4542	1 Sampson, Malissa ⁴³	First Named	40	F	Full	1896	Kiamitia	11509
4543	2 " Joseph ¹⁴	Son	11	M	"	1896	"	11510
	3							
	4							
	5	ENROLLMENT						
	6	OF NOS. 1 and 2 HEREON APPROVED BY THE SECRETARY						
	7	OF INTERIOR DEC 12 1902						
	8							
	9							
	10							
	11							
	12							
	13							
	14							
	15							
	16							
	17							

TRIBAL ENROLLMENT OF PARENTS

	Name of Father	Year	County	Name of Mother	Year	County
1	Alex Tolah	Dead	Towson	Sallie Tolah	Dead	Towson
2	Sam Sampson	"	Kiamitia	No 1		
3						
4						
5						
6		No1 on 1896 as Melessa Sampson				
7						
8						
9						
10						
11						
12						
13						
14						
15					Date of Application for Enrollment.	
16					5/11/99	
17						

104

Choctaw By Blood Enrollment Cards 1898-1914

RESIDENCE: Kiamitia   COUNTY. **Choctaw Nation**   **Choctaw Roll** CARD No.
POST OFFICE: Goodland, I.T.   *(Not Including Freedmen)* FIELD No. 1605

Dawes' Roll No.	NAME	Relationship to Person First Named	AGE	SEX	BLOOD	TRIBAL ENROLLMENT		
						Year	County	No.
4544	1 Ward, Allington ⁴⁵	First Named	42	M	Full	1896	Kiamitia	13743
	2							
	3							
	4							
	5	ENROLLMENT						
	6	OF NOS. 1 HEREON APPROVED BY THE SECRETARY						
	7	OF INTERIOR DEC 12 1902						
	8							
	9							
	10							
	11							
	12							
	13							
	14							
	15							
	16							
	17							

TRIBAL ENROLLMENT OF PARENTS

Name of Father	Year	County	Name of Mother	Year	County
1 Ish-lun-ka-by	Dead	Kiamitia	Ka-nun-te-ka	Dead	Kiamitia
2					
3					
4	Wife and Children on Chickasaw Card N 1422				
5					
6					
7					
8					
9					
10					
11					
12					
13					
14					
15				Date of Application for Enrollment	5/11/99
16					
17 No1 P.O. Hugo, I.T. 12/3⁰²					

P.O. Soper IT 6/14/04

Choctaw By Blood Enrollment Cards 1898-1914

RESIDENCE: Kiamitia   COUNTY. **Choctaw Nation**   **Choctaw Roll**   CARD No.

POST OFFICE: Goodland, I.T.   (Not Including Freedmen)   FIELD NO.   1606

Dawes' Roll No.	NAME		Relationship to Person	AGE	SEX	BLOOD	TRIBAL ENROLLMENT		
							Year	County	No.
4545	1 Coleman, Bond	36	First Named	33	M	Full	1896	Kiamitia	2692
4546	2 " Sukey	20	Dau	17	F	"	1896	"	2693
4547	3 " Emily	19	"	16	"	"	1896	"	2694
4548	4 " Silwee	10	"	7	"	"	1896	"	2695
	5								
	6								
	7	ENROLLMENT OF NOS. 1 2 3 and 4 HEREON APPROVED BY THE SECRETARY OF INTERIOR DEC 12 1902							
	8								
	9								
	10								
	11								
	12								
	13								
	14								
	15								
	16								
	17								

TRIBAL ENROLLMENT OF PARENTS

	Name of Father	Year	County	Name of Mother	Year	County
1	John Coleman	Dead	Towson	Lucy Coleman	Dead	Kiamitia
2	No 1			Manda Coleman	"	"
3	No 1			" "	"	"
4	No 1			" "	"	"
5						
6						
7						
8						
9						
10			No 4 on 1896 roll as Silvin Coleman			
11						
12			For child of No4 see NB (Mar 3rd 1905) Card #-104			
13						
14			No 3 now Allen 11/30/12			
15					Date of Application for Enrollment.	
16					5/11/99	
17						

Choctaw By Blood Enrollment Cards 1898-1914

RESIDENCE: Kiamitia   COUNTY. **Choctaw Nation**   **Choctaw Roll** *(Not Including Freedmen)*   CARD NO.

POST OFFICE: Goodland, I.T   FIELD NO.   1607

Dawes' Roll No.	NAME	Relationship to Person	AGE	SEX	BLOOD	TRIBAL ENROLLMENT		
						Year	County	No.
4549	₁ Jones, George ²⁶	First Named	23	M	Full	1893	Blue	27
4550	₂ " Frances ²⁷	Wife	24	F	"	1896	Kiamitia	5758
	3							
	4							
	5							
	6							
	7							
	8							
	9							
	10							
	11							
	12							
	13							
	14							
	15							
	16							
	17							

ENROLLMENT
OF NOS. 1 and 2 HEREON
APPROVED BY THE SECRETARY
OF INTERIOR DEC 12 1902

TRIBAL ENROLLMENT OF PARENTS

Name of Father	Year	County	Name of Mother	Year	County
₁ Peter Jefferson	1896	Cedar	Tennessee Jones	Dead	Kiamitia
₂ John Jacob	Dead	Kiamitia	Melvina Jacob	"	"
3					
4					
5					
6					
7					
8					
9			No 1 on 1893 Pay roll, Page 118, No 27, Blue Co.		
10					
11			No 2 on 1896 roll as Frances Heart.		
12					
13					
14				Date of Application for Enrollment.	
15					
16				5/11/99	
17					

Choctaw By Blood Enrollment Cards 1898-1914

RESIDENCE: Kiamitia   COUNTY. **Choctaw Nation**   **Choctaw Roll**   CARD NO.

POST OFFICE: Goodland, I.T   *(Not Including Freedmen)*   FIELD NO. **1608**

Dawes' Roll No.	NAME		Relationship to Person First Named	AGE	SEX	BLOOD	TRIBAL ENROLLMENT		
							Year	County	No.
4551	1 Coleman, Thompson	48	First Named	45	M	Full	1896	Kiamitia	2709
4552	2 " Jimmie	18	Son	15	"	"	1896	"	2711
4553	3 " Emma	15	Dau	12	F	"	1896	"	2712
4554	4 " William	8	Son	5	M	"	1896	"	2713
	5								
	6								
	7	ENROLLMENT OF NOS. 1 2 3 and 4 HEREON							
	8	APPROVED BY THE SECRETARY							
	9	OF INTERIOR DEC 12 1902							
	10								
	11								
	12								
	13								
	14								
	15								
	16								
	17								

TRIBAL ENROLLMENT OF PARENTS

	Name of Father	Year	County	Name of Mother	Year	County
1	John Coleman	Dead	Towson	Lucy Coleman	Dead	Kiamitia
2	No 1			Molsey Coleman	"	"
3	No 1			" "	"	"
4	No 1			" "	"	"
5						
6						
7						
8			For child of No. 1, see N.B. (Apr 26, 1906) Card No. 177			
9			" " " " 3 "	" " " " No. 784		
10						
11						
12						
13						
14					Date of Application for Enrollment.	
15					5/11/99	
16						
17	P.O. Lenton OK					

Choctaw By Blood Enrollment Cards 1898-1914

RESIDENCE: Kiamitia   COUNTY. **Choctaw Nation**   **Choctaw Roll** *(Not Including Freedmen)*   CARD NO.

POST OFFICE: Grant, I.T.   FIELD NO. **1609**

Dawes' Roll No.	NAME	Relationship to Person First Named	AGE	SEX	BLOOD	TRIBAL ENROLLMENT		
						Year	County	No.
4555	1 Roberts, Billy DIED PRIOR TO SEPTEMBER 25, 1902		45	M	Full	1896	Kiamitia	10836
4556	2 Ahekatubby, Emma 21	Dau	18	F	"	1896	"	10837
4557	3 Ahekatubby, Daniel 1	Gr Son	2½mo	M	"			
	4							
	5							
	6							
	7	ENROLLMENT						
	8	OF NOS. 1 2 and 3 HEREON APPROVED BY THE SECRETARY						
	9	OF INTERIOR DEC 12 1902						
	10							
	11							
	12							
	13							
	14							
	15							
	16							
	17							

TRIBAL ENROLLMENT OF PARENTS

	Name of Father	Year	County	Name of Mother	Year	County
1	Lullie Roberts	Dead	Kiamitia		Dead	Kiamitia
2	No 1			Minnie Robert	"	"
3	John Ahekatubby	1896	Kiamitia	No.2		
4						
5						
6	No.2 is now the wife of John Ahekoubbi[sic] on Choctaw card #652. Evidence					
7	of marriage filed March 27, 1902					
8	No.3 Born Jany. 9, 1902: enrolled March 27, 1902					
9	No 1 died Feb 9, 1902; proof of death filed Dec 8, 1902 No. 1 died Feb 9, 1902: Enrollment cancelled by Department July 8 1904					
10	For child of No.2, see N.B. (Apr 26, 1906) Card No. 87.					
11	" " " " " (March 3 1905) " " 1191.					
12						
13						
14						
15						#1&2
16					Date of Application for Enrollment	5/11/99
17						

Choctaw By Blood Enrollment Cards 1898-1914

RESIDENCE: Kiamitia   COUNTY: **Choctaw Nation**   **Choctaw Roll** (Not Including Freedmen)   CARD NO.

POST OFFICE: Grant, I.T.   FIELD NO. 1610

Dawes' Roll No.	NAME	Relationship to Person First Named	AGE	SEX	BLOOD	TRIBAL ENROLLMENT Year	County	No.
4558 ₁	Gooding, Basil L ³³	First Named	30	M	1/4	1896	Kiamitia	4834
I.W. 708 ₂	" Georgia A ²⁶	Wife	24	F	I.W.	1896	"	14572
4559 ₃	" Fannie ⁸	Dau	5	"	1/8	1896	"	4835
4560 ₄	" Jesse ⁶	Son	3	M	1/8	1896	"	4836
4561 ₅	" Governor L ⁵	"	1	"	1/8			
4562 ₆	Gooding, Never ③	Dau	4mo	F	1/8			
I.W. 994 ₇	" Henry L ⁵⁹	Father	59	M	I.W.	1896	Kiamitia	4573
₈								
₉								
₁₀								
₁₁	ENROLLMENT							
₁₂	OF NOS. 1 3 4 5 and 6 HEREON APPROVED BY THE SECRETARY							
₁₃	OF INTERIOR DEC 12 1902							
₁₄	ENROLLMENT							
₁₅	OF NOS. ~~ 2 ~~ HEREON APPROVED BY THE SECRETARY				ENROLLMENT			
₁₆	OF INTERIOR MAY -7 1904				OF NOS. ~~ 7 ~~ HEREON APPROVED BY THE SECRETARY			
₁₇					OF INTERIOR OCT 21 1904			

DIED PRIOR TO SEPTEMBER 25, 1902

TRIBAL ENROLLMENT OF PARENTS

	Name of Father	Year	County	Name of Mother	Year	County
₁	Henry L. Gooding	1896	Non Citz	Roseanna Gooding	Dead	Kiamitia
₂	Thos. Sprewell	1896	" "	Jennie Sprewell	1896	Non Citz
₃	No 1			No 2		
₄	No 1			No 2		
₅	No 1			No 2		
₆	No 1			No 2		
₇	Geo. C. Gooding	Dead	Non-citz	Esther Gooding	Dead	non-citz
₈						
₉		No2 See decision of March 2 '04				
₁₀		No4 on 1896 roll as Jessee Gooding				
₁₁		No.6 Enrolled June 23d, 1900				
₁₂		No5 Died July - 1899; proof of death filed Dec 8, 1902				
	No.5 died July – 1899; Enrollment cancelled by Department July 8, 1904					
₁₃	Nº7 married a Choctaw woman in 1863, lived with her in Choctaw Nation until her death in 1890. Subsequently					
₁₄	married a white woman by whom he has one child Ester May nine years old.					
₁₅	Nº7 transferred from Choctaw card "D148. See decision of August 31, 1904.		Sept. 15, 1904			Date of Application for Enrollment:
₁₆		- Have child born Nov. 11, 1902				5/11/99
₁₇	See Petition No W 57 58					

For child of Nos 1&2 see NB (Mar 3-1905) Card #52

Choctaw By Blood Enrollment Cards 1898-1914

RESIDENCE: Kiamitia   COUNTY.   **Choctaw Nation**   **Choctaw Roll**   CARD No.

POST OFFICE: Goodland, I.T   *(Not Including Freedmen)*   FIELD No. **1611**

Dawes' Roll No.	NAME	Relationship to Person	AGE	SEX	BLOOD	TRIBAL ENROLLMENT		
						Year	County	No.
4563	1 Parsons, Mary ^16^	First Named	13	F	1/2	1896	Kiamitia	10426
4564	2 " John ^13^	Bro	10	M	1/2	1896	"	10427
4565	3 " Daniel ^10^	"	7	"	1/2	1896	"	10428
	4							
	5							
	6							
	7							
	8							
	9							
	10							
	11	ENROLLMENT OF NOS. 1 2 and 3 HEREON						
	12	APPROVED BY THE SECRETARY						
	13	OF INTERIOR DEC 2 1902						
	14							
	15							
	16							
	17							

TRIBAL ENROLLMENT OF PARENTS

	Name of Father	Year	County	Name of Mother	Year	County
1	J. U. Parsons	1896	Non Citz	Liza Parsons	Dead	Kiamitia
2	" "	1896	" "	" "	"	"
3	" "	1896	" "	" "	"	"
4						
5						
6						
7			Names appear on 1896 roll as Parson.			
8						
9						
10						
11			Father of above children is John M[sic] Choctaw Card # 859			
12			No.1 is now the wife of Solomon Joel, Choctaw Card # 724.			
13						
14						
15						
16				Date of Application for Enrollment	5/11/99	
17						

111

Choctaw By Blood Enrollment Cards 1898-1914

RESIDENCE: Kiamitia   COUNTY. **Choctaw Nation**   **Choctaw Roll**   CARD No.

POST OFFICE: Frogville, I.T.   *(Not Including Freedmen)*   FIELD No. 1612

Dawes' Roll No.	NAME	Relationship to Person First Named	AGE	SEX	BLOOD	TRIBAL ENROLLMENT Year	County	No.
4566	1 Oakes, Samuel L ⁴⁸	First Named	45	M	1/8	1896	Kiamitia	9959
I.W. 638	2 " ", Cleora ²⁹	Wife	27	F	I.W.			
4567	3 " ", Tommie ²	Dau	1mo	F	1/16			
14685	4 " ", James G ¹	Son	2mo	M	1/16			
	5							
	6							
	7	ENROLLMENT						
	8	OF NOS. 1 and 3 HEREON APPROVED BY THE SECRETARY						
	9	OF INTERIOR DEC 12 1902						
	10							
	11	ENROLLMENT						
	12	OF NOS. 4 HEREON APPROVED BY THE SECRETARY						
	13	OF INTERIOR MAY 20 1903						
	14	ENROLLMENT						
	15	OF NOS. 2 HEREON APPROVED BY THE SECRETARY						
	16	OF INTERIOR MAR 26 1904						
	17							

TRIBAL ENROLLMENT OF PARENTS

Name of Father	Year	County	Name of Mother	Year	County
1 Thos. Oakes	Dead	Non Citz	Harriet Oakes	1896	Kiamitia
2 James W. Grant		Non-citizen	Eliza J. Grant		Non-citizen
3	No. 1		No. 2		
4	Nº1		Nº2		
5					
6		No.2 Enrolled Nov. 27th, 1900: see testimony			
7		of that date			
8		No.3 Enrolled November 27th, 1900.			
9		Nº4 Born Aug. 30, 1902: Enrolled Nov. 1, 1902			
		Evidence of marriage of Nos 1 and 2 filed Nov 27-1900			
10					
11		For child of Nos 1&2, see N.B. (Apr. 26, 1906) Card No. 120			
12					
13					
14			Date of Application for Enrollment.		
15					
16			5/11/99		
17					

112

RESIDENCE: Kiamitia   COUNTY. **Choctaw Nation**   **Choctaw Roll** CARD NO.
POST OFFICE: Frogville, I.T   *(Not Including Freedmen)*   FIELD NO. 1613

Dawes' Roll No.	NAME	Relationship to Person	AGE	SEX	BLOOD	TRIBAL ENROLLMENT		
						Year	County	No.
4568	1 Everidge, Martin V ⁴²	First Named	39	M	3/8	1896	Kiamitia	3774
I.W.84	2 " Minti ³⁷	Wife	34	F	I.W.	1896	"	14502
4569	3 Hutchings Willie L ¹⁸	Dau	15	"	3/16	1896	"	3776
4570	4 Everedge David C ¹¹	Son	8	M	3/16	1896	"	3777
I.W 1100	5 Hutchings, James W. ²⁹	Husband of No.3	29	M	I.W.			
16062	6 Everidge Floyd Wesley	Son	12	M	3/16	1893	Kiamitia	179
	7							
	8							
	9							
	10							
	11							
	12							
	13							
	14							
	15							
	16							
	17							

ENROLLMENT
OF NOS. 1 3 and 4 HEREON
APPROVED BY THE SECRETARY
OF INTERIOR DEC 12 1902

ENROLLMENT
OF NOS. 2 HEREON
APPROVED BY THE SECRETARY
OF INTERIOR JUN 13 1903

ENROLLMENT
OF NOS. 5 HEREON
APPROVED BY THE SECRETARY
OF INTERIOR NOV 16 1904

ENROLLMENT
OF NOS. 6 HEREON
APPROVED BY THE SECRETARY
OF INTERIOR NOV 23 1906

TRIBAL ENROLLMENT OF PARENTS

	Name of Father	Year	County	Name of Mother	Year	County
1	Joel Everidge	1896	Kiamitia	Sophie Everidge	Dead	Kiamitia
2	William Goswick	1896	Non Citz	Lutitia Goswick	"	Non Citz
3	No 1			No 2		
4	No 1			No 2		
5	Wᵐ PO. Hutchings	dead	non-citizen	Loucina Hutchings	dead	non-citizen
6	No 1			Sarah Ann Cochrum		"
7						
8						
9						

No1 on 1896 roll as M. V. Everidge
No4 " 1896 " " D. C.
No3 is now the wife of James W. Hutchings on Choctaw card #D.604.
Evidence of marriage of Nos 1 and2 filed Dec. 6, 1902   Jany 4, 1901
No.5 transferred from Choctaw card #D-1604, Oct. 31, 1904: See decision of Oct.15, 1903
No6 placed hereon under order of Commissioner to Five Civilized Tribes
of June 23 1906, holding that application was made for his enrollment
within the time provided by Act of July 1, 1902 (32 Stat 641)

GRANTED JUL 18 1906

Date of Application for Enrollment 5/11/99
1 to 4 inc

P.O. Hugo, I.T. 12/1/02

Choctaw By Blood Enrollment Cards 1898-1914

RESIDENCE: Kiamitia   COUNTY. **Choctaw Nation**   **Choctaw Roll** *(Not Including Freedmen)*   CARD No.
POST OFFICE: Grant, I.T.   FIELD No. 1614

Dawes' Roll No.	NAME	Relationship to Person First Named	AGE	SEX	BLOOD	TRIBAL ENROLLMENT Year	County	No.
4571	1 Fulton, William 31		28	M	Full	1896	Kiamitia	4245
4572	2 Jones, Sam 20	Ward	17	"	"	1896	"	7065
4573	3 " Edward 17	"	14	"	"	1896	"	7066
4574	4 Peters, Dixon ~~DIED PRIOR TO SEPTEMBER 25, 1902~~	"	16	"	"	1896	"	10430
4575	5 Crosby, Leander 10	"	7	"	"	1896	"	2730
4576	6 Pistokcha, Wilburn 10	"	7	"	"	1893	Jackson	190
	7							
	8							
	9	ENROLLMENT OF NOS. 1 2 3 4 5 and 6 HEREON APPROVED BY THE SECRETARY OF INTERIOR DEC 12 1902						
	10							
	11							
	12							
	13							
	14							
	15							
	16							
	17							

TRIBAL ENROLLMENT OF PARENTS

	Name of Father	Year	County	Name of Mother	Year	County
1	Charlison Fulton	Dead	Kiamitia	Liney Fulton	Dead	Kiamitia
2	Ed Jones	"	Non Citz	Mary Jones	"	"
3	" "	"	" "	" "	"	"
4	~~Isom Peters~~	"	~~Kiamitia~~	~~Leon Peters~~	"	"
5	Jacob Crosby	"	"	Susan Crosby	"	"
6	Gibson Pistokcha	"	"	Elsie Pistokcha	"	Jackson
7						
8						
9			No5 on 1896 roll as Landus Crosby			
10						
11			No6 on 1893 Pay roll as Wilson Pistukcha, Page 20, No 190, Jackson Co.			
12						
13			No2 also on 1896 roll, Page 156, No 6391 Sans Bois Co.			
14			as Sampson Jones			
15	No4 died April 18, 1899; proof of death filed Dec 6, 1902.				Date of Application for Enrollment.	
16	No.4 died April 18, 1899; Enrollment cancelled by Department July 8, 1904.				5/11/99	
17						

RESIDENCE: Kiamitia		COUNTY. **Choctaw Nation**				**Choctaw Roll** *(Not Including Freedmen)*		CARD NO. FIELD NO. **1615**	
POST OFFICE: Nelson, I.T.									

Dawes' Roll No.	NAME	Relationship to Person First Named	AGE	SEX	BLOOD	TRIBAL ENROLLMENT		
						Year	County	No.
4577	1 Sauls, Triffinnie 29	Named	26	F	1/2	1896	Kiamitia	11526
4578	2 " Wilson 9	Son	6	M	1/4	1896	"	11527
4579	3 " Oscar 6	"	3	"	1/4	1896	"	11528
4580	4 " Benjamin 5	"	17mo	"	1/4			
4581	5 " Bertha 3	Dau	4mo	F	1/4			
	6							
	7							
	8							
	9							
	10							
	11	ENROLLMENT OF NOS. 1 2 3 4 and 5 HEREON						
	12	APPROVED BY THE SECRETARY						
	13	OF INTERIOR Dec 12 1902						
	14							
	15							
	16							
	17							

TRIBAL ENROLLMENT OF PARENTS

	Name of Father	Year	County	Name of Mother	Year	County
1	Green Walker	1896	Kiamitia	Clara Walker	1896	Kiamitia
2	G. W. Sauls	1896	Non Citz	No 1		
3	" " "	1896	" "	No 1		
4	" " "	1896	" "	No 1		
5	" " "	1896	" "	No 1		
6						
7						
8			Surnames on 1896 roll as "Sols"			
9		No5 [sic]				
10			For child of No.1 see N.B. (Apr. 26 '06) No. 562			
11			" children " " " " " (Mar 3-1905) No 42			
12						
13						
14					#1 to 4 inc	
15				Date of Application for Enrollment		
16					5/11/99	
17				No5 enrolled Dec 14/99		

P.O. Soper I.T. 11/6/06

Choctaw By Blood Enrollment Cards 1898-1914

RESIDENCE: Kiamitia   COUNTY. **Choctaw Nation**   **Choctaw Roll** *(Not Including Freedmen)*   CARD NO.

POST OFFICE: Nelson, I.T.   FIELD NO. **1616**

Dawes' Roll No.	NAME		Relationship to Person	AGE	SEX	BLOOD	TRIBAL ENROLLMENT		
							Year	County	No.
4582	1 Walker, Green	57	First Named	54	M	1/2	1896	Kiamitia	13753
4583	2 " Clarissa	55	Wife	52	F	1/2	1896	"	13754
4584	3 " Wilson	31	Son	28	M	1/2	1896	"	13720
4585	4 " Green Jr	29	"	26	"	1/2	1896	"	13755
4586	5 " Martin	25	"	22	"	1/2	1896	"	13756
4587	6 " Jesse	16	"	13	"	1/2	1896	"	13757
4588	7 " Clarissa	13	Dau	10	F	1/2	1896	"	13758
	8								
	9								
	10								
	11	ENROLLMENT							
	12	OF NOS. 123456and7 HEREON APPROVED BY THE SECRETARY							
	13	OF INTERIOR DEC 12 1902							
	14								
	15								
	16								
	17								

TRIBAL ENROLLMENT OF PARENTS

	Name of Father	Year	County	Name of Mother	Year	County
1	William Walker	Dead	Creek Nation	Elsie Walker	Dead	Kiamitia
2	John Folsom	"	Blue		"	Blue
3	No 1			No 2		
4	No 1			No 2		
5	No 1			No 2		
6	No 1			No 2		
7	No 1			No 2		
8						
9			No6 on 1896 roll as Jessee Walker			
10			For child of No.5 see N.B. (Apr. 26, 1906) Card No. 187.			
11			" " " No 6 " " " " " " 1224			
12						
13						
14						
15					Date of Application for Enrollment.	
16					5/11/99	
17						

Choctaw By Blood Enrollment Cards 1898-1914

RESIDENCE: **Kiamitia**   COUNTY. **Choctaw Nation**   **Choctaw Roll**   CARD NO.
POST OFFICE: **Grant, I.T.**   *(Not Including Freedmen)*   FIELD NO.   **1617**

Dawes' Roll No.	NAME	Relationship to Person	AGE	SEX	BLOOD	TRIBAL ENROLLMENT		
						Year	County	No.
4589	1 Baxter, William ²⁹	First Named	26	M	Full	1893	Tobucksy	160
4590	2 ~~DIED PRIOR TO SEPTEMBER 25, 1902~~ Sibby	Wife	32	F	"	1896	Kiamitia	9976
	3							
	4							
	5							
	6							
	7							
	8	ENROLLMENT						
	9	OF NOS. 1 and 2 HEREON APPROVED BY THE SECRETARY						
	10	OF INTERIOR Dec 12, 1902						
	11							
	12							
	13							
	14							
	15							
	16							
	17							

TRIBAL ENROLLMENT OF PARENTS

	Name of Father	Year	County	Name of Mother	Year	County
1	Logan Baxter	Dead	Kiamitia	Phoebe Baxter	Dead	Tobucksy
2	~~Jos. Oklahambi~~	"	~~Red River~~	~~Lucy Greenwood~~	"	~~Kiamitia~~
3						
4						
5						
6			No 1 on 1893 Pay roll as Wᵐ Baxter, Page 15, No. 160			
7						
8			No 2 on 1896 roll as Sibby Oklahambi			
9			No.1 on Choctaw 1896 roll as Willie Bester; page 36, ⁴1446.			
10			No .2 died Sept. 23, 1899; Enrollment cancelled by Department July 8, 1904			
11						
12						
13						
14						
15				Date of Application for Enrollment.		
16					5/11/99	
17						

117

Choctaw By Blood Enrollment Cards 1898-1914

RESIDENCE: Kiamitia   COUNTY. **Choctaw Nation**   **Choctaw Roll** CARD NO.
POST OFFICE: Goodland, I.T.   *(Not Including Freedmen)* FIELD NO. **1618**

Dawes' Roll No.		NAME		Relationship to Person First Named	AGE	SEX	BLOOD	TRIBAL ENROLLMENT		
								Year	County	No.
I.W. 1292	1	Usray, James	54		51	M	I.W	1896	Kiamitia	15130
4591	2	" Lizzie	45	Wife	42	F	Full	1893	"	401
	3									
	4									
	5									
	6									
	7									
	8									
	9	ENROLLMENT OF NOS. 2 HEREON								
	10	APPROVED BY THE SECRETARY OF INTERIOR Dec 12 1902								
	11									
	12	ENROLLMENT								
	13	OF NOS. 1 HEREON								
	14	APPROVED BY THE SECRETARY OF INTERIOR Mar 14 1905								
	15									
	16									
	17									

TRIBAL ENROLLMENT OF PARENTS

	Name of Father	Year	County	Name of Mother	Year	County
1	Philip Usray	Dead	Non Citz	Harriet Usray	Dead	Non Citz
2	Bombo Lake	"	Kiamitia		"	Kiamitia
3						
4						
5						
6			No2 on 1893 Pay roll as Lizzie Lake, Page 50, No 401 Kiamitia Co.			
7			No.1 formerly husband of Malinda Usray (nee Roebuck),			
8			1885 Kiamitia, No. 901, and who died in 1887			
9						
10						
11						
12						
13						
14					Date of Application for Enrollment.	
15						
16					5/11/99	
17	P.O. Hugo, I.T.					

118

Choctaw By Blood Enrollment Cards 1898-1914

Choctaw Nation

Choctaw Roll
(Not Including Freedmen)

CARD NO.
FIELD NO. 1619

Dawes' Roll No.	NAME	Relationship to Person First Named	AGE	SEX	BLOOD	TRIBAL ENROLLMENT Year	County	No.
I.W. 1101	1 Hybarger, James C. 36	First Named	33	M	I.W.			
15406	2 " Mollie M 30	Wife	27	F	1/4	1893	Kiamitia	75
15407	3 " Eva L. 13	Dau	10	"	1/8	1893	"	76
15408	4 " Charlie 9	Son	6	M	1/8	1893	"	77
15409	5 " Willie R. 8	Dau	3	F	1/8			
15410	6 " Ruby M. 3	"	3wks	"	1/8			
	7					No.1	Choctaw residing in Chickasaw District	C.I. Roll 47
	8 No.2 on Choctaw roll as Mollie B. Hybarger					No.2	" "	CCR #2 259
	9 No.3 " " " " Eevie					No.3	" "	"
	10 No.4 " " " " Charlie					No.4	" "	"
	Dec 30/08 No.1 on C.C.R. No2 in pencil. Not on 1896 Choctaw roll.					No.5	" "	"
	12							
	13	No.2 1896 Chickasaw Dist 6200, as Mollie B Hightower						
	14	No.3 1896 " " 6205 " Evie Highberger						
	15 ENROLLMENT OF NOS. 2-3-4-5-6 HEREON APPROVED BY THE SECRETARY OF INTERIOR MAY 9 1904	No.4 1896 " " 6206 " Charlie "						
		No.5 1896 " " 6207 " Willie "						
		Marriage license destroyed. Affidavit of Judge Law to be supplied.						

TRIBAL ENROLLMENT OF PARENTS

	Name of Father	Year	County	Name of Mother	Year	County
1	John Hybarger	Dead	non-citizen	Minerva Hybarger	Dead	non-citz
2	Will Boswell	"	" "	Ellen Boswell	"	Kiamitia
3	No.1			No.2		
4	No.1	ENROLLMENT OF NOS. ~~~1~~~ HEREON		No.2		
5	No.1	APPROVED BY THE SECRETARY OF INTERIOR NOV 16 1904		No.2		
6	No.1			No.2		
7	All admitted to citizenship by Dawes Commission, Case No 1341, no appeal					
8	No.2 was admitted as Mollie Hybarger					
9	No.3 " " " Eva "					
10	No.4 " " " Charlie "					
11	No.5 " " " Willie "					
12	No.2 on 1893 pay roll, page 118, No. 75, Kiamitia Co, as Mollie Hybarger					
13	No.3 " 1893 " " " 119 " 76 " " " Eva "					
14	No.4 " 1893 " " " 119 " 77 " " " [sic]					
15	No.6 Affidavit of birth to be supplied. Recd. May 17/99					
16	Evidence of birth of No.5 received and filed Feby. 15, 1902.					
17						5/11/99

Choctaw By Blood Enrollment Cards 1898-1914

RESIDENCE:	Kiamitia	COUNTY.							
POST OFFICE:	Grant, I.T								

Choctaw Nation

Choctaw Roll (Not Including Freedmen)

CARD NO. FIELD NO. **1620**

Dawes' Roll No.	NAME		Relationship to Person First Named	AGE	SEX	BLOOD	TRIBAL ENROLLMENT		
							Year	County	No.
4592	1 Bohanan, Andrew	33	First Named	30	M	3/4	1896	Kiamitia	1453
I.W. 85	2 " Rosie D	25	Wife	22	F	I.W.	1896	"	14320
1593	3 ~~DIED PRIOR TO SEPTEMBER 25, 1902~~ Thomas Burton 3		Son	7wks	M	3/8			
	4								
	5								
	6								
	7								
	8								
	9								
	10		ENROLLMENT						
	11		OF NOS. 1 and 3 HEREON APPROVED BY THE SECRETARY						
	12		OF INTERIOR DEC 12 1902						
	13		ENROLLMENT OF NOS. ~~ 2 ~~ HEREON						
	14		APPROVED BY THE SECRETARY OF INTERIOR JUN 13 1903						
	15								
	16								
	17								

TRIBAL ENROLLMENT OF PARENTS

	Name of Father	Year	County	Name of Mother	Year	County
1	Joshua Bohanan	Dead	Kiamitia		Dead	Eagle
2	U. H. Nicks	"	Non Citz	Janie Nicks	1896	Non Citz
3	No.1			No.2		
4						
5						
6			No 2 on 1896 roll as Rosa D Bohanan			
7			No.3 Enrolled July 16, 1901			
8			~~No 3 died June 23, 1902, proof of death filed Dec 8, 1902~~ No.3 died June 23, 1902; Enrollment cancelled by Department July 8, 1904			
9			For child of Nos 1&2 see NB (March 3, 1905) #850			
10						
11						
12						
13						
14					Date of Application for Enrollment.	
15						
16					5/11/99	
17						

Choctaw By Blood Enrollment Cards 1898-1914

RESIDENCE: Jackson   COUNTY. **Choctaw Nation**   **Choctaw Roll**   CARD NO.
POST OFFICE: Bennington, I.T.   *(Not Including Freedmen)*   FIELD NO. **1621**

Dawes' Roll No.	NAME	Relationship to Person Named	AGE	SEX	BLOOD	TRIBAL ENROLLMENT Year	TRIBAL ENROLLMENT County	TRIBAL ENROLLMENT No.
4594 ₁	Loring, William H ³⁴	First Named	31	M	1/2	1893	Skullyville	336
15411 ₂	" Naomi ¹	Dau	8mo	F	1/4			
16204 ₃	Homer, Sissy	Sis	32	F	1/4	1893	Kiamitia	
₄								
₅	ENROLLMENT OF NOS. 3 HEREON APPROVED BY THE SECRETARY OF INTERIOR MAR 4- 1907							
₆								
₇								
₈								
₉	ENROLLMENT OF NOS. 1 HEREON APPROVED BY THE SECRETARY OF INTERIOR DEC 12 1902							
₁₀								
₁₁								
₁₂	ENROLLMENT OF NOS. ~~2~~ HEREON APPROVED BY THE SECRETARY OF INTERIOR MAY 9 1904							
₁₃								
₁₄								
₁₅								
₁₆								
₁₇								

TRIBAL ENROLLMENT OF PARENTS

	Name of Father	Year	County	Name of Mother	Year	County
₁	William Loring	Dead	Kiamitia	Mary Loring		Cherokee
₂	No 1			Sallie Loring		
₃	William Loring	dead	Kiamitia	Mary Loring		Cherokee
₄						
₅						
₆						
₇						
₈	No3 is wife of Silan Homer No1 on Choctaw card #1466, Feb. 20, 1907					
₉	No1 on 1893 Pay roll, Skullyville Co, Page 35, No. 336 as William Loring					
₁₀	For child of No.1 see NB (March 3,1905) #1074					
₁₁	~~Says his mother never lived in Cherokee Nation since his birth~~					
₁₂	~~Does not know that she was ever on those rolls. Was~~					
₁₃	~~never a resident of the Cherokee Nation, himself.~~					
	For child of No.3 see NB (March 3, 1905) #1072					
₁₄	~~No.1 is the husband of Lulie Loring on Choctaw card #D.609~~					
	No 2 born April 2, 1902; enrolled Dec 18, 1902					
₁₅	No 3 placed hereon under order of the Commissioner to Five Civilized Tribes of				Date of Application #1 for Enrollment.	
₁₆	Feb 20-1907 holding that application for her enrollment was made within the time provided				5/11/99	
₁₇	by the act of Congress approved Apr 26 1906					

121

Choctaw By Blood Enrollment Cards 1898-1914

RESIDENCE: Kiamitia   COUNTY   **Choctaw Nation**   Choctaw Roll _(Not Including Freedmen)_   CARD NO.
POST OFFICE: Grant, I. T.   FIELD NO. 1622

Dawes' Roll No.	NAME	Relationship to Person First Named	AGE	SEX	BLOOD	TRIBAL ENROLLMENT		
						Year	County	No.
14928	1 Robinson, Sam	Named	24	M	Full	1896	Kiamitia	10844
14929	2 " Mary	Wife	20	F	"	1896	"	10845
14930	3 " Julius	Son	19mo	M	"			
	4							
	5							
	6							
	7							
	8							
	9							
	10							
	11							
	12							
	13							
	14							
	15							
	16							
	17							

ENROLLMENT
OF NOS. 1, 2 and 3 HEREON
APPROVED BY THE SECRETARY
OF INTERIOR OCT 15 1903

TRIBAL ENROLLMENT OF PARENTS

	Name of Father	Year	County	Name of Mother	Year	County
1	Sam Robinson	Dead	Jackson	Sally Robinson	1896	Kiamitia
2	Henry Hayes	1896	Chick. Dist	Harriet Hayes	Dead	"
3	No. 1			No. 2		
4						
5						
6	No.3 Born May 16, 1901. Proof of birth filed Dec. 24, 1902					
7						
8						
9						
10						
11						
12						
13						
14						
15						#1&2
16				Date of Application for Enrollment 5/11/99		
17						

| RESIDENCE: Kiamitia | | COUNTY. | **Choctaw Nation** | | | | **Choctaw Roll** (Not Including Freedmen) | CARD No. FIELD No. | **1623** |
| POST OFFICE: Grant, I.T. | | | | | | | | | |

Dawes' Roll No.	NAME		Relationship to Person First Named	AGE	SEX	BLOOD	TRIBAL ENROLLMENT		
							Year	County	No.
4595	1 Choate, Ellis ~~DIED PRIOR TO SEPTEMBER 25, 1902~~		Named	62	M	Full	1896	Kiamitia	2697
4596	2 " Patsy	58	Wife	55	F	"	1896	"	2698
4597	3 Clark, Ella	18	Ward	15	"	"	1896	"	2702
	4								
	5								
	6								
	7								
	8	ENROLLMENT							
	9	OF NOS. 1 2 and 3 HEREON APPROVED BY THE SECRETARY							
	10	OF INTERIOR Dec 12 1902							
	11								
	12								
	13								
	14								
	15								
	16								
	17								

| | TRIBAL ENROLLMENT OF PARENTS | | | | | |

	Name of Father	Year	County	Name of Mother	Year	County
1	James Choate	Dead	Kiamitia	Betsy Choate	Dead	Kiamitia
2	John	"		Betsy Fry	"	Atoka
3	Adam Clark	"	Atoka	Jennie Clark	"	"
4						
5						
6						
7						
8						
9						
10						
11		No 1 died May 10, 1902; proof of death filed Dec 16, 1902.				
12		No.1 died May 10, 1902: Enrollment cancelled by Department July 8, 1904				
13						
14					Date of Application for Enrollment.	
15						
16					5/11/99	
17						

Choctaw By Blood Enrollment Cards 1898-1914

RESIDENCE: Kiamitia   COUNTY.   **Choctaw Nation**   Choctaw Roll   CARD NO.

POST OFFICE: Goodland, I.T.   *(Not Including Freedmen)*   FIELD NO.   1624

Dawes' Roll No.	NAME	Relationship to Person First Named	AGE	SEX	BLOOD	TRIBAL ENROLLMENT Year	County	No.
4598	1 Thomas, Benson ³¹	First Named	28	M	Full	1896	Jackson	12381
4599	2 DIED PRIOR TO SEPTEMBER 25, 1902 Fillis	Wife	27	F	"	1896	"	2780
4600	3 " Minnie ⁴	Dau	1	"	"			
	4							
	5							
	6							
	7 ENROLLMENT							
	8 OF NOS. 1 2 and 3 HEREON APPROVED BY THE SECRETARY							
	9 OF INTERIOR DEC 12 1902							
	10							
	11							
	12							
	13							
	14							
	15							
	16							
	17							

TRIBAL ENROLLMENT OF PARENTS

	Name of Father	Year	County	Name of Mother	Year	County
1	Johnson Onabby	Dead	Red River	Nancy Onabby	Dead	Eagle
2	Presley Fry	"	Blue	Ish-tu-na-tema	"	Blue
3	No 1			No 2		
4						
5						
6			No2 on 1896 roll as Fillis Crowder			
7		No.2 died Aug 4, 1901: Enrollment cancelled by Department July 8, 1904				
8		For child of No.1 see NB (March 3,1905) #1532				
9						
10						
11						
12						
13						
14						
15					Date of Application for Enrollment.	
16					5/11/99	
17	P.O. Soper IT					

124

Choctaw By Blood Enrollment Cards 1898-1914

RESIDENCE: Kiamitia
POST OFFICE: Goodland, I.T.

COUNTY. **Choctaw Nation**

Choctaw Roll *(Not Including Freedmen)*

CARD NO.
FIELD NO. 1625

Dawes' Roll No.	NAME	Relationship to Person	AGE	SEX	BLOOD	TRIBAL ENROLLMENT		
						Year	County	No.
4601	1 Cole, Joseph ²⁵	First Named	22	M	Full	1896	Blue	2908
	2							
	3							
	4							
	5							
	6							
	7							
	8							
	9							
	10							
	11	ENROLLMENT						
	12	OF NOS. 1 HEREON APPROVED BY THE SECRETARY						
	13	OF INTERIOR DEC 12 1902						
	14							
	15							
	16							
	17							

TRIBAL ENROLLMENT OF PARENTS

Name of Father	Year	County	Name of Mother	Year	County
1 John Cole	Dead	Kiamitia	Susie Cole	Dead	Kiamitia
2					
3					
4					
5	No. 1 is the husband of Selina Cole on Choctaw card #4247				
6					
7					
8					
9					
10					
11					
12					
13					
14					
15					
16			Date of Application for Enrollment	5/11/99	
17					

125

RESIDENCE: Kiamitia   COUNTY. **Choctaw Nation**   **Choctaw Roll**   CARD NO.

POST OFFICE: Goodland, I.T.   *(Not Including Freedmen)*   FIELD NO. 1626

Dawes' Roll No.	NAME	Relationship to Person First Named	AGE	SEX	BLOOD	TRIBAL ENROLLMENT Year	County	No.
4602	1 Price, Stewart DIED PRIOR TO SEPTEMBER 25 1902	Named	23	M	Full	1893	Blue	7
4603	2 Rhoda DIED PRIOR TO SEPTEMBER 25 1902	Wife	20	F	"	1893	Kiamitia	884
	3							
	4							
	5							
	6							
	7							
	8							
	9							
	10							
	11							
	12							
	13							
	14							
	15							
	16							
	17							

ENROLLMENT
OF NOS. 1 and 2 HEREON
APPROVED BY THE SECRETARY
OF INTERIOR DEC 12 1902

TRIBAL ENROLLMENT OF PARENTS

Name of Father	Year	County	Name of Mother	Year	County
1 Na-po-shubbee	Dead	Towson	O-che-ha-na-	Dead	Towson
2 John Williams	"	Kiamitia	Mary Williams	"	Kiamitia
3					
4					
5					
6					
7					
8					
9					
10					
11					
12					
13					
14					
15					
16				5/11/99	
17					

Choctaw By Blood Enrollment Cards 1898-1914

| RESIDENCE: Kiamitia | COUNTY. | Choctaw Nation | Choctaw Roll | CARD NO. |
| POST OFFICE: Grant, I.T. | | | (Not Including Freedmen) | FIELD NO. 1627 |

| Dawes' Roll No. | NAME | Relationship to Person | AGE | SEX | BLOOD | TRIBAL ENROLLMENT | | |
						Year	County	No.
4604	1 Sunney, James ³²	First Named	29	M	Full	1896	Kiamitia	11497
	2							
	3							
	4							
	5							
	6							
	7							
	8							
	9							
	10							
	11	ENROLLMENT						
	12	OF NOS. 1 HEREON APPROVED BY THE SECRETARY						
	13	OF INTERIOR DEC 12 1902						
	14							
	15							
	16							
	17							

TRIBAL ENROLLMENT OF PARENTS

Name of Father	Year	County	Name of Mother	Year	County
1 Wesley Sunney	Dead	Kiamitia	Susan Sunney	Dead	Kiamitia
2					
3					
4					
5	For child of No.1 see NB (March 3, 1905) #1528				
6					
7					
8					
9					
10					
11					
12					
13					
14					
15				Date of Application for Enrollment	5/11/99
16					
17 P.O. Bennington I.T.					

Choctaw By Blood Enrollment Cards 1898-1914

RESIDENCE: Kiamitia   COUNTY.

POST OFFICE: Goodland, I.T.

Choctaw Nation

Choctaw Roll *(Not Including Freedmen)*

CARD NO.

FIELD NO. 1628

Dawes' Roll No.	NAME		Relationship to Person First Named	AGE	SEX	BLOOD	TRIBAL ENROLLMENT		
							Year	County	No.
4605	1 Battiest, Solomon	45	Named	42	M	Full	1896	Kiamitia	1429
4606	2 " Winnie	43	Wife	40	F	"	1896	"	1430
4607	3 " John	13	Son	10	M	"	1896	"	1431
	4								
	5								
	6								
	7								
	8								
	9								
	10								
	11	ENROLLMENT							
	12	OF NOS. 1 2 and 3 HEREON APPROVED BY THE SECRETARY							
	13	OF INTERIOR DEC 12 1902							
	14								
	15								
	16								
	17								

TRIBAL ENROLLMENT OF PARENTS

	Name of Father	Year	County	Name of Mother	Year	
1	John Battiest	Dead	Kiamitia		Dead	Kiamitia
2	Jesse Bohanan	"	Red River	Nancy Bohanan	"	Red River
3	No 1			Ellen Battiest	1896	Kiamitia
4						
5						
6						
7						
8						
9						
10						
11						
12						
13						
14						
15						
16				Date of Application for Enrollment	5/11/99	
17	P.O. Hugo, I.T.					

Choctaw By Blood Enrollment Cards 1898-1914

RESIDENCE: Kiamitia
POST OFFICE: Antlers, I.T.

COUNTY: **Choctaw Nation**

Choctaw Roll *(Not Including Freedmen)*

CARD No. 1629
FIELD No. 1629

Dawes' Roll No.	NAME		Relationship to Person	AGE	SEX	BLOOD	TRIBAL ENROLLMENT		
							Year	County	No.
4608	1 Parker, Gabriel E	25	First Named	20	M	1/8	1896	Kiamitia	10450
4609	2 " James W.	18	Bro.	15	"	1/8	1896	"	10452
4610	3 " Lue	13	Sister	10	F	1/8	1896	"	10453
4611	4 " Cora	11	"	8	"	1/8	1896	"	10454
4612	5 " Georgia O	7	"	4	"	1/8	1896	"	10455
I.W.639	6 " Louise E.	22	Wife	22	F	I.W.			
	7								
	8								
	9	ENROLLMENT OF NOS. 1 2 3 4 and 5 HEREON							
	10	APPROVED BY THE SECRETARY OF INTERIOR Dec 12 1902							
	11								
	12	ENROLLMENT OF NOS. 6 HEREON							
	13	APPROVED BY THE SECRETARY OF INTERIOR Mar 26 1904							
	14								
	15								
	16								
	17								

TRIBAL ENROLLMENT OF PARENTS

	Name of Father	Year	County	Name of Mother	Year	County
1	J.C. Parker	1896	Non Citz	Eliza E. Parker	Dead	Kiamitia
2	" "	1896	" "	" " "	"	"
3	" "	1896	" "	" " "	"	"
4	" "	1896	" "	" " "	"	"
5	" "	1896	" "	" " "	"	"
6	John B. George		non citizen	Louise B. George		non citizen
7						
8						
9						
10	No2 on 1896 roll as Jim W. Parker					
11	No3 " 1896 " " Lula "			For child of Nos 1&6 see NB (Mar3'05) #699		
12	No4 " 1896 " " Cora G. "					
	No5 " 1896 " " George O. "					
13	No 1 appeared before Commission this day and states that					
	his age is 23 years, December 26, 1900					1 to 5 inc
14	No 1 is the husband of Louise E Parker on Choctaw Card #D603 Dec 26, 1900					
15	John C. Parker father of children on this card is on Choctaw card #D797, Sept. 22, 1902					
16	No 6 transferred from Choctaw card D603 January 25, 1904.			Date of Application for Enrollment.		5/11/99
17	See decision of January 7, 1904.					

129

Choctaw By Blood Enrollment Cards 1898-1914

RESIDENCE: **Kiamitia** COUNTY. **Choctaw Nation** **Choctaw Roll** *(Not Including Freedmen)* CARD NO. FIELD NO. **1630**
POST OFFICE: **Goodland, I.T.**

Dawes' Roll No.	NAME		Relationship to Person First Named	AGE	SEX	BLOOD	TRIBAL ENROLLMENT		
							Year	County	No.
4613	1 Cole, Willy	28	First Named	25	M	Full	1896	Kiamitia	2739
4614	2 " Missie	26	Wife	23	F	"	1896	"	2740
4615	3 James, Charles	11	S.Son	8	M	"	1896	"	7087
14686	4 Cole, Nelson	2	Son	2	M	"			
14687	5 " Susan	1	Dau	7wks	F	"			
	6								
	7	ENROLLMENT							
	8	OF NOS. 1 2 and 3 HEREON APPROVED BY THE SECRETARY							
	9	OF INTERIOR Dec 20 1903							
	10								
	11	ENROLLMENT							
	12	OF NOS. 4 and 5 HEREON APPROVED BY THE SECRETARY							
	13	OF INTERIOR May 20 1903							
	14								
	15								
	16								
	17								

TRIBAL ENROLLMENT OF PARENTS

	Name of Father	Year	County	Name of Mother	Year	County
1	John Cole	Dead	Kiamitia	Liney Cole	Dead	Kiamitia
2	Johnson Webster	"	Jackson	Mary Webster	"	"
3	John James	1896	Kiamitia	No 2		
4	No 1			No 2		
5	No 1			No 2		
6						
7			No4 Born Aug 27, 1900 Enrolled Nov. 5, 1902			
8			Nᵒ.5 Born Sept. 15, 1902 Enrolled Nov. 5, 1902			
9			For child of Nos 1&2 see N.B (Apr. 26, 1906) Card No. 162			
10						
11						
12						
13						
14					#1 to 3	
15					Date of Application for Enrollment.	
16					5/11/99	
17						

Choctaw By Blood Enrollment Cards 1898-1914

RESIDENCE: Kiamitia
POST OFFICE: Grant, I.T.

COUNTY. **Choctaw Nation**

Choctaw Roll (Not Including Freedmen)

CARD No.
FIELD NO. 1631

Dawes' Roll No.	NAME	Relationship to Person First Named	AGE	SEX	BLOOD	TRIBAL ENROLLMENT Year	TRIBAL ENROLLMENT County	TRIBAL ENROLLMENT No.
4614	1 Bohanan, Thomas B. 31	First Named	28	M	1/4	1896	Kiamitia	1422
I.W. 86	2 " Alice 27	Wife	24	F	I.W.	1896	"	14317
4617	3 " Bertha M 8	Dau	5	"	1/8	1896	"	1423
4618	4 " Harmon J 2	Son	2mo	M	1/8			
	5							
	6							
	7	ENROLLMENT						
	8	OF NOS. 1 3 and 4 HEREON APPROVED BY THE SECRETARY						
	9	OF INTERIOR DEC 12 1902						
	10							
	11							
	12	ENROLLMENT						
	13	OF NOS. ~~~ 2 ~~~ HEREON APPROVED BY THE SECRETARY						
	14	OF INTERIOR JUN 13 1903						
	15							
	16							
	17							

TRIBAL ENROLLMENT OF PARENTS

	Name of Father	Year	County	Name of Mother	Year	County
1	Joshua Bohanan	Dead	Kiamitia	Eliz. Bohanan	Dead	Non Citz
2	B.S. Middleton	1896	Non Citz	Eliz. Middleton	1896	" "
3	No 1			No 2		
4	No. 1			No 2		
5						
6	Evidence of marriage of parents of No1 taken in					
7	case of other members of family, satisfactory.					
8	No.4 Enrolled March 28, 1901					
9	For child of Nos 1 &2 see NB (Mar 3-1905) Card #36					
10						
11						
12						
13						#1 to 3
14					Date of Application for Enrollment.	
15						
16					5/11/99	
17						

Choctaw By Blood Enrollment Cards 1898-1914

RESIDENCE: Kiamitia   COUNTY. **Choctaw Nation**   **Choctaw Roll**   CARD No.
POST OFFICE: Goodland, I.T   *(Not Including Freedmen)*   FIELD No. **1632**

Dawes' Roll No.		NAME	Relationship to Person	AGE	SEX	BLOOD	TRIBAL ENROLLMENT		
							Year	County	No.
4619	1	Morris, Israel ~~DIED PRIOR TO SEPTEMBER 25, 1902~~	First Named	25	M	Full	1896	Kiamitia	8711
	2								
	3								
	4								
	5								
	6	ENROLLMENT							
	7	OF NOS. 1 HEREON APPROVED BY THE SECRETARY							
	8	OF INTERIOR DEC 12 1902							
	9								
	10								
	11								
	12								
	13								
	14								
	15								
	16								
	17								

TRIBAL ENROLLMENT OF PARENTS

	Name of Father	Year	County	Name of Mother	Year	County
1	Gilbert Morris	Dead	Kiamitia	Lucy Morris	Dead	Kiamitia
2						
3						
4						
5						
6	No1 died in Nov. 1900. Proof of death filed Dec 30, 1902					
7	No.1 died Nov 1-1900: Enrollment cancelled by Department July 8, 1904					
8						
9						
10						
11						
12						
13						
14						
15						
16			Date of Application for Enrollment.	5/11/99		
17						

Choctaw By Blood Enrollment Cards 1898-1914

RESIDENCE: Kiamitia   COUNTY: **Choctaw Nation**   **Choctaw Roll**   CARD NO.
POST OFFICE: Goodland, I.T.   *(Not Including Freedmen)*   FIELD NO. **1633**

Dawes' Roll No.	NAME	Relationship to Person First Named	AGE	SEX	BLOOD	TRIBAL ENROLLMENT Year	TRIBAL ENROLLMENT County	TRIBAL ENROLLMENT No.
4620	1 James, Benjamin ³²	First Named	29	M	Full	1896	Kiamitia	7088
4621	2 " Winnie ²²	Wife	19	F	"	1896	"	7089
4622	3 ~~Fannie~~ DIED PRIOR TO SEPTEMBER 25, 1902	Dau	7mo	"	"			
4623	4 Coleman, Louisa ¹²	Sister in Law	9	"	"	1896	Kiamitia	2706
	5							
	6							
	7							
	8							
	9							
	10							
	11	ENROLLMENT						
	12	OF NOS. 1 2 3 and 4 HEREON APPROVED BY THE SECRETARY						
	13	OF INTERIOR Dec 12 1902						
	14							
	15							
	16							
	17							

TRIBAL ENROLLMENT OF PARENTS

	Name of Father	Year	County	Name of Mother	Year	County
1	George James	Dead	Jackson	Manda James	Dead	Jackson
2	Lon Coleman	"	Kiamitia	Viney Coleman	"	Kiamitia
3	No 1			No 2		
4	Lon Coleman	Dead	Kiamitia	Viney Coleman	Dead	Kiamitia
5						
6						
7			Nº3 Died Oct. 14, 1901, proof of death filed Feby. 21, 1903.			
8			No.3 died Oct. 14, 1901: Enrollment cancelled by Department July 8, 1904. For child of Nos 1&2 see NB (March 3, 1905) #1083			
9						
10						
11						
12						
13						
14						
15				Date of Application for Enrollment.	5/11/99	
16						
17	P.O. Soper I.T. 4/11/05					

Choctaw By Blood Enrollment Cards 1898-1914

RESIDENCE: Kiamitia COUNTY.
POST OFFICE: Goodland, I.T

Choctaw Nation

Choctaw Roll
(Not Including Freedmen)

CARD No.
FIELD No. 1634

Dawes' Roll No.	NAME	Relationship to Person	AGE	SEX	BLOOD	TRIBAL ENROLLMENT		
						Year	County	No.
4624	1 Skelton, Alexander ³¹	First Named	28	M	Full	1896	Kiamitia	11515
4625	2 " Mollie ⁴⁷	Wife	44	F	"	1896	"	11516
	3							
	4							
	5							
	6							
	7							
	8							
	9							
	10							
	11	ENROLLMENT						
	12	OF NOS. 1 and 2 HEREON APPROVED BY THE SECRETARY						
	13	OF INTERIOR DEC 12 1902						
	14							
	15							
	16							
	17							

TRIBAL ENROLLMENT OF PARENTS

	Name of Father	Year	County	Name of Mother	Year	County
1	Morgan Skelton	Dead	Jackson	Winey Skelton	Dead	Jackson
2	Ko-li-che	"	"	Sallie	1896	Kiamitia
3						
4						
5						
6	Nos 1 and 2 have separated					
7	No.1 is Husband of Ellen Austin, Choctaw Card #1671					
8						
9						
10						
11						
12						
13						
14					Date of Application for Enrollment.	
15						
16					5/11/99	
17						

Choctaw By Blood Enrollment Cards 1898-1914

Dawes' Roll No.	NAME	Relationship to Person First Named	AGE	SEX	BLOOD	TRIBAL ENROLLMENT		
						Year	County	No.
4626	1 Alexander, Isaac ⁶³	First Named	60	M	Full	1896	Kiamitia	337
4627	2 " , Sallie ~~DIED PRIOR TO SEPTEMBER 25 1902~~	Wife	40	F	"	1896	"	338
4628	3 Peter, Lucy ¹²	S.Dau	15	"	"	1896	"	339
4629	4 " , Edward ¹⁰	S.Son	7	M	"	1896	"	340
	5							
	6							
	7							
	8							
	9							
	10							
	11	ENROLLMENT OF NOS. 1 2 3 and 4 HEREON						
	12	APPROVED BY THE SECRETARY OF INTERIOR Dec 12, 1902.						
	13							
	14							
	15							
	16							
	17							

TRIBAL ENROLLMENT OF PARENTS

	Name of Father	Year	County	Name of Mother	Year	County
1	Alex. Alexander	Dead	Towson	I-yo-ko-mat-una	Dead	Towson
2	~~Na-kish-ho-yaby~~	"	~~Kiamitia~~		"	~~Kiamitia~~
3	Isom Peter	"	"	No 2		
4	" "	"	"	No 2		
5						
6		No.3 on 1896 roll as Lucy Alexander.				
7		No.4 " 1896 " " Edward "				
		~~No.2 died Aug-1899; Proof of death filed Dec. 6, 1902.~~				
8		No.2 died Aug-1899; Enrollment cancelled by Department July 8, 1904.				
9		For child of No.3 See NB (Apr. 26, 1906) Card No. 177.				
10						
11						
12						
13						
14						
15						
16				Date of Application for Enrollment.	5/11/99	
17	P.O. Lenton, I.T. 3/13/07					

Choctaw By Blood Enrollment Cards 1898-1914

RESIDENCE: Kiamitia   COUNTY. **Choctaw Nation**   Choctaw Roll *(Not Including Freedmen)*   CARD No.

POST OFFICE: Grant, I.T   FIELD No. 1636

Dawes' Roll No.	NAME		Relationship to Person First Named	AGE	SEX	BLOOD	TRIBAL ENROLLMENT		
							Year	County	No.
4630	1 Greenwood, Hall	55	First Named	52	M	Full	1896	Kiamitia	4812
4631	2 Morris, Gilbert	7	Ward	4	"	"	1896	"	8710
	3								
	4								
	5								
	6								
	7								
	8								
	9	ENROLLMENT							
	10	OF NOS. 1 and 2 HEREON APPROVED BY THE SECRETARY							
	11	OF INTERIOR DEC 12 1902							
	12								
	13								
	14								
	15								
	16								
	17								

TRIBAL ENROLLMENT OF PARENTS

	Name of Father	Year	County	Name of Mother	Year	County
1	Greenwood	Dead	Kiamitia	Chom-pa	Dead	Jackson
2	Amos Morris	"	"	Frances Johnson	"	Kiamitia
3						
4						
5						
6	No 1 is legal guardian of No 2. Certified copy of guardianship					
7	papers filed May 25, 1903.					
8	No 1 was married to Maggie Ward Choctaw card #949 Jany 1, 1903.					
9	For child of No.1 see NB (March 3, 1905) #11202 " " " " " " (April 26, 1906) #844					
10						
11						
12						
13						
14						
15						
16				Date of Application for Enrollment.	5/11/99	
17						

Choctaw By Blood Enrollment Cards 1898-1914

RESIDENCE: Kiamitia   COUNTY. **Choctaw Nation**   **Choctaw Roll**   CARD NO.
POST OFFICE: Grant, I.T.   _(Not Including Freedmen)_   FIELD NO.   1637

Dawes' Roll No.	NAME	Relationship to Person First Named	AGE	SEX	BLOOD	TRIBAL ENROLLMENT Year	County	No.
4632	1 Battiest, Osborne ³⁷	First Named	34	M	Full	1896	Kiamitia	1441
4633	2 " Louisa ²³	Wife	20	F	"	1893	Jackson	602
4634	3 DIED PRIOR TO SEPTEMBER 25, 1902 Robert	Son	1	M	"			
4635	4 DIED PRIOR TO SEPTEMBER 25, 1902 Ellison	Son	4mo	M	"			
14688	5 " Davis ¹	Son	6mo	M	"			
	6							
	7							
	8	ENROLLMENT OF NOS. 1 2 3 and 4 HEREON						
	9	APPROVED BY THE SECRETARY OF INTERIOR DEC 12 1902						
	10							
	11	ENROLLMENT						
	12	OF NOS. 5 HEREON						
	13	APPROVED BY THE SECRETARY OF INTERIOR MAY 20 1903						
	14							
	15							
	16							
	17							

TRIBAL ENROLLMENT OF PARENTS

	Name of Father	Year	County	Name of Mother	Year	County
1	Israel Battiest	Dead	Kiamitia	Tennessee Battiest	Dead	Towson
2	Jos. Tanetubbee	"	Jackson	Sophie Tanetubbee	1896	Kiamitia
3	No 1			No 2		
4	No.1			No.2		
5	No 1			No 2		
6						
7			No2 on 1893 Pay roll as Lawash Tanetubee, Page 70, No 602			
8			Jackson Co			
9			For child of Nos 1&2 see NB (March 3, 1905) #1193			
10						
11						
12			No.4 Enrolled June 27th, 1900.			
13			No3 died March 2, 1901; proof of death filed Dec 6, 1902			
14			No4 " November – 1900; " " " " " " "		Date of Application for Enrollment. #1 to 3 inc
15			No5 born June 2, 1902; enrolled Dec. 9, 1902			
16						5/11/99
17			No. 3 died March 2, 1901; No. 4 died Nov - 1900; Enrollment cancelled by Department July 8, 1904			

137

Choctaw By Blood Enrollment Cards 1898-1914

RESIDENCE: Kiamitia   COUNTY. **Choctaw Nation**   **Choctaw Roll**   CARD No.

POST OFFICE: Goodland, I.T.   *(Not Including Freedmen)*   FIELD NO. 1638

Dawes' Roll No.	NAME	Relationship to Person First Named	AGE	SEX	BLOOD	TRIBAL ENROLLMENT Year	County	No.
4636	1 Austin, Sillen ~~DIED PRIOR TO SEPTEMBER 25 1902~~		54	F	Full	1896	Kiamitia	9964
	2							
	3							
	4							
	5							
	6							
	7							
	8							
	9							
	10							
	11	ENROLLMENT						
	12	OF NOS. 1 HEREON APPROVED BY THE SECRETARY						
	13	OF INTERIOR DEC 12 1902						
	14							
	15							
	16							
	17							

TRIBAL ENROLLMENT OF PARENTS

	Name of Father	Year	County	Name of Mother	Year	County
1	John Battiest	Dead	Kiamitia		Dead	Kiamitia
2						
3						
4						
5						
6			On 1896 roll as Silly Oston			
7						
8		No.1 died July – 1901 : Enrollment cancelled by Department May 2-1906				
9						
10						
11						
12						
13						
14						
15						
16					Date of Application for Enrollment.	5/11/99
17						

RESIDENCE: Kiamitia   COUNTY. **Choctaw Nation**   **Choctaw Roll**   CARD NO.
POST OFFICE: Grant, I.T.   *(Not Including Freedmen)*   FIELD NO. **1639**

Dawes' Roll No.	NAME	Relationship to Person First Named	AGE	SEX	BLOOD	TRIBAL ENROLLMENT Year	County	No.
4637	1 McIntosh, Silvey ²⁸	First Named	25	F	Full	1896	Kiamitia	9391
4638	2 " John G. ²⁵	S Son	22	M	1/2	1896	"	9392
4639	3 " Alexander ²³	"	20	"	1/2	1896	"	9393
4640	4 " William R ¹⁸	"	15	"	1/2	1896	"	9394
4641	5 " Rutha ¹³	S Dau	10	F	1/2	1896	"	9395
I.W. 1498	6 " John G.	Hus	52	M	I.W.	1896	"	14873
	7							
	8							
	9	ENROLLMENT OF NOS. 1 2 3 4 and 5 HEREON APPROVED BY THE SECRETARY OF INTERIOR						
	10							
	11							
	12	ENROLLMENT						
	13	OF NOS. ~~~ 6 ~~~ HEREON APPROVED BY THE SECRETARY						
	14	OF INTERIOR Nov 27, 1905						
	15							
	16							
	17							

TRIBAL ENROLLMENT OF PARENTS

	Name of Father	Year	County	Name of Mother	Year	County
1	Jesse Roberts	Dead	Kiamitia	Mary Roberts	Dead	Kiamitia
2	J.G. McIntosh	1896	Non Citz	Mary Roberts	"	"
3	" "	1896	" "	" "	"	"
4	" "	1896	" "	" "	"	"
5	" "	1896	" "	" "	"	"
6	Louis McIntosh	Dead	Creek	Ruth McIntosh	"	Cherokee
7						
8						
9						
10	No.3 on 1896 roll as Alex A. McIntosh					
11	No.4 " 1896 " " William "					
12	Husband of No.1 and father of children on this card is					
13	~~John G. McIntosh on Choctaw Card #D942.~~					
14	No.6 also on 1885 Choctaw Census Roll Kiamitia County No 418					
15	No.6 transferred from Choctaw Card D.942 October 20, 1905. See					
16	decision of October 4, 1905.			#1 to 5		
17				Date of Application for Enrollment 5/11/99		

Choctaw By Blood Enrollment Cards 1898-1914

RESIDENCE: Kiamitia	COUNTY.	Choctaw Nation	Choctaw Roll (Not Including Freedmen)	CARD NO.
POST OFFICE: Goodland, I.T				FIELD NO. 1640

Dawes' Roll No.	NAME		Relationship to Person First Named	AGE	SEX	BLOOD	TRIBAL ENROLLMENT		
							Year	County	No.
4642	1 Holton, Sally	86	First Named	83	F	Full	1896	Kiamitia	2685
	2								
	3								
	4								
	5								
	6								
	7								
	8								
	9								
	10								
	11								
	12								
	13								
	14								
	15								
	16								
	17								

ENROLLMENT
OF NOS. 1 HEREON
APPROVED BY THE SECRETARY
OF INTERIOR DEC 12 1902

TRIBAL ENROLLMENT OF PARENTS

	Name of Father	Year	County	Name of Mother	Year	County
1	A-pok-sha-nubbee	Dead	in Mississippi	Sah-le-o	Dead	Towson
2						
3						
4						
5						
6						
7		On 1896 roll as Sally Colton				
8						
9						
10						
11						
12						
13						
14					Date of Application for Enrollment.	
15						
16					5/11/99	
17						

Choctaw By Blood Enrollment Cards 1898-1914

RESIDENCE: Kiamitia   COUNTY. **Choctaw Nation**   **Choctaw Roll**   CARD NO.
POST OFFICE: Goodland, I.T   *(Not Including Freedmen)*   FIELD NO.   1641

Dawes' Roll No.	NAME	Relationship to Person Named	AGE	SEX	BLOOD	TRIBAL ENROLLMENT Year	County	No.
4643	1 Webster, Daniel ³¹	First Named	28	M	Full	1896	Kiamitia	13721
4644	2 " Lucy ²⁸	Wife	25	F	"	1896	"	13722
	3							
	4							
	5	ENROLLMENT						
	6	OF NOS. 1 and 2 HEREON APPROVED BY THE SECRETARY						
	7	OF INTERIOR DEC 12 1902						
	8							
	9							
	10							
	11							
	12							
	13							
	14							
	15							
	16							
	17							

TRIBAL ENROLLMENT OF PARENTS

Name of Father	Year	County	Name of Mother	Year	County
1 Johnson Webster	Dead	Jackson	Mollie Webster	1896	Kiamitia
2 John Wilson	"		Lucinda Wilson	Dead	"
3					
4					
5					
6		For child of No1 see NB (March 3, 1905) #1212			
7					
8					
9					
10					
11					
12					
13					
14				Date of Application for Enrollment.	
15					
16				5/11/99	
17 Hugo, I.T. 11/5/07					

141

Choctaw By Blood Enrollment Cards 1898-1914

RESIDENCE: Kiamitia
POST OFFICE: Grant, I.T.
COUNTY.
Choctaw Nation
Choctaw Roll
(Not Including Freedmen)
CARD NO.
FIELD NO. **1642**

Dawes' Roll No.	NAME	Relationship to Person First Named	AGE	SEX	BLOOD	TRIBAL ENROLLMENT Year	County	No.
4645	1 ~~DIED PRIOR TO SEPTEMBER 25, 1902~~ ~~Morris, Sena~~	~~First Named~~	~~25~~	~~F~~	~~Full~~	~~1893~~	~~Jackson~~	~~204~~
4646	2 ~~DIED PRIOR TO SEPTEMBER 25, 1902~~ ~~, Liza~~	~~Dau~~	~~10mo~~	"	"			
14689	3 Fulton, Rilda	1 Dau	12mo	"	"			
	4							
	5							
	6							
	7							
	8	ENROLLMENT OF NOS. 1 and 2 HEREON						
	9	APPROVED BY THE SECRETARY						
	10	OF INTERIOR Dec 12, 1902						
	11							
	12							
	13	ENROLLMENT OF NOS. 3 HEREON						
	14	APPROVED BY THE SECRETARY						
	15	OF INTERIOR May 20, 1903						
	16							
	17							

	TRIBAL ENROLLMENT OF PARENTS					
	Name of Father	Year	County	Name of Mother	Year	County
1	~~Joseph Tanitobe~~	~~Dead~~	~~Jackson~~	~~Sophia Tanitobe~~	~~1896~~	~~Kiamitia~~
2	~~Amos Morris~~	"	~~Kiamitia~~	~~No 1~~		
3	William Fulton			No 1		
4						
5						
6						
7						
8						
9		No.1 on 1893 Pay roll as Sinie Fry, Page 24, No.204, Jackson Co.				
10						
11						
12		No1 died Feb 19, 1902: Proof of death filed Dec 6, 1902				
13		No2 " May 14, 1900: " " " " " "				
13		No3 Born Dec. 19, 1901. Proof of birth filed Dec. 24, 1902				
14		Father of No.3 is No1 on Choc 1614				
15		No.1 died Feb.19,1902: No.2 died May14,1900: Enrollment cancelled by Department July 8,1904				
16					Date of Application for Enrollment. a#1&2 5/11/99	
17						

142

Choctaw By Blood Enrollment Cards 1898-1914

RESIDENCE: Kiamitia   COUNTY. **Choctaw Nation**   **Choctaw Roll** *(Not Including Freedmen)*   CARD NO.

POST OFFICE: Grant, I.T.   FIELD NO. **1643**

Dawes' Roll No.	NAME	Relationship to Person First Named	AGE	SEX	BLOOD	TRIBAL ENROLLMENT Year	County	No.
4647	1 Tanitobe, Sophia DIED PRIOR TO SEPTEMBER 25 1902	First Named	50	F	Full	1893	Jackson	600
	2							
	3							
	4							
	5							
	6							
	7							
	8							
	9							
	10							
	11							
	12							
	13							
	14							
	15							
	16							
	17							

ENROLLMENT
OF NOS. 1 HEREON
APPROVED BY THE SECRETARY
OF INTERIOR DEC 12 1902

TRIBAL ENROLLMENT OF PARENTS

Name of Father	Year	County	Name of Mother	Year	County
1 John Hale	Dead			Dead	
2					
3					
4					
5	On 1893 Pay roll as Sophia Tanetubee, Page 70, No 600, Jackson Co				
6					
7	No.1 died in 1900; Enrollment cancelled by Department May 2 1906				
8					
9					
10					
11					
12					
13					
14					
15					
16			Date of Application for Enrollment.	5/11/99	
17					

143

Choctaw By Blood Enrollment Cards 1898-1914

RESIDENCE: Red River COUNTY. **Choctaw Nation** **Choctaw Roll** CARD No.
POST OFFICE: Shawneetown, I.T (Not Including Freedmen) FIELD No. 1644

Dawes' Roll No.	NAME	Relationship to Person First Named	AGE	SEX	BLOOD	TRIBAL ENROLLMENT		
						Year	County	No.
4648	Hayes, Pitman DIED PRIOR TO SEPTEMBER 25 1902		43	M	Full	1896	Red River	5655
2								
3								
4								
5								
6								
7								
8								
9								
10								
11	ENROLLMENT							
12	OF NOS. 1 HEREON APPROVED BY THE SECRETARY							
13	OF INTERIOR DEC 12 1902							
14								
15								
16								
17								

TRIBAL ENROLLMENT OF PARENTS

	Name of Father	Year	County	Name of Mother	Year	County
1	Wesley Hayes	Dead	Red River		Dead	Bok Tuklo
2						
3						
4						
5	No. 1 died July 1899; Enrollment cancelled by Department May 3 1906					
6	Is slightly insane					
7						
8	Also on 1896 roll Kiamitia Co, Page 140,					
9	No 5771					
10						
11						
12						
13						
14						
15						
16				Date of Application for Enrollment.	5/11/99	
17						

144

Choctaw By Blood Enrollment Cards 1898-1914

RESIDENCE: Kiamitia   COUNTY. **Choctaw Nation**   **Choctaw Roll**   CARD NO.
POST OFFICE: Grant, I.T.   *(Not Including Freedmen)*   FIELD NO.   1645

Dawes' Roll No.	NAME		Relationship to Person First Named	AGE	SEX	BLOOD	TRIBAL ENROLLMENT		
							Year	County	No.
4649	1 Tanitubbi, Charles	26	First Named	23	M	Full	1896	Kiamitia	12354
4650	2 " Amelia	21	Wife	18	F	"	1893	Atoka	151
14690	3 " Jennie	2	Dau	2	F	"			
	4								
	5								
	6	ENROLLMENT							
	7	OF NOS. 1 and 2 HEREON							
	8	APPROVED BY THE SECRETARY OF INTERIOR DEC 12 1902							
	9								
	10	ENROLLMENT							
	11	OF NOS. 3 HEREON							
	12	APPROVED BY THE SECRETARY OF INTERIOR MAY 20 1903							
	13								
	14								
	15								
	16								
	17								

TRIBAL ENROLLMENT OF PARENTS

	Name of Father	Year	County	Name of Mother	Year	County
1	Sam Tanitubbi	1896	Kiamitia	Elsie Tanitubbi	1896	Kiamitia
2	Adam Clark	Dead	Atoka	Jane Clark	Dead	Blue
3	Nº1			Nº2		
4						
5						
6			Sam and Elsin Tanitubbi card #533			
7						
8						
9			No2 on 1893 Pay roll as Amelia Clark Page 14, No 151 Atoka Co.			
10			Nº3 Born Sept. 9, 1900, enrolled Dec. 24, 1902			
11						
12						
13						
14						#1&2 inc
15					Date of Application for Enrollment.	
16					5/11/99	
17						

145

Choctaw By Blood Enrollment Cards 1898-1914

RESIDENCE: Jacks Fork COUNTY. **Choctaw Nation** **Choctaw Roll** CARD NO.
POST OFFICE: Stringtown, I.T. (Not Including Freedmen) FIELD NO. **1646**

Dawes' Roll No.	NAME	Relationship to Person First Named	AGE	SEX	BLOOD	TRIBAL ENROLLMENT		
						Year	County	No.
4651	1 Fobb, Namon DIED ABOUT SEPTEMBER 25, 1902		24	M	Full	1896	Jacks Fork	4559
4652	2 " Benjamin 19	Bro	16	"	"	1896	" "	4510
	3							
	4							
	5							
	6							
	7							
	8							
	9							
	10							
	11							
	12							
	13							
	14							
	15							
	16							
	17							

> ENROLLMENT
> OF NOS. 1 and 2 HEREON
> APPROVED BY THE SECRETARY
> OF INTERIOR Dec. 12, 1902.

TRIBAL ENROLLMENT OF PARENTS

Name of Father	Year	County	Name of Mother	Year	County
1 Frank Fobb	Dead	Jacks Fork	Lottie Fobb	Dead	Jacks Fork
2 " "	"	" "	" "	"	" " "
3					
4					
5	No.1 on 1896 roll as Lyman Fobb.				
6					
7	No1 died Nov. 25, 1899; Proof of death filed Dec. 5, 1902				
8	No2 is husband of Louisa Anderson, Choctaw card #1939, Jany 22, 1903				
9	No.1 died Nov. 25, 1899; Enrollment cancelled by Department July 8, 1904.				
10					
11					
12					
13					
14					
15					
16			Date of Application for Enrollment.		5/11/99
17	P.O. Kosoma[sic], I.T. 12/1 '02				

Choctaw By Blood Enrollment Cards 1898-1914

RESIDENCE: Kiamitia POST OFFICE: Grant, I.T. COUNTY, **Choctaw Nation** **Choctaw Roll** *(Not Including Freedmen)* CARD NO. FIELD NO. **1647**

Dawes' Roll No.	NAME	Relationship to Person First Named	AGE	SEX	BLOOD	TRIBAL ENROLLMENT Year	TRIBAL ENROLLMENT County	TRIBAL ENROLLMENT No.
4653	1 Bohanan, Anthony 60	First Named	57	M	Full	1896	Kiamitia	1417
4654	2 " , Lizzie 53	Wife	50	F	"	1896	"	1418
DEAD	3 " , Style	Son	13	M	"	1896	"	1420
4655	4 " , Elsie 7	Ward	4	F	"	1896	"	1421
	5							
	6							
	7	ENROLLMENT						
	8	OF NOS. 1 2 and 4 HEREON						
	9	APPROVED BY THE SECRETARY OF INTERIOR Dec. 12, 1902						
	10							
	11							
	12	No.3 hereon dismissed under order of						
	13	the Commission to the Five Civilized						
	14	Tribes of March 31, 1905.						
	15							
	16							
	17							

TRIBAL ENROLLMENT OF PARENTS

Name of Father	Year	County	Name of Mother	Year	County
1 Jesse Bohanan	Dead	Red River	Nancy Bohanan	Dead	Red River
2 Robinson Timehala	"	"	Amy Timehala	1896	"
3 No 1			No 2		
4 Unknown			Ella Byington	1896	Kiamitia
5					
6					
7					
8	No3 died Aug. 11, 1900. Proof of death filed Nov. 3, 1902.				
9					
10					
11					
12					
13					
14					
15				Date of Application for Enrollment.	
16				5/11/99	
17					

147

Choctaw By Blood Enrollment Cards 1898-1914

RESIDENCE: Kiamitia COUNTY. **Choctaw Nation** **Choctaw Roll** (Not Including Freedmen) CARD No. FIELD No. **1648**
POST OFFICE: Grant, I.T.

Dawes' Roll No.	NAME		Relationship to Person First Named	AGE	SEX	BLOOD	TRIBAL ENROLLMENT		
							Year	County	No.
4656	1 Bohanan, Frances	28	First Named	25	F	Full	1896	Kiamitia	1419
4657	2 Lenox, Lena	2	Dau	2mo	F	1/2	New born		
4658	3 " Wilson	1	Son	4mo	M	1/2			
	4								
	5								
	6								
	7	ENROLLMENT OF NOS. 1 2 and 3 HEREON							
	8	APPROVED BY THE SECRETARY OF INTERIOR DEC 12 1902							
	9								
	10								
	11								
	12								
	13								
	14								
	15								
	16								
	17								

TRIBAL ENROLLMENT OF PARENTS

	Name of Father	Year	County	Name of Mother	Year	County
1	Anthony Bohanan	1896	Kiamitia	Lizzie Bohanan	1896	Kiamitia
2	Will Lenox			No.1		
3	" "		non-citizen	Nº1		
4						
5						
6						
7	No 2 Illegitimate. Enrolled, June 8, 1900					
8	Nº3 Born March 24, 1902, enrolled Aug. 6, 1902					
9	For child of No.1 see NB (March 3, 1905) #1134					
10						
11						
12						
13						
14					Date of Application for Enrollment.	
15						
16					5/11/99	
17						

Choctaw By Blood Enrollment Cards 1898-1914

RESIDENCE: Jackson   COUNTY. **Choctaw Nation**   **Choctaw Roll**   CARD NO.

POST OFFICE: Mayhew, I.T.   (Not Including Freedmen)   FIELD NO. **1649**

Dawes' Roll No.	NAME		Relationship to Person First Named	AGE	SEX	BLOOD	TRIBAL ENROLLMENT		
							Year	County	No.
4659	1 Bench, Sam	23	First Named	20	M	Full	1896	Jackson	1527
4660	2 " , Mollie	36	Wife	33	F	"	1896	"	4306
4661	3 Frazier, Ben DIED PRIOR TO SEPTEMBER 25 1902		Bro in Law	3	M	"	1896	"	4307
4662	4 McCoy, John	12	Step-Son	9	"	"	1896	"	9407
	5								
	6								
	7								
	8								
	9								
	10								
	11	ENROLLMENT							
	12	OF NOS. 1 2 3 and 4 HEREON APPROVED BY THE SECRETARY							
	13	OF INTERIOR Dec. 12, 1902							
	14								
	15								
	16								
	17								

TRIBAL ENROLLMENT OF PARENTS

	Name of Father	Year	County	Name of Mother	Year	County
1	Chris Bench	Dead	Jackson	Winnie Bench	Dead	Jackson
2	Deborn Frazier	1896	"	Sophy Frazier	1896	"
3	"	1896	"	"	1896	"
4	Nelson McCoy	Dead	Blue	No 2		
5						
6						
7						
8	No 2 on 1896 roll as Mollie Frazier					
9	No.4 also on Choctaw 1896 Census Roll, P.10, #373, as John Allen					
10	No.2 is now wife of Dave Homer 11/2 '02 No.2 is 28 years old.					
11	For child of No.2 see NB (March 3, 1905) #851					
12	No.3 died in 1900; Proof of death filed Nov. 26, 1902					
13	No3 died - - 1900; Enrollment cancelled by Department July 8, 1904.					
14	For child of No.1 see NB (March 3, 1905) #1101					
15					9/25/16	as to Nos 1 2&3
16					Date of Application for Enrollment	5/11/99
17	P.O. Jackson, I.T. 11/21/02				9/25/16	as to No.4
					Date of Application for Enrollment	Aug 22/99.

149

Choctaw By Blood Enrollment Cards 1898-1914

RESIDENCE: Kiamitia
POST OFFICE: Goodland, I.T.
COUNTY: **Choctaw Nation**
Choctaw Roll *(Not Including Freedmen)*
CARD NO.
FIELD NO. **1650**

Dawes' Roll No.	NAME		Relationship to Person First Named	AGE	SEX	BLOOD	TRIBAL ENROLLMENT		
							Year	County	No.
4663	1 Spring, Samuel B.	28	First Named	25	M	3/4	1896	Kiamitia	11475
I.W. 640	2 " , Maud M.	23	Wife	20	F	I.W.	1896	"	15049
4664	3 " , Ethel	3	Dau	8mo	F	3/8			
	4								
	5								
	6	ENROLLMENT							
	7	OF NOS. 1 and 3 HEREON APPROVED BY THE SECRETARY							
	8	OF INTERIOR Dec. 12, 1902							
	9	ENROLLMENT OF NOS. 2 HEREON							
	10	APPROVED BY THE SECRETARY OF INTERIOR Mar. 26, 1904							
	11								
	12								
	13								
	14								
	15								
	16								
	17								

TRIBAL ENROLLMENT OF PARENTS

	Name of Father	Year	County	Name of Mother	Year	County
1	Levi Spring	1896	Kiamitia	Bessie Spring	Dead	Kiamitia
2	J.J. Terry	1896	"	Phoebe Terry	"	Mississippi
3	No.1			No.2		
4						
5			No. 2 enrolled as Maude Spring.			
6						
7			No3 Enrolled April 7th, 1900.			
8						
9						
10						
11						
12						
13						
14						
15				9/25/16		as to Nos1&2
16				Date of Application for Enrollment		5/11/99
17	P.O. Hugo I.T. 12/4/02					

150

Choctaw By Blood Enrollment Cards 1898-1914

RESIDENCE: Kiamitia   COUNTY: **Choctaw Nation**   **Choctaw Roll** (Not Including Freedmen)   CARD NO.

POST OFFICE: Grant I.T.   FIELD NO. **1651**

Dawes' Roll No.	NAME	Relationship to Person First Named	AGE	SEX	BLOOD	TRIBAL ENROLLMENT		
						Year	County	No.
4665	1 Alexander, Eastman 45	First Named	42	M	Full	1896	Kiamitia	341
4666	2 " Lila 44	Wife	41	F	"a	1896	"	342
	3							
	4							
	5							
	6	ENROLLMENT						
	7	OF NOS. 1 and 2 HEREON APPROVED BY THE SECRETARY						
	8	OF INTERIOR DEC 12 1902						
	9							
	10							
	11							
	12							
	13							
	14							
	15							
	16							
	17							

TRIBAL ENROLLMENT OF PARENTS

	Name of Father	Year	County	Name of Mother	Year	County
1	Alexander Itolla	Dead	Towson	Sallie Itolla	Dead	Towson
2	Chalatubbee	"	Kiamitia	Polly	"	Kiamitia
3						
4						
5						
6						
7		No.2 enrolled as Lillie Alexander				
8						
9						
10						
11						
12						
13						
14						
15						
16			Date of Application for Enrollment.	5/11/99		
17						

151

Choctaw By Blood Enrollment Cards 1898-1914

RESIDENCE: **Kiamitia** COUNTY. **Choctaw Nation** **Choctaw Roll** CARD NO.

POST OFFICE: **Nelson I.T.** (Not Including Freedmen) FIELD NO. **1652**

Dawes' Roll No.	NAME	Relationship to Person	AGE	SEX	BLOOD	TRIBAL ENROLLMENT		
						Year	County	No.
~~4667~~	1 ~~Oklabe Joseph~~ DIED PRIOR TO SEPTEMBER 28 1902	First Named	~~35~~	~~M~~	~~Full~~	~~1896~~	~~Kiamitia~~	~~9965~~
~~4668~~	2 ~~Simeon~~ DIED PRIOR TO SEPTEMBER 28 1902	Son	~~7~~	~~M~~	"	~~1896~~	"	~~9967~~
	3							
	4							
	5							
	6							
	7							
	8	ENROLLMENT OF NOS. 1 and 2 HEREON						
	9	APPROVED BY THE SECRETARY						
	10	OF INTERIOR DEC 12 1902						
	11							
	12							
	13							
	14							
	15							
	16							
	17							

TRIBAL ENROLLMENT OF PARENTS

	Name of Father	Year	County	Name of Mother	Year	County
1	~~Davis Oklabe~~	~~1896~~	~~Kiamitia~~		~~Dead~~	~~Kiamitia~~
2	~~No 1~~			~~Sunaly Oklabe~~	"	"
3						
4						
5			No 2 enrolled as Oklobbe			
6			No1 died August 8,1902; No2 died July 26,1902· Enrollment cancelled by Department			
7	May 2-1906					
8						
9						
10						
11						
12						
13						
14						
15						
16				Date of Application for Enrollment.		5/11/99
17						

Choctaw By Blood Enrollment Cards 1898-1914

RESIDENCE: Kiamitia
POST OFFICE: Grant, I.T.

COUNTY. **Choctaw Nation**

Choctaw Roll
(Not Including Freedmen)

CARD NO.
FIELD NO. 1653

Dawes' Roll No.	NAME		Relationship to Person First Named	AGE	SEX	BLOOD	TRIBAL ENROLLMENT		
							Year	County	No.
4669	1 Skelton, Noel	31	First Named	28	M	Full	1896	Kiamitia	11545
4670	2 " Jincy	30	Wife	27	F	"	1896	"	11546
	3								
	4								
	5								
	6								
	7								
	8								
	9								
	10								
	11								
	12								
	13								
	14								
	15								
	16								
	17								

ENROLLMENT
OF NOS. 1 and 2 HEREON
APPROVED BY THE SECRETARY
OF INTERIOR   DEC 12 1902

TRIBAL ENROLLMENT OF PARENTS

	Name of Father	Year	County	Name of Mother	Year	County
1	Morgan Skelton	Dead	Jackson	Winey Skelton	Dead	Jackson
2	Sam Tanetubbee	1896	Kiamitia	Elsie Tanetubbee	1896	Kiamitia
3						
4						
5	For child of Nos 1&2 see NB (Apr 26-06) Card #854					
6						
7						
8						
9						
10						
11						
12						
13						
14						
15					Date of Application for Enrollment.	
16					5/11/99	
17						

153

Choctaw By Blood Enrollment Cards 1898-1914

RESIDENCE: Kiamitia   COUNTY. **Choctaw Nation**   **Choctaw Roll** (*Not Including Freedmen*)   CARD No.

POST OFFICE: Grant, I.T.   FIELD No. 1654

Dawes' Roll No.	NAME	Relationship to Person First Named	AGE	SEX	BLOOD	TRIBAL ENROLLMENT		
						Year	County	No.
4671	1 Coleman, Thomas [19]	First Named	16	M	Full	1896	Kiamitia	2705
	2							
	3							
	4							
	5	ENROLLMENT						
	6	OF NOS. 1 HEREON APPROVED BY THE SECRETARY						
	7	OF INTERIOR DEC 12 1902						
	8							
	9							
	10							
	11							
	12							
	13							
	14							
	15							
	16							
	17							

TRIBAL ENROLLMENT OF PARENTS

	Name of Father	Year	County	Name of Mother	Year	County
1	Lon Coleman	Dead	Kiamitia	Fannie Coleman	Dead	Kiamitia
2						
3						
4						
5						
6						
7						
8						
9						
10						
11						
12						
13						
14						
15						
16					Date of Application for Enrollment 5/11/99	
17						

Choctaw By Blood Enrollment Cards 1898-1914

RESIDENCE: Kiamitia   COUNTY. **Choctaw Nation**   **Choctaw Roll**   CARD NO.
POST OFFICE: Goodland, I.T.   *(Not Including Freedmen)*   FIELD NO. **1655**

Dawes' Roll No.	NAME	Relationship to Person First Named	AGE	SEX	BLOOD	TRIBAL ENROLLMENT Year	County	No.
DEAD	1 McKinney, Edmund T	Named	47	M	Full	1896	Kiamitia	9370
4672	2 " , Martha 49	Wife	46	F	"	1896	"	9371
4673	3 DIED PRIOR TO SEPTEMBER 25 1902 " , Nancy	Dau	19	"	"	1896	"	9372
4674	4 " , Laura E. 16	"	13	"	"	1896	"	9375
4675	5 " , Sallie 12	"	9	"	"	1896	"	9376
4676	6 " , Ida 10	"	7	"	"	1896	"	9377
4677	7 " , Joseph 7	Son	4	M	"	1896	"	9378
4678	8 DIED PRIOR TO SEPTEMBER 25, 1902 " , Samuel	"	1	"	"			
4679	9 " , Isaac 21	Ward	18	"	"	1896	Kiamitia	9373
4680	10 " , Eli 18	"	15	"	"	1896	"	9374
	11							
	12	ENROLLMENT OF NOS. 23456789and10 HEREON APPROVED BY THE SECRETARY				No.1 hereon dismissed under order of		
	13	OF INTERIOR Dec. 12, 1902				the Commission to the Five Civilized		
	14					Tribes of March 31, 1905.		
	15 No3 died-1901: No8 died-1900: Enrollment cancelled by							
	16							
	17 Department July 8, 1904.							

TRIBAL ENROLLMENT OF PARENTS

	Name of Father	Year	County	Name of Mother	Year	County
1	Tan-tubbee	Dead	Kiamitia	Eliza Tantubbee	Dead	Kiamitia
2	Jane Coat	"	"	Phoebe Wilson	"	"
3	No 1			No 2		
4	No 1			No 2		
5	No 1			No 2		
6	No 1			No 2		
7	No 1			No 2		
8	No 1			No 2		
9	Solomon Tantubbee	Dead	Atoka		Dead	Atoka
10	" "	"	"		"	"
11	No10 is duplicate of No3 on Choctaw Card #4399 approved roll No. 12269					
12	Enrollment hereon cancelled by Department April 5, 1906 (I.T.D.5252-1906) D.C.13102-1906.					
	No1 on 1896 roll as Edmund McKinney					
13	No3 " 1896 " " Nannie "					
14	No10 " 1896 " " Ely "					
15	No1 died July 2, 1900: Proof of death filed Oct. 15, 1902.			Date of Application for Enrollment.		
16	No3 died in 1901: Proof of death filed Dec. 12, 1902. No8 " " 1900: " " " " " " "			5/11/99		
17	P.O. Hugo, I.T. 12/10/06					

Choctaw By Blood Enrollment Cards 1898-1914

RESIDENCE: Jacks Fork   COUNTY. **Choctaw Nation**   **Choctaw Roll** (Not Including Freedmen)   CARD NO. FIELD NO. 1656
POST OFFICE: Antlers, I.T.

Dawes' Roll No.	NAME	Relationship to Person First Named	AGE	SEX	BLOOD	TRIBAL ENROLLMENT		
						Year	County	No.
4681	1 Reuben, Isaac DIED PRIOR TO SEPTEMBER 25 1902	First Named	26	M	Full	1893	Cedar	392
	2							
	3							
	4							
	5							
	6							
	7							
	8							
	9							
	10							
	11	ENROLLMENT						
	12	OF NOS. 1 HEREON						
	13	APPROVED BY THE SECRETARY OF INTERIOR						
	14							
	15							
	16							
	17							

TRIBAL ENROLLMENT OF PARENTS

	Name of Father	Year	County	Name of Mother	Year	County
1	A-pa-la-tubbee	Dead	Kiamitia		Dead	Kiamitia
2						
3						
4						
5						
6	No. 1 died October 18, 1899. Enrollment cancelled by Department Mar. 2, 1906					
7						
8	On 1893 Pay roll, Page 36, No 392, Cedar Co					
9						
10	In penitentiary, Name of mother unknown					
11						
12						
13						
14						
15						
16				Date of Application for Enrollment	5/11/99	
17						

Choctaw By Blood Enrollment Cards 1898-1914

RESIDENCE: Jackson   COUNTY. **Choctaw Nation**   **Choctaw Roll**   CARD No.
POST OFFICE: Mayhew, I.T.   *(Not Including Freedmen)*   FIELD No.   1657

Dawes' Roll No.	NAME	Relationship to Person First Named	AGE	SEX	BLOOD	TRIBAL ENROLLMENT		
						Year	County	No.
4682	1 Battiest, Ratio 33	First Named	30	M	Full	1893	Kiamitia	39
	2							
	3							
	4							
	5							
	6							
	7							
	8							
	9							
	10							
	11	ENROLLMENT						
	12	OF NOS. 1 HEREON APPROVED BY THE SECRETARY						
	13	OF INTERIOR DEC 12 1902						
	14							
	15							
	16							
	17							

TRIBAL ENROLLMENT OF PARENTS

	Name of Father	Year	County	Name of Mother	Year	County
1	Chasie Battiest	Dead	Cedar	Malissie Battiest	Dead	Kiamitia
2						
3						
4						
5						
6		On 1893 Pay roll, Page 6, No 39, Kiamitia Co				
7						
8						
9						
10						
11	*"Died prior to Sept 25, 1902; Not entitled to land or money."					
12		See I.O.L.-G.F. #931-1911				
13						
14						
15						
16				Date of Application for Enrollment.	5/11/99	
17						

Choctaw By Blood Enrollment Cards 1898-1914

Dawes' Roll No.	NAME		Relationship to Person	AGE	SEX	BLOOD	TRIBAL ENROLLMENT		
							Year	County	No.
4683	1	Smith, Silas ~~DIED PRIOR TO SEPTEMBER 25 1902~~	First Named	58	M	Full	1896	Kiamitia	11544
4684	2	" Jane 43	Wife	40	F	"	1893	Cedar	201
	3								
	4								
	5								
	6								
	7								
	8								
	9								
	10	ENROLLMENT							
	11	OF NOS. 1 and 2 HEREON APPROVED BY THE SECRETARY							
	12	OF INTERIOR Dec. 12, 1902							
	13								
	14								
	15								
	16								
	17								

TRIBAL ENROLLMENT OF PARENTS

	Name of Father	Year	County	Name of Mother	Year	County
1	Solomon Smith	Dead	Kiamitia	Pisally Smith	Dead	Kiamitia
2	Washington	"	Cedar		"	Cedar
3						
4						
5						
6						
7						
8		No 2 on 1893 Pay roll as Jancy Hayes, Page 18, No.201 Cedar Co				
9		as Janey Hayes also on 1896 roll page 132 No.5425 Jency				
10		Hayes, Cedar Co.				
11						
12		No.1 died Mch or Apr 1900: Proof of death filed Dec. 6, 1902.				
13		No.1 died April 1900: Enrollment cancelled by Department July 8, 1904.				
14						
15						
16				Date of Application for Enrollment	5/11/99	
17						

158

Choctaw By Blood Enrollment Cards 1898-1914

RESIDENCE: Kiamitia   COUNTY. **Choctaw Nation**   Choctaw Roll   CARD NO.
POST OFFICE: Grant, I.T.   *(Not Including Freedmen)*   FIELD NO. **1659**

Dawes' Roll No.	NAME		Relationship to Person	AGE	SEX	BLOOD	TRIBAL ENROLLMENT		
							Year	County	No.
4685	1 Boatman, Simon	47	First Named	44	M	Full	1896	Kiamitia	1434
4686	2 " , Sibbie	41	Wife	38	F	"	1896	"	1435
	3								
	4								
	5								
	6								
	7								
	8								
	9								
	10								
	11	ENROLLMENT OF NOS. 1 and 2 HEREON APPROVED BY THE SECRETARY OF INTERIOR Dec. 12, 1902.							
	12								
	13								
	14								
	15								
	16								
	17								

TRIBAL ENROLLMENT OF PARENTS

	Name of Father	Year	County	Name of Mother	Year	County
1	Wᵐ Boatman	Dead	Towson	Sallie Boatman	Dead	Kiamitia
2	Ish-tut-tubbee	"	"	Ya-tu-na	"	Towson
3						
4						
5						
6						
7						
8						
9						
10						
11						
12						
13						
14					Date of Application for Enrollment.	
15						
16					5/11/99	
17						

Choctaw By Blood Enrollment Cards 1898-1914

RESIDENCE: **Kiamitia**
POST OFFICE: **Grant, I.T.**

COUNTY. **Choctaw Nation**

Choctaw Roll
(Not Including Freedmen)

CARD NO.
FIELD NO. **1660**

Dawes' Roll No.	NAME	Relationship to Person First Named	AGE	SEX	BLOOD	TRIBAL ENROLLMENT		
						Year	County	No.
4687	1 Boatman, Abraham 79	First Named	76	M	Full	1896	Kiamitia	1463
4688	2 Vicey DIED PRIOR TO SEPTEMBER 25 1902	Wife	70	F	"	1896	"	1464
	3							
	4							
	5							
	6							
	7							
	8							
	9							
	10							
	11	ENROLLMENT						
	12	OF NOS. 1 and 2 HEREON APPROVED BY THE SECRETARY						
	13	OF INTERIOR DEC 12 1902						
	14							
	15							
	16							
	17							

TRIBAL ENROLLMENT OF PARENTS

	Name of Father	Year	County	Name of Mother	Year	County
1	Ho-pi-ye-e-ma-taha	Dead	Towson	I-yok-kle	Dead	Towson
2	Ho-pi-ye	"	"	E-ma-ho-tu-na	"	"
3						
4						
5						
6		No1 on 1896 roll as Abram Boardman				
7		No2 " 1896 " " Sophia "				
8		No 2 died Oct 11, 1901: proof of death filed Dec 16, 1902				
9		No2 died Oct. 11, 1901: Enrollment cancelled by Department July 8, 1904				
10						
11						
12						
13						
14						
15				Date of Application for Enrollment		
16					5/11/99	
17						

Choctaw By Blood Enrollment Cards 1898-1914

RESIDENCE: Kiamitia   COUNTY. **Choctaw Nation**   Choctaw Roll   CARD NO.
POST OFFICE: Grant, I.T   *(Not Including Freedmen)*   FIELD NO. 1661

Dawes' Roll No.	NAME	Relationship to Person First Named	AGE	SEX	BLOOD	TRIBAL ENROLLMENT Year	County	No.
4689	1 Tanitubbi, Allen ³³	Named	30	M	Full	1896	Kiamitia	12359
	2							
	3							
	4							
	5							
	6							
	7							
	8							
	9							
	10							
	11							
	12							
	13							
	14							
	15							
	16							
	17							

ENROLLMENT
OF NOS. 1 HEREON
APPROVED BY THE SECRETARY
OF INTERIOR DEC 12 1902

TRIBAL ENROLLMENT OF PARENTS

Name of Father	Year	County	Name of Mother	Year	County
1 Adam Tanitubbi	Dead	Kiamitia	Lucy Tanitubbi	1896	Kiamitia
2					
3					
4					
5					
6					
7					
8					
9					
10					
11					
12					
13					
14				Date of Application for Enrollment.	
15					
16				5/11/99	
17					

Choctaw By Blood Enrollment Cards 1898-1914

RESIDENCE: Kiamitia
POST OFFICE: Goodland, I.T
COUNTY. **Choctaw Nation**
Choctaw Roll *(Not Including Freedmen)*
CARD No. FIELD No. 1662

Dawes' Roll No.	NAME		Relationship to Person First Named	AGE	SEX	BLOOD	TRIBAL ENROLLMENT		
							Year	County	No.
14931	1 Hatcher, William	29	First Named	26	M	1/4	1896	Kiamitia	5745
	2								
	3								
	4								
	5								
	6								
	7								
	8								
	9								
	10								
	11								
	12								
	13								
	14								
	15								
	16								
	17								

ENROLLMENT
OF NOS. ~~1~~ HEREON
APPROVED BY THE SECRETARY
OF INTERIOR OCT 15 1903

TRIBAL ENROLLMENT OF PARENTS

	Name of Father	Year	County	Name of Mother	Year	County
1	Dol Hatcher	Dead	Non Citz	Eliza Trevino	1896	Kiamitia
2						
3						
4						
5						
6						
7						
8						
9		Born and lived in Texas until eleven years of age				
10		when he came to Choctaw Nation where he has				
11		resided ever since. See evidence.				
12				Mother of No. 1 on Choc card D.146		
13		1893 Payroll Kiamitia Co page 95 No 786				
14						
15				Date of Application for Enrollment.		
16				5/11/99		
17						

Choctaw By Blood Enrollment Cards 1898-1914

RESIDENCE: Kiamitia   COUNTY. **Choctaw Nation**   **Choctaw Roll**   CARD NO.

POST OFFICE: Grant I.T.   *(Not Including Freedmen)*   FIELD NO. 1663

Dawes' Roll No.	NAME		Relationship to Person First Named	AGE	SEX	BLOOD	TRIBAL ENROLLMENT		
							Year	County	No.
4690	1	Skelton James	26 First Named	23	M	Full	1896	Kiamitia	11517
	2								
	3								
	4								
	5								
	6								
	7								
	8	ENROLLMENT							
	9	OF NOS. 1 HEREON APPROVED BY THE SECRETARY							
	10	OF INTERIOR DEC 12 1902							
	11								
	12								
	13								
	14								
	15								
	16								
	17								

TRIBAL ENROLLMENT OF PARENTS

	Name of Father	Year	County	Name of Mother	Year	County
1	Morgan Skelton	Ded	Jackson	Winey Skelton	Ded	Jackson
2						
3						
4						
5						
6						
7						
8						
9						
10						
11						
12						
13						
14						
15						
16				Date of Application for Enrollment	May 11 "99	
17						

Choctaw By Blood Enrollment Cards 1898-1914

RESIDENCE: Kiamitia COUNTY. **Choctaw Nation** Choctaw Roll *(Not Including Freedmen)* CARD NO.

POST OFFICE: Grant, I.T. FIELD NO. **1664**

Dawes' Roll No.	NAME	Relationship to Person First Named	AGE	SEX	BLOOD	TRIBAL ENROLLMENT Year	TRIBAL ENROLLMENT County	No.
4691	1 Woods, Simmie ~~DIED PRIOR TO SEPTEMBER 25 1902~~	First Named	25	M	Full	1896	Jackson	13826
4692	2 " Emily	Wife	22	F	"	1896	"	13827
4693	3 " Cyrus	Son	2	M	"			
4694	4 Pistokachi, Mary ~~DIED PRIOR TO SEPTEMBER 25 1902~~	Ward	10	F	"	1896	Jackson	10462
	5							
	6							
	7							
	8							
	9	ENROLLMENT						
	10	OF NOS. 1 2 3 and 4 HEREON APPROVED BY THE SECRETARY						
	11	OF INTERIOR Ded 12 1902						
	12							
	13							
	14							
	15							
	16							
	17							

TRIBAL ENROLLMENT OF PARENTS

	Name of Father	Year	County	Name of Mother	Year	County
1	~~Basil McCann~~	~~Dead~~	~~Kiamitia~~	~~Mulscy~~	~~Dead~~	~~Kiamitia~~
2	Coleman Jones	"	Jacksaon	Winnie Pistokachi	"	Jackson
3	No 1			No 2		
4	~~Willie Pistokachi~~	~~Dead~~	~~Jackson~~	~~Winnie Pistokachi~~	~~Dead~~	~~Jackson~~
5						
6						
7			No 1 on 1896 roll as Summie Wood			
8			No 2 " 1896 " " Emily "			
9		No.1 died Oct. 22, 1900: Enrollment cancelled by Department July 8, 1904				
10		~~No4 died before Sept. 25, 1902: Enrollment cancelled by Department May 2, 1906~~				
11						
12						
13						
14						
15						
16				Date of Application for Enrollment.	5/12/99	
17						

Choctaw By Blood Enrollment Cards 1898-1914

RESIDENCE: Kiamitia   COUNTY, **Choctaw Nation**

POST OFFICE: ~~Hampton~~, I.T.

Field No. 1665

Choctaw Roll
(Not Including Freedmen) FIE

Dawes' Roll No.		NAME Hamden	Relationship to Person	AGE	SEX	BLOOD	TRIBAL ENROLLMENT		
							Year	County	No.
4695	1	Williams, Forbis ³⁸	First Named	35	M	Full	1896	Kiamitia	13782
4696	2	" Melissa ¹³	Dau	10	F	"	1896	"	13784
	3								
	4								
	5								
	6								
	7	ENROLLMENT OF NOS. 1 and 2 HEREON							
	8	APPROVED BY THE SECRETARY OF INTERIOR DEC 12 1902							
	9								
	10								
	11								
	12								
	13								
	14								
	15								
	16								
	17								

TRIBAL ENROLLMENT OF PARENTS

	Name of Father	Year	County	Name of Mother	Year	County
1	Williams	Dead	Games[sic]	Molsey Williams	Dead	Kiamitia
2	No 1			Elizabeth Williams	"	"
3						
4						
5						
6						
7						
8						
9						
10						
11						
12						
13						
14						
15						
16				Date of Application for Enrollment	5/12/99	
17						

165

Choctaw By Blood Enrollment Cards 1898-1914

RESIDENCE: Atoka   COUNTY. **Choctaw Nation**   **Choctaw Roll**   CARD NO.
POST OFFICE: Coalgate, I.T.   *(Not Including Freedmen)*   FIELD NO. **1666**

Dawes' Roll No.	NAME		Relationship to Person First Named	AGE	SEX	BLOOD	TRIBAL ENROLLMENT		
							Year	County	No.
I.W.896	1 Wiltsey, John M	(43)	First Named	40	M	I.W.			
4697	2 " Annie	25	Wife	22	F	Full	1896	Kiamitia	13735
4698	3 " Mary E	4	Dau	6mo	"	1/2			
4699	4 Wade, Ben	7	S.Son	3	M	Full	1896	Kiamitia	13736
	5								
	6	ENROLLMENT							
	7	OF NOS. 2 – 3 and 4 HEREON							
	8	APPROVED BY THE SECRETARY OF INTERIOR Dec 12 1902							
	9								
	10								
	11	ENROLLMENT OF NOS 1 HEREON							
	12	APPROVED BY THE SECRETARY OF INTERIOR Aug 3 1904							
	13								
	14								
	15								
	16	No4 lives with Osborne Frazier, on Choctaw #3767							
	17	No.3: Correct name is Mary A. Wiltsey							

TRIBAL ENROLLMENT OF PARENTS

	Name of Father	Year	County	Name of Mother	Year	County
1	Jas. B. Wiltsey	Dead	Non Citz	Almena Wiltsey	1896	Non Citz
2	Ellis Wade	"	Jackson	Mary Wade	Dead	Kiamitia
3	No 1			No 2		
4	John James	1896	Kiamitia	No 2		
5						
6						
7	No2 on 1896 roll as Annie Wade					
8	For child of Nos 1&2 see NB (Mar 3, 1905) #688					
9						
10						
11						
12						
13						
14				Date of Application for Enrollment.		
15						
16				5/12/99		
17						

166

Choctaw By Blood Enrollment Cards 1898-1914

RESIDENCE: Jackson
POST OFFICE: Mayhew, I.T.

COUNTY. **Choctaw Nation**

Choctaw Roll
(Not Including Freedmen)

CARD NO.
FIELD NO. **1667**

Dawes' Roll No.	NAME		Relationship to Person	AGE	SEX	BLOOD	TRIBAL ENROLLMENT		
							Year	County	No.
4700	1 Durant, Wilson	63	First Named	60	M	Full	1896	Jackson	3494
4701	2 Cole, Edward	15	Ward	12	"	"	1896	"	3496
4702	3 Durant, Bessie	6	"	3	F	"	1896	"	3497
I.W.1102	4 " Dora	22	Wife	19	"	I.W.			
4703	5 " Rachel	3	Dau	23mo	F	1/2			
	6								
	7								
	8	ENROLLMENT OF NOS. 1 2 3 and 5 HEREON APPROVED BY THE SECRETARY OF INTERIOR Dec 12 1902							
	9								
	10								
	11								
	12	ENROLLMENT OF NOS. ~~~ 4 ~~~ HEREON APPROVED BY THE SECRETARY OF INTERIOR Nov 16 1904							
	13								
	14								
	15								
	16								
	17								

TRIBAL ENROLLMENT OF PARENTS

	Name of Father	Year	County	Name of Mother	Year	County
1	Geo. Durant	Dead	Bok Tuklo	Mollie Durant	Dead	Jackson
2	Allen Cole	"	Jackson	Lucy Cole	"	"
3	Fisher Frazier	1896	"	Susan Frazier	1896	"
4	Jack Butler		Non Citz	Sallie Butler		Non Citz
5	No 1			No 2		
6						
7	No5 Enrolled August 1, 1901					
8	No4 has left No 1 12/1/02					
9	For child of Nos 1&4 see N.B. (Apr 26, 1906) Card No. 30.					
10	No2 Name changed under Departmental instructions of July 28, 1904 (D.C. #27366-1904).					
11	For child of No4 see NB (Apr 26-06) #1153					
12						
13						
14						#1 to 3
15						Date of Application for Enrollment.
16						5/12/99
17	P.O. Address of No4 Boswell I.T. 7/25/04			No4 enrolled Aug 21/99		

Choctaw By Blood Enrollment Cards 1898-1914

RESIDENCE: **Kiamitia**   COUNTY. **Choctaw Nation**   **Choctaw Roll** CARD No.

POST OFFICE: **Grant, I.T.**   *(Not Including Freedmen)* FIELD No. **1668**

Dawes' Roll No.	NAME	Relationship to Person First Named	AGE	SEX	BLOOD	TRIBAL ENROLLMENT Year	County	No.
4704	1 Chronic, Emma ³³	First Named	35	F	Full	1893	Kiamitia	143
4705	2 Grubbs, George ²¹	Son	18	M	"	1896	"	4811
	3							
	4							
	5	ENROLLMENT						
	6	OF NOS. 1 and 2 HEREON APPROVED BY THE SECRETARY						
	7	OF INTERIOR DEC 12 1902						
	8							
	9							
	10							
	11							
	12							
	13							
	14							
	15							
	16							
	17							

TRIBAL ENROLLMENT OF PARENTS

	Name of Father	Year	County	Name of Mother	Year	County
1	Larry Roberts	Dead	Kiamitia		Dead	Kiamitia
2	John Grubbs	"	"	No 1		
3						
4						
5	No 1 on 1893 Pay roll, Page 17, No 143, Kiamitia Co as Emy Chronic					
6	No 2 " 1893 " " " 17 " 144 " " " George Grubb					
7	No.1 on 1896 Choctaw roll as Emma Roberts page 278: #10851					
8						
9						
10						
11						
12						
13						
14					Date of Application for Enrollment	5/12/99
15						
16						
17						

Choctaw By Blood Enrollment Cards 1898-1914

RESIDENCE: Nashoba   COUNTY. **Choctaw Nation**   **Choctaw Roll**   CARD NO.
POST OFFICE: Tushkahomma[sic], I.T.   *(Not Including Freedmen)*   FIELD NO.   **1669**

Dawes' Roll No.	NAME		Relationship to Person First Named	AGE	SEX	BLOOD	TRIBAL ENROLLMENT		
							Year	County	No.
DEAD	1	Pickens, Nicholas	Named	45	M	Full	1896	Nashoba	10369
4706	2	" Paulie [51]	Wife	48	F	"	1896	"	10370
4707	3	" Frances [13]	Dau	10	"	"	1896	"	10371
4708	4	" Sallie [11]	"	8	"	"	1896	"	10372
4709	5	" Johnson [9]	Son	6	M	"	1896	"	10373
	6								
	7	ENROLLMENT							
	8	OF NOS. 2 3 4 and 5 HEREON APPROVED BY THE SECRETARY							
	9	OF INTERIOR Dec 12 1902							
	10								
	11	No.1 hereon dismissed under order of							
	12	the Commission to the Five Civilized							
	13	Tribes of March 31, 1905.							
	14								
	15								
	16								
	17								

TRIBAL ENROLLMENT OF PARENTS

	Name of Father	Year	County	Name of Mother	Year	County
1	Campbelle[sic] Pickens	Dead	Bok Tuklo	Emily Pickens	Dead	Bok Tuklo
2	Jimpson Nelson	"	Cedar		"	Cedar
3	No 1			No 2		
4	No 1			No 2		
5	No 1			No 2		
6						
7						
8	No4 on 1896 roll as Saillie[sic] Pickens					
9	No.1 also on 1896 roll; page 262; #10321, as Nicholas Pickens					
10	Nº1 Died Nov. 9, 1901, proof of death filed March 9, 1903.					
11						
12						
13						
14					Date of Application for Enrollment.	
15						
16					5/12/99	
17						

RESIDENCE: Blue
COUNTY. **Choctaw Nation**
POST OFFICE: Durant, I.T.

Choctaw Roll CARD NO.
(Not Including Freedmen) FIELD NO. 1670

Dawes' Roll No.	NAME	Relationship to Person First Named	AGE	SEX	BLOOD	TRIBAL ENROLLMENT		
						Year	County	No.
15283	1 Human, John B ³⁴	First Named	31	M	1/32			
I.W. 799	2 " Mary J ㉝	Wife	30	F	I.W.			
15284	3 " Pearl ¹⁴	Dau	11	"	1/64			
15285	4 " Floy ¹¹	"	8	"	1/64			
15286	5 " Myrtle Ola ⁸	"	5	"	1/64			
15287	6 " Winona ⁵	"	2	"	1/64			
	7 ENROLLMENT							
	8 OF NOS. 2 HEREON APPROVED BY THE SECRETARY							
	9 OF INTERIOR MAY 9 1904							
	Nos 1to 5 incl Admitted by C.C.C.C. March 21 '04							
	No 6 (Jurisdiction) dismissed							
	12							
	13							
	14 ENROLLMENT							
	15 OF NOS. 1-3-4-5-6 HEREON APPROVED BY THE SECRETARY							
	16 OF INTERIOR MAY 9 1904							
	17							

TRIBAL ENROLLMENT OF PARENTS

	Name of Father	Year	County	Name of Mother	Year	County
1	J. G. Human	1896	Non Citz	Pearly Human	Dead	Non Citz
2	H. H. Austin	1896	" "	Lizzie Austin	"	" "
3	No 1			No 2		
4	No 1			No 2		
5	No 1			No 2		
6	No 1			No 2		
7	Judgment of U.S. Ct. Admitting Nos 1 to 5 incl vacated and set aside by [illegible] Nos 1 to 6 inclusive now in C.C.C.C. Case #95					
8	Nos4&5 Denied in 96 in Case #1346 and No2 in 414; [remaining illegible]					
9	Nos1 to 5 were admitted by the U.S. Court, Central District,					
10	Indian Territory, August 26, 1897. Case No24 No2 was admitted as Mary Human					
11	No5 " " " Myrtle Ola "					
12						
13	Moved to Choctaw Nation from Texas about August 1897					
14						
15	No6 Affidavit of birth to be supplied: Recd Oct 6/99				5/12/99	
16						
17	For child of No1 & 2 see NB (Mar 3-05) Card #105					

Choctaw By Blood Enrollment Cards 1898-1914

RESIDENCE: Kiamitia COUNTY. **Choctaw Nation** **Choctaw Roll** CARD NO.
POST OFFICE: Goodland, I.T. *(Not Including Freedmen)* FIELD NO. 1671

Dawes' Roll No.	NAME	Relationship to Person First Named	AGE	SEX	BLOOD	TRIBAL ENROLLMENT Year	County	No.
4710	₁ Austin, Ellen ⁴⁶	First Named	43	F	Full	1896	Kiamitia	9766
4711	₂ Calister, Jane ⁷	Dau	4	F	"	1896	"	9768
	3							
	4							
	5							
	6	ENROLLMENT						
	7	OF NOS. 1 and 2 HEREON APPROVED BY THE SECRETARY						
	8	OF INTERIOR DEC 12 1902						
	9							
	10							
	11							
	12							
	13							
	14							
	15							
	16							
	17							

TRIBAL ENROLLMENT OF PARENTS

	Name of Father	Year	County	Name of Mother	Year	County
1	Austin	Dead	Kiamitia	Ilis Austin	Dead	Kiamitia
2	Jacob Calister	"	"	No 1		
3						
4						
5			No1 on 1896 roll as Elen Nichodemus			
6			No2 " 1896 " " Jane "			
7			No.1 is wife of Alexander Skelton Choc. #1634			
8						
9						
10						
11						
12						
13						
14						
15				Date of Application for Enrollment.	5/12/99	
16						
17						

Choctaw By Blood Enrollment Cards 1898-1914

RESIDENCE: **Kiamitia** COUNTY. **Choctaw Nation** **Choctaw Roll** (Not Including Freedmen) CARD NO. FIELD NO. **1672**
POST OFFICE: **Grant, I.T.**

Dawes' Roll No.	NAME		Relationship to Person First Named	AGE	SEX	BLOOD	TRIBAL ENROLLMENT		
							Year	County	No.
4712	1 Roberts, Eastman	29	First Named	26	M	Full	1896	Kiamitia	10833
4713	2 " Ella	40	Wife	37	F	"	1896	"	12277
4714	3 Thorpe, Grover	16	S.Son	13	M	1/2	1896	"	12278
4715	4 " Leta	13	S.Dau	10	F	1/2	1896	"	12279
~~4716~~	~~5 Roberts, Kelly~~ DIED PRIOR TO SEPTEMBER 25 1902		~~Sister~~	~~16~~	~~"~~	~~Full~~	~~1896~~	~~"~~	~~10834~~
	6								
	7								
	8								
	9								
	10								
	11	ENROLLMENT OF NOS. 1 2 3 4 and 5 HEREON APPROVED BY THE SECRETARY OF INTERIOR DEC 12 1902							
	12								
	13								
	14								
	15								
	16								
	17								

TRIBAL ENROLLMENT OF PARENTS

	Name of Father	Year	County	Name of Mother	Year	County
1	Jesse Roberts	Dead	Kiamitia	Mary Roberts	Dead	Kiamitia
2	Wallace Byington	"	"	Hannah Byington	"	"
3	Edward Thorpe	"	Non Citz	No 2		
4	" "	"	" "	No 2		
5	~~Jesse Roberts~~	"	~~Kiamitia~~	~~Mary Roberts~~	"	~~Kiamitia~~
6						
7						
8						
9		No 2 on 1896 roll as Ella Thorpe				
10		No 4 " 1896 " " Seta "				
11		No 5 died Sept. – 1899; proof of death filed Dec 8, 1902				
12		No.5 died Sept. – 1899: Enrollment cancelled by Department July 8, 1904				
13						
14						
15						
16				Date of Application for Enrollment.	5/12/99	
17						

172

Choctaw By Blood Enrollment Cards 1898-1914

RESIDENCE: Chickasaw Nation Pontotoc COUNTY. **Choctaw Nation**

POST OFFICE: New Castle, I.T

Choctaw Roll *(Not Including Freedmen)*

CARD NO.

FIELD NO. 1673

Dawes' Roll No.	NAME	Relationship to Person	AGE	SEX	BLOOD	TRIBAL ENROLLMENT		
						Year	County	No.
4717	1 Oxford, Josephine 26	First Named	23	F	1/2	1896	Kiamitia	9966
4718	2 Thomas, William T. 12	Son	9	M	1/4	1896	"	1447
	3							
	4							
	5							
	6							
	7	ENROLLMENT OF NOS. 1 and 2 HEREON APPROVED BY THE SECRETARY OF INTERIOR DEC 12 1902						
	8							
	9							
	10							
	11							
	12							
	13							
	14							
	15							
	16							
	17							

TRIBAL ENROLLMENT OF PARENTS

	Name of Father	Year	County	Name of Mother	Year	County
1	Christ. Bench	Dead	Jackson	Nancy Bench	Dead	Jackson
2	William Thomas	"	Non Citz	No1		
3						
4						
5						
6						
7	No 2 on 1896 roll as Willy T. Bench					
8						
9						
10						
11						
12						
13						
14						
15						
16				Date of Application for Enrollment	5/12/99	
17						

Choctaw By Blood Enrollment Cards 1898-1914

RESIDENCE: Kiamitia   COUNTY. **Choctaw Nation**   **Choctaw Roll**   CARD NO.
POST OFFICE: Goodland, I.T.   *(Not Including Freedmen)*   FIELD NO.   1674

Dawes' Roll No.	NAME		Relationship to Person First Named	AGE	SEX	BLOOD	TRIBAL ENROLLMENT		
							Year	County	No.
4719	1 Battiest, Josiah	42		39	M	Full	1896	Kiamitia	1539
4720	2 " Melissa	20	Wife	17	F	"	1896	"	8712
4721	3 " Martha	12	Dau	9	"	"	1896	"	1440
4722	4 " Mary	12	Dau	9	"	"	1893	"	37
	5								
	6								
	7								
	8								
	9								
	10								
	11	ENROLLMENT							
	12	OF NOS. 1 2 3 and 4 HEREON APPROVED BY THE SECRETARY							
	13	OF INTERIOR DEC 12 1902							
	14								
	15								
	16								
	17								

TRIBAL ENROLLMENT OF PARENTS

	Name of Father	Year	County	Name of Mother	Year	County
1	Johnson Battiest	Dead	Kiamitia	Losen Battiest	Dead	Kiamitia
2	Forbis Miashaya	"	"	Melissa Miashaya	"	"
3	No 1			Sillen Bacon	"	"
4	No 1			" "	"	"
5						
6						
7	No 2 on 1896 roll as Melissa Mishaya					
8	No 4 " 1893 Pay roll, Page 6, No 37, Kiamitia Co.					
9						
10						
11						
12						
13						
14					Date of Application for Enrollment.	
15						
16					5/12/99	
17						

174

Choctaw By Blood Enrollment Cards 1898-1914

RESIDENCE: Kiamitia   COUNTY: **Choctaw Nation**   **Choctaw Roll**   CARD No.
POST OFFICE: Antlers, I.T.   *(Not Including Freedmen)*   FIELD No. 1675

Dawes' Roll No.	NAME	Relationship to Person	AGE	SEX	BLOOD	TRIBAL ENROLLMENT Year	County	No.
4723	1 Frazier, Harris ²³	First Named	20	M	3/4	1896	Kiamitia	4240
	2							
	3							
	4							
	5							
	6							
	7							
	8	ENROLLMENT						
	9	OF NOS. 1 HEREON APPROVED BY THE SECRETARY						
	10	OF INTERIOR DEC 12 1902						
	11							
	12							
	13							
	14							
	15							
	16							
	17							

TRIBAL ENROLLMENT OF PARENTS

	Name of Father	Year	County	Name of Mother	Year	County
1	Stephen Frazier	Dead	Cedar	Louisa Frazier	Dead	Kiamitia
2						
3						
4						
5						
6						
7						
8						
9						
10						
11		No.1 is the husband and father of Joanna				
12		Frazier and Clara Frazier on Chickasaw card 1426				
13					Feby 26, 1900.	
14		No1 is divorced from Joanna Frazier; see his letter filed Dec. 23, 1902.				
15						
16				Date of Application for Enrollment.	5/12/99	
17						

Choctaw By Blood Enrollment Cards 1898-1914

RESIDENCE: Kiamitia
POST OFFICE: Grant, I.T.
COUNTY: **Choctaw Nation**
Choctaw Roll (Not Including Freedmen)
CARD NO.
FIELD NO. **1676**

Dawes' Roll No.	NAME	Relationship to Person First Named	AGE	SEX	BLOOD	TRIBAL ENROLLMENT Year	County	No.
I.W. 87	₁ Walters, Charles W ⁴¹	First Named	38	M	I.W.			
4724	₂ " Isabel ²²	Wife	19	F	Full	1893	Kiamitia	46
4725	₃ ~~Buckner~~ DIED PRIOR TO SEPTEMBER 25, 2902	~~Son~~	~~2mo~~	~~M~~	~~1/2~~			
	₄							
	₅							
	₆							
	₇	ENROLLMENT ~~OF NOS. 2 and 3~~ HEREON APPROVED BY THE SECRETARY OF INTERIOR Dec 12 1902						
	₈							
	₉							
	₁₀	ENROLLMENT OF NOS. I ~~~~ HEREON APPROVED BY THE SECRETARY OF INTERIOR						
	₁₁							
	₁₂							
	₁₃							
	₁₄							
	₁₅							
	₁₆							
	₁₇							

TRIBAL ENROLLMENT OF PARENTS

	Name of Father	Year	County	Name of Mother	Year	County
₁	Jacob Walters	Dead	Non Citz	Mary Walters	Dead	Non Citz
₂	Aiken John	1896	Towson	Isabelle John	"	Towson
₃	~~No. 1~~			~~No. 2~~		
₄						
₅						
₆						
₇						
₈		No2 on 1893 Pay roll as Zibbil John, Page 6, No. 46, Kiamitia Co				
₉		No.2 on 1896 Choctaw roll as Sibil Johnson, page 174, #7090.				
₁₀		Evidence of marriage to be supplied Recd May 18/99				
₁₁						
₁₂		No. 3 Enrolled June 23d 1900				
₁₃		N°3 Died Feb. 4, 1901: Proof of death filed Nov. 1, 1902.				
₁₄		No.3 died Feb. 4, 1901: Enrollment cancelled by Department July 8, 1904.				
₁₅						Date of Application for Enrollment.
₁₆		For child of Nos 1&2 see NB (Mar 3ʳᵈ 1905) Card #107.				5/12/99
₁₇	P.O. Ardmore, I.T. 12/30/02					

Choctaw By Blood Enrollment Cards 1898-1914

RESIDENCE: **Kiamitia**
POST OFFICE: **Grant, I.T.**

COUNTY. **Choctaw Nation**

Choctaw Roll
(Not Including Freedmen)

CARD NO.
FIELD NO. **1677**

Dawes' Roll No.	NAME	Relationship to Person First Named	AGE	SEX	BLOOD	TRIBAL ENROLLMENT		
						Year	County	No.
VOID.	1 Patterson, Thomas	Named	16	M	Full	1893	Kiamitia	109
	2							
	3							
	4							
	5							
	6							
	7							
	8							
	9							
	10							
	11							
	12							
	13							
	14							
	15							
	16							
	17							

TRIBAL ENROLLMENT OF PARENTS

Name of Father	Year	County	Name of Mother	Year	County
1 Jefferson Homma	Dead	Kiamitia	Isabelle Homma	Dead	Kiamitia
2					
3					
4					
5	On 1893 Pay roll at Tom Iabella[sic], Page 13 No 109, Kiamitia Co				
6					
7					
8					
9					
10					
11					
12					
13					
14					
15					
16				Date of Application for Enrollment	5/12/99
17					

Duplicate of Thomas Patterson or Choctaw card No. 1700. Sept. 10, 1902.

177

RESIDENCE: Kiamitia   COUNTY. **Choctaw Nation**   **Choctaw Roll**   CARD No.

POST OFFICE: Goodland, I.T.   *(Not Including Freedmen)*   FIELD No. 1678

Dawes' Roll No.	NAME	Relationship to Person First Named	AGE	SEX	BLOOD	TRIBAL ENROLLMENT		
						Year	County	No.
VOID.	1 Gooding, Charles H		36	M	1/8	1896	Kiamitia	4815
VOID.	2 " Louis L.	Son	12	"	1/2	1896	"	4816
VOID.	3 " Josephine A	Dau	10	F	1/2	1896	"	4817
VOID.	4 " Henry L Jr	Son	8	M	1/2	1896	"	4818
	5							
	6							
	7							
	8							
	9							
	10							
	11							
	12							
	13							
	14							
	15							
	16							
	17							

TRIBAL ENROLLMENT OF PARENTS

	Name of Father	Year	County	Name of Mother	Year	County
1	H. L. Gooding		Kiamitia	Roseana Gooding		Kiamitia
2	No 1			Annie Gooding	Dead	"
3	No 1			" "	"	"
4	No 1			" "	"	"
5						
6	No 1 on 1896 roll as Chas. H. Gooding					
7	No 2 " 1896 "	" Louis "				
8	No 3 " 1896 "	" Josephine "				
9	No 4 " 1896 "	" Henry " Jr.				
10	All on Choctaw card #1479.					
11						
12						
13						
14				Date of Application for Enrollment.		
15					5/12/99	
16						
17						

CANCELLED

Sept. 2, 1902.

Choctaw By Blood Enrollment Cards 1898-1914

RESIDENCE: Kiamitia
POST OFFICE: Nelson, I.T.
COUNTY. **Choctaw Nation**
Choctaw Roll *(Not Including Freedmen)*
CARD NO.
FIELD NO. 1679

Dawes' Roll No.	NAME	Relationship to Person First Named	AGE	SEX	BLOOD	TRIBAL ENROLLMENT		
						Year	County	No.
4726	1 Williams, Henry ³⁵	First Named	32	M	1/4	1896	Kiamitia	13751
	2							
	3							
	4							
	5							
	6							
	7							
	8							
	9							
	10							
	11	ENROLLMENT OF NOS. 1 HEREON APPROVED BY THE SECRETARY OF INTERIOR DEC 12 1902						
	12							
	13							
	14							
	15							
	16							
	17							

TRIBAL ENROLLMENT OF PARENTS

	Name of Father	Year	County	Name of Mother	Year	County
1	Wᵐ Williams	Dead	Non Citz	Emily Williams	1896	Kiamitia
2						
3						
4						
5						
6	For child of No 1 see NB (March 3-1905) Card No 41					
7						
8						
9						
10						
11						
12						
13						
14						
15						
16				DATE OF APPLICATION FOR ENROLLMENT. 5/15/99		
17						

179

Choctaw By Blood Enrollment Cards 1898-1914

RESIDENCE: Kiamitia   COUNTY. **Choctaw Nation**   **Choctaw Roll**   CARD No.

POST OFFICE: Nelson, I.T.   *(Not Including Freedmen)*   FIELD No. 1680

Dawes' Roll No.	NAME	Relationship to Person First Named	AGE	SEX	BLOOD	TRIBAL ENROLLMENT Year	County	No.
DEAD.	1 Williams, Emily **DEAD.**	Named	54	F	1/2	1896	Kiamitia	13750
	2							
	3							
	No. 1 HEREON DISMISSED UNDER ORDER OF THE COMMISSION TO THE FIVE CIVILIZED TRIBES OF MARCH 31, 1905. 6							
	7							
	8							
	9							
	10							
	11							
	12							
	13							
	14							
	15							
	16							
	17							

TRIBAL ENROLLMENT OF PARENTS

	Name of Father	Year	County	Name of Mother	Year	County
1	John Smallwood	Dead	Kiamitia	Nancy Perry	Dead	Kiamitia
2						
3						
4						
5	Nº1 Died Feby. 6, 1902; proof of death filed April 2, 1902					
6						
7						
8						
9						
10						
11						
12						
13						
14						
15						
16				Date of Application for Enrollment.	5/15/99	
17						

CANCELLED

Died prior to Sept. 25, 1902

Choctaw By Blood Enrollment Cards 1898-1914

RESIDENCE: Kiamitia		COUNTY. **Choctaw Nation**				**Choctaw Roll** *(Not Including Freedmen)*	CARD NO.	
POST OFFICE: Nelson, I.T							FIELD NO.	1681

Dawes' Roll No.	NAME	Relationship to Person Named	AGE	SEX	BLOOD	TRIBAL ENROLLMENT		
						Year	County	No.
4727	1 Roebuck, William ⁴³	First Named	40	M	1/8	1896	Kiamitia	10848
4728	2 " David E ²¹	Son	18	M	9/16	1896	"	10849
	3							
	4							
	5							
	6							
	7							
	8							
	9							
	10							
	11	ENROLLMENT						
	12	OF NOS. 1 and 2 HEREON APPROVED BY THE SECRETARY						
	13	OF INTERIOR DEC 12 1902						
	14							
	15							
	16							
	17							

TRIBAL ENROLLMENT OF PARENTS

	Name of Father	Year	County	Name of Mother	Year	County
1	Ben Roebuck	Dead	Non Citz	Clarissa Roebuck	Dead	Kiamitia
2	No 1			Sophia Smallwood	"	"
3						
4						
5						
6						
7						
8						
9						
10						
11	No.1 is now husband of Isabella Kelly on Choctaw Card #1410, July 8, 1901. Correct name					
12	of No.2 is David Elexander Roebuck. See letter filed with evidence of marriage					
13	with Choctaw card #1768, Aug 10, 1901.					
	No.2 is now the husband of Carrie Fowler on Choctaw Card #1768, Aug. 10, 1901.					
14	For child of No.1 see N.B. (Apr. 26, 1906) Card No. 204.					
15	" " " No 2 " " (March 3, 1905) " " 1173					
16	" " " No 1 " " " " " " 1226					
17				Date of Application for Enrollment.	5/15/99	

181

Choctaw By Blood Enrollment Cards 1898-1914

RESIDENCE: Kiamitia   COUNTY. **Choctaw Nation**   **Choctaw Roll** CARD NO.
POST OFFICE: Nelson, I.T.   *(Not Including Freedmen)* FIELD NO. 1682

Dawes' Roll No.	NAME	Relationship to Person	AGE	SEX	BLOOD	TRIBAL ENROLLMENT		
						Year	County	No.
4729	1 Luce, Solomon 36	First Named	33	M	Full	1896	Kiamitia	8105
	2							
	3							
	4							
	5							
	6							
	7	ENROLLMENT						
	8	OF NOS. 1 HEREON APPROVED BY THE SECRETARY						
	9	OF INTERIOR DEC 12 1902						
	10							
	11							
	12							
	13							
	14							
	15							
	16							
	17							

TRIBAL ENROLLMENT OF PARENTS

	Name of Father	Year	County	Name of Mother	Year	County
1	Moses Luce	Dead	Red River	Agnes Luce	Dead	Red River
2						
3						
4						
5						
6						
7						
8						
9						
10						
11						
12						
13						
14						
15				Date of Application for Enrollment.		
16				5/15/99		
17						

Choctaw By Blood Enrollment Cards 1898-1914

RESIDENCE: Jacks Fork
POST OFFICE: Antlers, I.T.

COUNTY. **Choctaw Nation**

Choctaw Roll
(Not Including Freedmen)

CARD NO.
FIELD NO. 1683

Dawes' Roll No.	NAME	Relationship to Person First Named	AGE	SEX	BLOOD	TRIBAL ENROLLMENT		
						Year	County	No.
4730	1 Underwood, Watkin 31		28	M	3/4	1893	Jacks Forks	723
4731	2 " Isabella 32	Wife	29	F	Full	1893	" "	724
4732	3 DIED PRIOR TO SEPTEMBER 25, 1902 Charley	Son	8	M	7/8	1893	" "	725
	4							
	5							
	6							
	7	ENROLLMENT						
	8	OF NOS. 1 2 and 3 HEREON APPROVED BY THE SECRETARY						
	9	OF INTERIOR DEC 12 1902						
	10							
	11							
	12							
	13							
	14							
	15							
	16							
	17							

TRIBAL ENROLLMENT OF PARENTS

	Name of Father	Year	County	Name of Mother	Year	County
1	Mullen Underwood	1896	Jacks Fork	Abie Underwood	1896	Jacks Fork
2	Jackson Deney	Dead	" "	Sinie Jackson	Dead	" "
3	No 1			No 2		
4						
5						
6	No1 on 1893 Pay Roll Page 81, No 723, Jacks Fork County					
7	No2 " 1893 " " " 81 " 724 " " "					
8	No3 " 1893 " " " 81 " 725 " " "					
9						
10	No3 died Sept. 2, 1901; proof of death filed Dec 5, 1902					
11	No3 died Sept. 2, 1901; Enrollment cancelled July 8, 1904					
12						
13						
14						
15						
16				Date of Application for Enrollment	5/15/99	
17						

183

Choctaw By Blood Enrollment Cards 1898-1914

RESIDENCE: Jacks Fork   COUNTY. **Choctaw Nation**   **Choctaw Roll**   CARD NO.

POST OFFICE: Antlers, I.T.   *(Not Including Freedmen)*   FIELD NO. **1684**

Dawes' Roll No.	NAME	Relationship to Person First Named	AGE	SEX	BLOOD	TRIBAL ENROLLMENT Year	County	No.
4733	1 Wesley, Edmond ³⁰	First Named	27	M	Full	1893	Jacks Fork	755
4734	2 " Rhoda ³¹	Wife	28	F	"	1893	" "	579
4735	3 " Edith ²	Dau	5m	F	"			
4736	4 " Thompson ¹	Son	1mo	M	"			
	5							
	6							
	7							
	8							
	9							
	10							
	11	ENROLLMENT						
	12	OF NOS. 1 2 3 and 4 HEREON APPROVED BY THE SECRETARY						
	13	OF INTERIOR Dec 12 1902						
	14							
	15							
	16							
	17							

TRIBAL ENROLLMENT OF PARENTS

	Name of Father	Year	County	Name of Mother	Year	County
1	Thompson Wesley	Dead	Jacks Fork	Ellen Wesley	1896	Jacks Fork
2	Gooden Nelson	"	" "	Mulsey Nelson	1896	" "
3	No. 1			No. 2		
4	No. 1			No. 2		
5						
6						
7	No1 on 1893 Pay roll Page 85, No 755, Jacks Fork Co					
8	No2 " 1893 " " " 65 " 579 " " " as Rhodie Nelson					
9	No.3 Enrolled January 16, 1901 ~~No4 Born Dec. 2, 1901; enrolled Jan. 3, 1902~~					
10	For child of Nos. 1 and 2 see NB (March 3 1905) #1279					
11						
12						
13						
14						
15				#1&2		
16				Date of Application for Enrollment.	5/15/99	
17						

184

Choctaw By Blood Enrollment Cards 1898-1914

RESIDENCE: Kiamitia   COUNTY: **Choctaw Nation**   **Choctaw Roll** CARD NO.
POST OFFICE: Nelson, I.T.   (Not Including Freedmen)   FIELD NO. 1685

Dawes' Roll No.	NAME	Relationship to Person First Named	AGE	SEX	BLOOD	TRIBAL ENROLLMENT		
						Year	County	No.
I.W. 641	1 McKee, John D 40	First Named	38	M	I.W.	1896	Kiamitia	14871
4737	2 " Mary A 35	Wife	32	F	1/4	1896	"	9379
4738	3 " Mary L 14	Dau	11	"	1/8	1896	"	9380
4739	4 " Martin 11	Son	8	M	1/8	1896	"	9381
4740	5 " George 10	"	7	"	1/8	1896	"	9382
4741	6 " Andrew J 9	"	6	"	1/8	1896	"	9383
4742	7 " Lula 7	Dau	4	F	1/8	1896	"	9384
4743	8 " John D 4	Son	5mo	M	1/8			
4744	9 " Isaac 14	Ward	11	"	1/2	1893	Kiamitia	479
	10							
	11 ENROLLMENT OF NOS. 2345678and9 HEREON				DECI ARED			
	12 APPROVED BY THE SECRETARY OF INTERIOR DEC 12 1902							
	13 No 9 also on 1896 Census Roll No. 8095							
	14 as Isaac Leflore							
	15 ENROLLMENT							
	16 OF NOS. 1 HEREON APPROVED BY THE SECRETARY							
	17 OF INTERIOR MAR 26 1904							

TRIBAL ENROLLMENT OF PARENTS

	Name of Father	Year	County	Name of Mother	Year	County
1	G. W. McKee	Dead	Non Citz	Mary McKee	Dead	Non Citz
2	W. M. Smallwood	1896	Kiamitia	Narcissa Smallwood	1896	Kiamitia
3	No 1			No 2		
4	No 1			No 2		
5	No 1			No 2		
6	No 1			No 2		
7	No 1			No 2		
8	No 1			No 2		
9				Tinie Smallwood	Dead	Kiamitia
10						
11						
12	No1 on 1896 roll as Jno. D. McKee					
13	No2 " 1896 " " Mary McKee			For child of Nos. 1&2 see NB (March 3,1905) #1178.		
14	No3 " 1896 " " Jackson " No6 " 1896 " " Jackson "					
15	No9 on 1893 Pay roll Page 58, No 479, Kiamitia County			Date of Application for Enrollment.		
16	Mother of No9 died when he was but two day of age			5/15/99		
17	Child is illegitimate. Name of father unknown.					

Choctaw By Blood Enrollment Cards 1898-1914

RESIDENCE: Jacks Fork   COUNTY. **Choctaw Nation**   **Choctaw Roll** CARD NO.

POST OFFICE: Stringtown, I.T.   *(Not Including Freedmen)*   FIELD NO. 1686

Dawes' Roll No.	NAME	Relationship to Person	AGE	SEX	BLOOD	TRIBAL ENROLLMENT		
						Year	County	No.
4745	1 Noah, David C DIED PRIOR TO SEPTEMBER 25, 1902	First Named	53	M	Full	1896	Jacks Fork	9859
	2							
	3							
	4							
	5							
	6							
	7							
	8	ENROLLMENT						
	9	OF NOS. 1 HEREON APPROVED BY THE SECRETARY						
	10	OF INTERIOR DEC 12 1902						
	11							
	12							
	13							
	14							
	15							
	16							
	17							

TRIBAL ENROLLMENT OF PARENTS

	Name of Father	Year	County	Name of Mother	Year	County
1	Charles Noah	Dead	Nashoba	Ish-ta-hok	Dead	Nashoba
2						
3						
4						
5						
6						
7		No 1 died Dec 28, 1899: proof of death filed Nov 25, 1902.				
8		No 1 died Dec. 28, 1899.			July 1, 1904	
9						
10						
11						
12						
13						
14						
15						
16				Date of Application for Enrollment.	5/15/99	
17						

186

Choctaw By Blood Enrollment Cards 1898-1914

RESIDENCE: Jacks Fork	COUNTY.	**Choctaw Nation**	**Choctaw Roll**	CARD No.
POST OFFICE: Stringtown, I.T.			*(Not Including Freedmen)*	FIELD NO. 1687

Dawes' Roll No.	NAME		Relationship to Person First Named	AGE	SEX	BLOOD	TRIBAL ENROLLMENT		
							Year	County	No.
4746	1	Noah, Rogers	24	First Named	21	M	Full	1896	Jacks Fork	9861
4747	2	" Selina	21	Wife	18	F	"	1896	" "	1930
	3								
	4								
	5								
	6								
	7	ENROLLMENT OF NOS. 1 and 2 HEREON							
	8	APPROVED BY THE SECRETARY							
	9	OF INTERIOR DEC 12 1902							
	10								
	11								
	12								
	13								
	14								
	15								
	16								
	17								

TRIBAL ENROLLMENT OF PARENTS

	Name of Father	Year	County	Name of Mother	Year	County
1	David C. Noah	1896	Jacks Fork	Lucy Noah	Dead	Jacks Fork
2	Haken Benjamin	Dead	" "	Mariah Benjamin	"	" "
3						
4						
5						
6						
7			No1 on 1896 roll as Roggers Noah			
8			No2 " 1896 " " Selina Benjamin			
9						
10						
11						
12						
13						
14					Date of Application for Enrollment.	
15					5/15/99	
16						
17						

Choctaw By Blood Enrollment Cards 1898-1914

RESIDENCE: Jacks Fork   COUNTY. **Choctaw Nation**   **Choctaw Roll** *(Not Including Freedmen)*   CARD NO. 1688

POST OFFICE: Antlers, I.T.   FIELD NO. 1688

Dawes' Roll No.	NAME		Relationship to Person First Named	AGE	SEX	BLOOD	TRIBAL ENROLLMENT		
							Year	County	No.
4748	1 Onubby Robert L	24	First Named	21	M	Full	1896	Jacks Fork	10027
	2								
	3								
	4								
	5								
	6								
	7	ENROLLMENT							
	8	OF NOS. 1 HEREON							
		APPROVED BY THE SECRETARY							
	9	OF INTERIOR DEC 12 1902							
	10								
	11								
	12								
	13								
	14								
	15								
	16								
	17								

TRIBAL ENROLLMENT OF PARENTS

	Name of Father	Year	County	Name of Mother	Year	County
1	Sismon Onubby		Dead in Mississippi	Susan Onubby		Dead in Mississippi
2						
3						
4						
5						
6	On 1896 roll as Robert Onubbe					
7	N°1 is also known by name of Robert E Lee. See letter Gen of file #5394-1902					
8	For child of No.1 see NB (Mar. 3,1905) #483					
9						
10						
11						
12						
13						
14						
15					Date of Application for Enrollment.	
16						5/15/99
17	PO Leflore IT 4/12/05					

188

Choctaw By Blood Enrollment Cards 1898-1914

RESIDENCE: Jacks Fork   COUNTY, **Choctaw Nation**   **Choctaw Roll**   CARD NO.
POST OFFICE: Antlers, I.T.   *(Not Including Freedmen)*   FIELD NO.   1689

Dawes' Roll No.	NAME		Relationship to Person	AGE	SEX	BLOOD	TRIBAL ENROLLMENT		
							Year	County	No.
4749	1 Nelson, Stephen	52	First Named	49	M	3/4	1896	Jacks Fork	9872
4750	2 " Lula	32	Wife	29	F	1/2	1896	" "	9873
4751	3 " James	14	Son	11	M	5/8	1896	" "	9874
4752	4 " Cole	7	"	4	"	5/8	1896	" "	9875
4753	5 " Mitchell ~~DIED PRIOR TO SEPTEMBER 25 1902~~		"	3	"	5/8	1896	" "	9876
4754	6 " Eden	1	Son	1mo	M	5/8			
	7								
	8								
	9								
	10								
	11	ENROLLMENT OF NOS. 1 2 3 4 5 and 6 HEREON							
	12	APPROVED BY THE SECRETARY							
	13	OF INTERIOR DEC 12 1902							
	14								
	15								
	16								
	17								

TRIBAL ENROLLMENT OF PARENTS

	Name of Father	Year	County	Name of Mother	Year	County
1	Gooden Nelson	Dead	Jacks Fork	Molsey Nelson	1896	Jacks Fork
2	King Ashford	"	Non Citz	Elizabeth Perkins	1896	Kiamitia
3	No 1			No 2		
4	No 1			No 2		
5	No 1			No 2		
6	No.1			No.2		
7						
8						
9	No.6 born Aug. 31, 1901 and enrolled Oct. 15, 1901					
10	For child of Nos 1&2 see N.B. (Apr. 26, 1906) Card No 26.					
11	No.5 died October 1, 1900; proof of death filed Dec. 5, 1902					
12	~~No.5 died Oct. 1, 1900. Enrollment cancelled by Department July 8, 1904~~					
13						
14						
15						
16				Date of Application for Enrollment.	5/15/99	
17						

189

RESIDENCE: Jacks Fork   COUNTY. **Choctaw Nation**   Choctaw Roll   CARD No.
POST OFFICE: Antlers, I.T.   *(Not Including Freedmen)*   FIELD No. 1690

Dawes' Roll No.	NAME	Relationship to Person First Named	AGE	SEX	BLOOD	TRIBAL ENROLLMENT Year	TRIBAL ENROLLMENT County	TRIBAL ENROLLMENT No.
4755	1 Nelson, Hardy DIED PRIOR TO SEPTEMBER 25 1902	First Named	23	M	Full	1896	Jacks Fork	9879
4756	2 " Sisty 30	Wife	27	F	"	1896	" "	9880
	3							
	4							
	5							
	6	ENROLLMENT						
	7	OF NOS. 1 and 2 HEREON						
	8	APPROVED BY THE SECRETARY OF INTERIOR DEC 12 1902						
	9							
	10							
	11							
	12							
	13							
	14							
	15							
	16							
	17							

TRIBAL ENROLLMENT OF PARENTS

	Name of Father	Year	County	Name of Mother	Year	County
1	Gabriel Nelson	1896	Kiamitia	Selina Barlin	1896	Kiamitia
2	Missen Noah	Dead	Jacks Fork	Isabelle Noah	Dead	Jacks Fork
3						
4						
5						
6						
7		No2 on 1896 roll as Sisty Noah				
8						
9						
10		No.1 died Dec. – 900: Enrollment cancelled by Department July 8, 1904.				
11						
12						
13						
14						
15						
16				Date of Application for Enrollment 5/15/99		
17						

RESIDENCE: Kiamitia   COUNTY. **Choctaw Nation**   **Choctaw Roll**   CARD NO.
POST OFFICE: Antlers, I.T   *(Not Including Freedmen)*   FIELD NO. 1691

Dawes' Roll No.	NAME	Relationship to Person	AGE	SEX	BLOOD	TRIBAL ENROLLMENT		
						Year	County	No.
4757	1 Simpson, Isaac 45	First Named	42	M	Full	1896	Jacks Fork	11710
4758	2 " Sarah 21	Wife	18	F	3/4	1893	Kiamitia	422
4759	3 " John 15	Son	12	M	Full	1896	Jacks Fork	11711
14914	4 Ketcham, Thomas S 14	"	11	"	"	1896	" "	11712
4760	5 Simpson, Leo ~~DIED PRIOR TO SEPTEMBER 25, 1902~~	Son	9mo	M	7/8			
	6							
	7	ENROLLMENT	No 1 admitted by act of Council of Oct. 30, 1890					
	8	OF NOS. 1 2 3 and 5 HEREON						
	9	APPROVED BY THE SECRETARY OF INTERIOR DEC 12 1902						
	10							
	11							
	12	ENROLLMENT						
	13	OF NOS. 4 HEREON						
	14	APPROVED BY THE SECRETARY OF INTERIOR MAY 21 1903						
	15							
	16							
	17							

TRIBAL ENROLLMENT OF PARENTS

	Name of Father	Year	County	Name of Mother	Year	County
1	Simpson John	Dead	in Mississippi	Anie John	Dead	in Mississippi
2	Alfred Nelson	"	Kiamitia	Nancy Nelson	1896	Kiamitia
3	No 1			Margaret Simpson	Dead	Jacks Fork
4	No 1			" "	"	" "
5	~~No.1~~			~~No.2~~		
6						
7						
8						
9						
10	No2 on 1893 Pay Roll, Page 52, No 422, Kiamitia Co as Sarah Nelson					
11	No.5 Enrolled Oct. 26th, 1900					
12	No 4 Legally adopted by Father Wm H. Ketcham, April 8th 1901 See copy of order of Court filed May 3-1901, and his name					
13	changed to Thomas Simpson Ketcham May 3 1901					
14	~~No 5 died Dec 26, 1901; proof of death filed Dec 8, 1902~~				#1 to 4 Date of Application for Enrollment	
15	~~No. 5 died Dec. 26, 1901; Enrollment cancelled by Department July 8, 1904~~					
16					5/15/99	
17	For child of Nos 1&2 see NB (Mar 3-1905) Card No 40.					

Choctaw By Blood Enrollment Cards 1898-1914

Dawes' Roll No.	NAME	Relationship to Person First Named	AGE	SEX	BLOOD	TRIBAL ENROLLMENT Year	County	No.
I.W. 241	1 Cornelius, Benjamin F 50	First Named	45	M	I.W	1896	Jacks Fork	14429
4761	2 " Ella M 41	Wife	38	F	1/2	1896	" "	3028
4762	3 " Anna M 19	Dau	16	"	1/4	1896	" "	3029
4763	4 " Emmet D 17	Son	14	M	1/4	1896	" "	3030
4764	5 " Lorenzo F 15	"	12	"	1/4	1896	" "	3031
4765	6 " Willie M 14	"	11	"	1/4	1896	" "	3032
4766	7 " Bessie I. 10	Dau	7	F	1/4	1896	" "	3033
4767	8 " Jesse P 8	Son	5	M	1/4	1896	" "	3034
4768	9 " Oliver H 6	"	3	"	1/4	1896	" "	3035
	10							
	11	ENROLLMENT OF NOS. 2 3 4 5 6 7 8 and 9 HEREON APPROVED BY THE SECRETARY OF INTERIOR DEC 12 1902						
	12							
	13							
	14	ENROLLMENT OF NOS. 1 HEREON APPROVED BY THE SECRETARY OF INTERIOR SEP 13 1903						
	15							
	16							
	17							

TRIBAL ENROLLMENT OF PARENTS

	Name of Father	Year	County	Name of Mother	Year	County
1	E. C. Cornelius	1896	Non Citz	Anna Cornelius	1896	Non Citz
2	L.G. Harris	Dead	" "	Betsey Harris	Dead	Jacks Fork
3	No1			No2		
4	No1			No2		
5	No1			No2		
6	No1			No2		
7	No1			No2		
8	No1			No2		
9	No1			No2		
10						
11						
12	No1 on 1896 roll as Ben F. Cornelius. Was also admitted by Dawes Commission as an Intermarried Choctaw Dec 2/96. Case No 733					
13						
14	No3 on 1896 roll as May Cornelius				Date of Application for Enrollment.	
15	No4 " 1896 " " Emit "					
16	No5 " 1896 " " Frank L "					
	No7 " 1896 " " Bessie " Date of application for enrollment 5/15/99					
17	No8 " 1896 " " Jessee "					

P.O. Davis, I.T. 10/22/02

Choctaw By Blood Enrollment Cards 1898-1914

| RESIDENCE: Jacks Fork | COUNTY. | Choctaw Nation | Choctaw Roll | CARD No. |
| POST OFFICE: Antlers, I.T. | | | (Not Including Freedmen) | FIELD No. 1693 |

Dawes' Roll No.	NAME	Relationship to Person First Named	AGE	SEX	BLOOD	TRIBAL ENROLLMENT		
						Year	County	No.
1	Nash, Henry C	Named	39	M	I.W	1896	Jacks Fork	14906
2								
3								
4								
5								
6								
7								
8								
9								
10								
11								
12								
13								
14								
15								
16								
17								

TRIBAL ENROLLMENT OF PARENTS

	Name of Father	Year	County	Name of Mother	Year	County
1	F. H. Nash	1896	Non Citz	Frances Nash	1896	Non Citz
2						
3						
4						
5						
6						
7						
8		On 1896 roll as H.C. Nash. Was also admitted by Dawes				
9		Commission Case No 1139. No appeal.				
10		Admitted as a Choctaw I.W.				
11		Wife and child on Chickasaw Card No 1427				
12		On 1897 Chickasaw Roll of Chickasaws residing in				
13		Choctaw Nation, Second District, Page 82, as H.C. Nash.				
14						
15						
16				Date of Application for Enrollment 5/15/99		
17						

CANCELLED

MAR 29 1904

and No 1 transferred to Chickasaw Card #427

193

Choctaw By Blood Enrollment Cards 1898-1914

RESIDENCE: Kiamitia
POST OFFICE: Antlers, I.T.
COUNTY. **Choctaw Nation**
Choctaw Roll (*Not Including Freedmen*)
CARD NO.
FIELD NO. 1694

Dawes' Roll No.	NAME		Relationship to Person First Named	AGE	SEX	BLOOD	TRIBAL ENROLLMENT		
							Year	County	No.
4769	1 Turner, James	38	First Named	35	M	1/2	1896	Jacks Fork	12511
4770	2 " Tina	43	Wife	40	F	Full	1896	" "	12512
4771	3 " Silas	11	Son	8	M	3/4	1896	" "	12513
4772	4 Parish, Eliza	17	Ward	14	F	Full	1896	" "	8376
4773	5 William, Levina	15	"	12	"	"	1896	" "	8377
4774	6 Parish, Eli	1	Son of Nº4	8mo	M	7/8			
	7								
	8								
	9								
	10								
	11	ENROLLMENT OF NOS. 1 2 3 4 5 and 6 HEREON							
	12	APPROVED BY THE SECRETARY OF INTERIOR DEC 12 1902							
	13								
	14								
	15								
	16								
	17								

TRIBAL ENROLLMENT OF PARENTS

	Name of Father	Year	County	Name of Mother	Year	County
1	James Turner	Dead	Non Citz	Sallie Turner	Dead	Jacks Fork
2	William Farlis	"	Atoka	Sallie A. Farlis		" "
3	No 1			Sarah Turner	Dead	" "
4	Edmund William		Jacks Fork	Bicey William	"	" " "
5	" "		" "	" "	"	" " "
6	Elias Parish	1893	" "	Nº4		
7						
8						
9	No2 on 1896 roll as Sinie Turner					
10	Nº4 is now the wife of Elias Parish on Choctaw card #1715, evidence of					
11	marriage filed Aug. 6, 1902.					
12	Nº6 Born Dec. 23, 1902: enrolled Aug. 6, 1902. For child of No 4 see NB (March 3, 1905) #1207					
13						
14						#1 to 5
15					Date of Application for Enrollment.	
16					5/15/99	
17						

Choctaw By Blood Enrollment Cards 1898-1914

RESIDENCE: Jacks Fork   COUNTY. **Choctaw Nation**   **Choctaw Roll** *(Not Including Freedmen)*   CARD NO.

POST OFFICE: Antlers, I.T.   FIELD NO. 1695

Dawes' Roll No.	NAME		Relationship to Person First Named	AGE	SEX	BLOOD	TRIBAL ENROLLMENT		
							Year	County	No.
4775	1 Underwood, Mullen		DIED PRIOR TO SEPTEMBER 25, 1902	60	M	Full	1896	Jacks Fork	12586
4776	2 " Aby	53	Wife	50	F	"	1896	" "	12587
4777	3 " John	15	Son	12	M	"	1896	" "	12588
	4								
	5								
	6								
	7	ENROLLMENT							
	8	OF NOS. 1 2 and 3 HEREON APPROVED BY THE SECRETARY							
	9	OF INTERIOR DEC 12 1902							
	10								
	11								
	12								
	13								
	14								
	15								
	16								
	17								

TRIBAL ENROLLMENT OF PARENTS

	Name of Father	Year	County	Name of Mother	Year	County
1	Pehtchie Underwood	Dead	Jacks Fork	Tennessee Underwood	Dead	Jacks Fork
2	Ta-ho-nubbee	"	Cedar	Oh-na-te-hoyo	"	Cedar
3	No 1			No 2		
4						
5						
6						
7	No2 on 1896 roll as Abbey Underwood					
8						
9	No1 died March 20, 1902; proof of death filed Dec 5, 1902.					
10	No. 1 died March 20, 1902; Enrollment cancelled by Department July 8, 1904					
11						
12						
13						
14					Date of Application for Enrollment.	
15		.				
16					5/15/99	
17						

Choctaw By Blood Enrollment Cards 1898-1914

RESIDENCE: Jacks Fork COUNTY. **Choctaw Nation** Choctaw Roll CARD No.
POST OFFICE: Antlers, I.T. (Not Including Freedmen) FIELD No. **1696**

Dawes' Roll No.	NAME	Relationship to Person First Named	AGE	SEX	BLOOD	TRIBAL ENROLLMENT Year	County	No.
4778	1 Baldwin, George W. 58	First Named	55	M	Full	1893	Cedar	36
4779	2 " Selina 53	Wife	50	F	"	1893	"	37
4780	3 DIED PRIOR TO SEPTEMBER 25, 1902 " Samuel	Son	18	M	"	1893	"	38
4781	4 " Mary 15	Dau	12	F	"	1893	"	39
15412	5 " Eliza 12	"	9	"	"			
4782	6 " Jesse 10	Son	7	M	"	1893	Cedar	40
	7							
	8 For child of No.4 see NB (March 3 1905) #1332.							
	9							
	10 ENROLLMENT OF NOS. 1 2 3 4 and 6 HEREON							
	11 APPROVED BY THE SECRETARY							
	OF INTERIOR Dec 12 1902							
	12							
	13							
	14 ENROLLMENT OF NOS. 5 HEREON							
	15 APPROVED BY THE SECRETARY							
	OF INTERIOR May 9 1904							
	16							
	17							

TRIBAL ENROLLMENT OF PARENTS

	Name of Father	Year	County	Name of Mother	Year	County
1	David Baldwin	Dead	Kiamitia	Jennie Baldwin	Dead	Cedar
2	Harlin Perry	"	Cedar	Fa-la-mah	"	Cedar
3	No 1			No 2		
4	No 1			No 2		
5	No 1			No 2		
6	No 1			No 2		
7						
8	No1 on 1893 Pay roll Page 4 No.36, Cedar County as Washington Baldwin					
9	No2 " 1893 " " " 4 " 37 " "					
10	No3 " 1893 " " " 4 " 38 " "					
	No4 " 1893 " " " 4 " 39 " "					
11	No6 " 1893 " " " 4 " 40 " "					
12	No.3 died Nov. – 1901. Enrollment cancelled by Department July 8, 1904					
	No5 not found on roll. See testimony of No1, her father.					
13	No4 is duplicate of No5 on Choctaw card #3283.					
14	No3 died November 1901; proof of death filed Dec 19/02					
15	one affidavit" See testimonony[sic] as to why the name of	Date of Application for Enrollment.				
16	No5 is not on 1893 or 1896 Roll – Dec. 2, 1902	5/15/99				
17	No4 PO Arpelar IT 4/1/05					

196

Choctaw By Blood Enrollment Cards 1898-1914

RESIDENCE: Jacks Fork
POST OFFICE: Antlers, I.T.

COUNTY. **Choctaw Nation**

Choctaw Roll
(Not Including Freedmen)

CARD No.
FIELD No. **1697**

Dawes' Roll No.	NAME	Relationship to Person	AGE	SEX	BLOOD	TRIBAL ENROLLMENT		
						Year	County	No.
4783	1 Weaver, Jackson DIED PRIOR TO SEPTEMBER 25, 1902	First Named	23	M	Full	1896	Jacks Fork	14110
4784	2 " Mary 23	Wife	20	F	"	1896	" "	10591
	3							
	4							
	5							
	6							
	7	ENROLLMENT OF NOS. 1 and 2 HEREON						
	8	APPROVED BY THE SECRETARY OF INTERIOR Dec 12 1902						
	9							
	10							
	11							
	12							
	13							
	14							
	15							
	16							
	17							

TRIBAL ENROLLMENT OF PARENTS

Name of Father	Year	County	Name of Mother	Year	County
1 Calvin Jackson	Dead	Atoka	Sallie Jackson	Dead	Atoka
2 Nicholas Patterson	"	Jacks Fork	Emma Patterson	"	Jacks Fork
3					
4					
5					
6	No2 on 1896 roll [sic] Mary Patterson				
7	No 1 died Nov – 1899: Enrollment cancelled by Department July 8, 1904.				
8					
9					
10					
11					
12					
13					
14			Date of Application for Enrollment.		
15					
16			5/15/99		
17					

197

Choctaw By Blood Enrollment Cards 1898-1914

RESIDENCE: Kiamitia   COUNTY. **Choctaw Nation**   **Choctaw Roll**   CARD No.
POST OFFICE: Nelson, I.T.   *(Not Including Freedmen)*   FIELD No. **1698**

Dawes' Roll No.	NAME	Relationship to Person	AGE	SEX	BLOOD	TRIBAL ENROLLMENT Year	County	No.
4785	1 Cartubbee, Selina DIED PRIOR TO SEPTEMBER 25 1902	First Named	32	F	Full	1896	Kiamitia	2719
4786	2 " Frank ⁸	Son	5	M	"	1896	"	2721
	3							
	4							
	5							
	6							
	7							
	8							
	9							
	10							
	11							
	12							
	13							
	14							
	15							
	16							
	17							

ENROLLMENT
OF NOS. 1 and 2 HEREON
APPROVED BY THE SECRETARY
OF INTERIOR Dec 12 1902

TRIBAL ENROLLMENT OF PARENTS

	Name of Father	Year	County	Name of Mother	Year	County
1	Bob Robert	Dead	Towson	Sally Robert	Dead	Kiamitia
2	Thos. Cartubbee	"	Kiamitia	No 1		
3						
4						
5						
6	No.1 died – – ,1899: Enrollment cancelled by Department July 8, 1904					
7						
8						
9						
10						
11						
12						
13						
14						
15					Date of Application for Enrollment.	
16					5/15/99	
17						

198

OFFICE: Antlers, I.T.	Choctaw Nation (Not Including Freedmen)						FIELD NO. 1699	

es' No.	NAME	Relationship to Person First Named	AGE	SEX	BLOOD	TRIBAL ENROLLMENT Year	County	No.
87	1 Graman, Jackson 31	First Named	28	M	Full	1896	Wade	4713
88	2 " Sallie 32	Wife	29	F	"	1896	"	4714
89	3 " Emerson 14	Son	11	M	"	1896	"	4715
90	4 " Agnes 12	Dau	9	F	"	1896	"	4716
91	5 " Molsy 10	"	7	"	"	1896	"	4717
92	6 " Petross 7	Son	3	M	"	1896	"	4718
93	7 " Levicey 4	Dau	5mo	F	"			
94	8 " Gibson 1	Son	5mo	M	"			
	9							
	10							
	11	ENROLLMENT OF NOS. 12345678 HEREON						
	12	APPROVED BY THE SECRETARY						
	13	OF INTERIOR DEC 12 1902						
	14							
	15							
	16							
	17							

TRIBAL ENROLLMENT OF PARENTS

	Name of Father	Year	County	Name of Mother	Year	C
1	Ala-sho-ma	Dead	Wade	Amy	Dead	Wade
2	Jno. McIntosh	"	Jacks Fork	Selina Creman	"	Jacks F
3	No1			No2		
4	No1			No2		
5	No1			No2		
6	No1			No2		
7	No1			No2		
8	Nº1			Nº2		
9						
10	No6 on 1896 roll as Patmos Graman					
11	Nº8 Born Jany. 17, 1902: enrolled June 2, 1902					
12	For child of Nos. 1 and 2 see NB (March 3 1905) #1249					
13						
14					#1 to 7 inc	
15				Date of Application for Enrollment.		
16					5/15/99	
17						

Choctaw By Blood Enrollment Cards 1898-1914

RESIDENCE: Jackson COUNTY.
POST OFFICE: Kosoma, I.T.

Choctaw Nation

Choctaw Roll *(Not Including Freedmen)*

CARD NO.
FIELD NO. **1700**

Dawes' Roll No.	NAME		Relationship to Person	AGE	SEX	BLOOD	TRIBAL ENROLLMENT		
							Year	County	No.
4795	1 Cole, Wilson	37	First Named	34	M	Full	1896	Jacks Fork	3009
4796	2 DIED PRIOR TO SEPTEMBER 25 1902 Betsy		Wife	32	F	"	1896	" "	3010
4797	3 " Titus	16	Son	13	M	"	1896	" "	3011
4798	4 DIED PRIOR TO SEPTEMBER 25 1902 Lizzie		Dau	8	F	"	1896	" "	3012
4799	5 " Louisiana	11	"	8	"	"	1896	" "	3013
4800	6 " Amy	8	"	5	"	"	1896	" "	3014
4801	7 " Anice	4	Son	3mo	M	"			
	8								
	9								
	10								
	11	ENROLLMENT OF NOS. 1234567 HEREON APPROVED BY THE SECRETARY OF INTERIOR Dec 12 1902							
	12								
	13								
	14								
	15								
	16								
	17								

TRIBAL ENROLLMENT OF PARENTS

	Name of Father	Year	County	Name of Mother	Year	County
1	Peter Cole	Dead	Cedar	Mulsey Cole	Dead	Jacks Fork
2	Iok la nubbee	"	Nashoba	Siney Hudson	"	" " "
3	No 1			No 2		
4	No 1			No 2		
5	No 1			No 2		
6	No 1			No 2		
7	No 1			No 2		
8						
9			No2 on 1896 roll as Bincey Cole			
10			No 6 " 1896 " " Annie "			
11			No2 died Nov. 2, 1899: proof of death filed Dec. 8, 1902			
12			No4 " Feb. – 1902: " " " " " " "			
13		No.2 died Nov. 2, 1899: No.4 died Feb.-1901: Enrollment cancelled by Department July 8, 1904				
14						
15			No.7 is now living with Culberson Hudson Choc. Card #1723		Date of Application for Enrollment.
16						5/15/99
17	Zoraya, I.T. 7/11/06					

Choctaw By Blood Enrollment Cards 1898-1914

RESIDENCE: Kiamitia
POST OFFICE: Nelson, I.T.

COUNTY. **Choctaw Nation**

Choctaw Roll
(Not Including Freedmen)

CARD NO.
FIELD NO. 1701

Dawes' Roll No.	NAME	Relationship to Person	AGE	SEX	BLOOD	TRIBAL ENROLLMENT		
						Year	County	No.
4802	1 Durant, Sallie 56	First Named	53	F	Full	1896	Kiamitia	10850
	2							
	3							
	4							
	5							
	6							
	7							
	8							
	9							
	10							
	11	ENROLLMENT OF NOS. 1 HEREON APPROVED BY THE SECRETARY OF INTERIOR DEC 12 1902						
	12							
	13							
	14							
	15							
	16							
	17							

TRIBAL ENROLLMENT OF PARENTS

	Name of Father	Year	County	Name of Mother	Year	County
1	Posha Roberts	Dead	Bok Tuklo	Melisa Roberts	Dead	Bok Tuklo
2						
3						
4						
5						
6			On 1896 roll as Sallie Roberts			
7						
8						
9						
10						
11						
12						
13						
14						
15						
16				Date of Application for Enrollment.	5/15/99	
17						

Choctaw By Blood Enrollment Cards 1898-1914

RESIDENCE: Jacks Fork
POST OFFICE: Antlers, I.T.

COUNTY. **Choctaw Nation**

Choctaw Roll
(Not Including Freedmen)

CARD NO.

FIELD NO. 1702

Dawes' Roll No.	NAME		Relationship to Person First Named	AGE	SEX	BLOOD	TRIBAL ENROLLMENT		
							Year	County	No.
4803	1 Jones, Willis	37	First Named	34	M	Full	1896	Jacks Fork	7361
4804	2 " Louisa	34	Wife	31	F	"	1896	" "	7362
	3								
	4								
	5								
	6								
	7	ENROLLMENT							
	8	OF NOS. 1 and 2 HEREON							
	9	APPROVED BY THE SECRETARY OF INTERIOR DEC 12 1902							
	10								
	11								
	12								
	13								
	14								
	15								
	16								
	17								

TRIBAL ENROLLMENT OF PARENTS

Name of Father	Year	County	Name of Mother	Year	County
1 Jones Hoteka	Dead	Jacks Fork	Pekie Hoteka	Dead	Jacks Fork
2 Dixon Wade	"	Atoka	Susie Wade	"	" "
3					
4					
5					
6					
7	No 2 is now wife of Simeon Tom Choctaw card #1720 evidence of				
8	marriage filed Dec. 8, 1902				
9					
10	No.1 in Penitentiary at Atlanta Ga.				
11					
12					
13					
14					
15					
16			Date of Application for Enrollment.	5/15/99	
17					

Choctaw By Blood Enrollment Cards 1898-1914

RESIDENCE: Kiamitia   COUNTY. **Choctaw Nation**   **Choctaw Roll** C.
POST OFFICE: Antlers, I.T.   *(Not Including Freedmen)*   FIELD No. 1703

Dawes' Roll No.	NAME		Relationship to Person	AGE	SEX	BLOOD	TRIBAL ENROLLMENT		
							Year	County	No.
4805	1 Nelson, Eden	36	First Named	33	M	3/4	1896	Jacks Fork	9883
4806	2 " Laura	28	Wife	25	F	1/4	1896	" "	9885
4807	3 " Isham	8	Son	4	M	1/2	1896	" "	9884
4808	4 " Gooding	7	"	3	"	1/2	1896	" "	9886
4809	5 " Osborne	6	"	2	"	1/2			
4810	6 " Jerusha	4	Dau	2mo	F	1/2			
4811	7 " David	1	Son	1mo	M	1/2			
	8								
	9								
	10								
	11	ENROLLMENT							
	12	OF NOS. 123456and7 HEREON APPROVED BY THE SECRETARY							
	13	OF INTERIOR DEC 12 1902							
	14								
	15								
	16								
	17								

TRIBAL ENROLLMENT OF PARENTS

	Name of Father	Year	County	Name of Mother	Year	County
1	Gooden Nelson	Dead	Jacks Fork	Mulsey Nelson	1896	Jacks Fork
2	King Ashford	"	Non Citz	Elizabeth Perkins	1896	Kiamitia
3	No1			No2		
4	No1			No2		
5	No1			No2		
6	No1			No2		
7	No.1			No.2		
8						
9			No.7 Enrolled July 26, 1901.			
10			For child of Nos 1 and 2 see NB (March 3,1905) #1280			
11						
12						
13						
14				Date of Application for Enrollment.		
15						
16				5/15/99		
17						

RESIDENCE: Jacks Fork	COUNTY.				Choctaw Roll		CARD NO.	
POST OFFICE: Antlers, I.T	Choctaw Nation				(Not Including Freedmen)		FIELD NO. 1704	

Dawes' Roll No.	NAME		Relationship to Person	AGE	SEX	BLOOD	TRIBAL ENROLLMENT		
							Year	County	No.
4812	1 Camp, Martin	25	First Named	22	M	Full	1896	Jacks Fork	3058
DEAD.	2 " Annie		Wife	37	F	"	1893	" "	397
4813	3 " Waitie	4	Son	6mo	M	"			
4814	4 Anontubbee, Eliza DIED PRIOR TO SEPTEMBER 29, 1902		S. Dau	16	F	"	1893	Jacks Fork	398
	5								
	6								
	7	ENROLLMENT							
	8	OF NOS. 1 3 and 4 HEREON							
	9	APPROVED BY THE SECRETARY OF INTERIOR DEC 12 1902							
	10								
	11								
	12	No. 2 HEREON DISMISSED UNDER							
	13	ORDER OF THE COMMISSION TO THE FIVE CIVILIZED TRIBES OF MARCH 31, 1905.							
	14								
	15								
	16								
	17								

TRIBAL ENROLLMENT OF PARENTS

	Name of Father	Year	County	Name of Mother	Year	County
1	Amos Camp	1896	Jacks Fork	Siney Camp	Dead	Jacks Fork
2	Harkin	Dead	Cedar	Sallie Harkin	"	Cedar
3	No1			No2		
4	Harris Anontubbee	Dead	Cedar	No2		
5						
6						
7	No 2 on 1893 Pay roll Page 43, No 397, Jacks Fork Co as Aimie Harkin					
8	No 4 " 1893 " " " 43 " 398 " " " " Eliza Harkin					
9	No 4 also on 1896 " " 149 " 6134 " " " " Eliza Harris					
	No 2 died Nov. – 1899; proof of death filed Dec 8, 1902.					
10	No 4 " Sept. – 1900; " " " " " " "					
11	No 4 died Sept – 1900. Enrollment cancelled by Department July 8, 1904					
12	No.1 is husband of Mary Jefferson Choc. Card #1795					
13						
14					Date of Application for Enrollment.	
15						
16					5/15/99	
17						

Choctaw By Blood Enrollment Cards 1898-1914

RESIDENCE: Cedar	COUNTY.					CARD NO.		
POST OFFICE: Rodney, I.T.				**Choctaw Nation**		Choctaw Roll *(Not Including Freedmen)*	FIELD NO. 1705	

Dawes' Roll No.	NAME	Relationship to Person Named	AGE	SEX	BLOOD	TRIBAL ENROLLMENT		
						Year	County	No.
4815	₁ Sherred, John ⁵⁹	First Named	56	M	Full	1896	Cedar	11351
4816	₂ Becky DIED PRIOR TO SEPTEMBER 25 1902	Wife	43	F	"	1896	"	11352
	₃							
	₄							
	₅							
	₆	ENROLLMENT						
	₇	OF NOS. 1 and 2 HEREON APPROVED BY THE SECRETARY						
	₈	OF INTERIOR DEC 12 1902						
	₉							
	10							
	11							
	12							
	13							
	14							
	15							
	16							
	17							

TRIBAL ENROLLMENT OF PARENTS

	Name of Father	Year	County	Name of Mother	Year	County
₁	Tick-bot-tubbee	Dead	Cedar	Co-ne-ha-ma	Dead	Jacks Fork
₂	Amos Hotekubbee	"	"	Ma-ha-che-tona	"	Cedar
₃						
₄						
₅						
₆						
₇		No2 on 1896 roll as Bikie Sherred				
₈		No1 " 1896 " " John M. "				
₉						
10		No1 died October, 1899; proof of death filed Dec 5, 1902				
11		No.1 died Oct. – 1899; Enrollment cancelled by Department July 8, 1904				
12						
13						
14						
15						
16			Date of Application for Enrollment.	5/15/99		
17						

Choctaw By Blood Enrollment Cards 1898-1914

Choctaw Nation   Choctaw Roll   CARD NO.

POST OFFICE: Antlers, I.T.   *(Not Including Freedmen)*   FIELD NO. 1706

Dawes' Roll No.		NAME		Relationship to Person First Named	AGE	SEX	BLOOD	TRIBAL ENROLLMENT		
								Year	County	No.
4817	1	Greenwood, Hattie	48	Named	45	F	Full	1896	Jacks Fork	4997
4818	2	" Allen	24	Son	21	M	"	1896	" "	4999
4819	3	" Myatt	19	"	16	"	"	1896	" "	4998
	4									
	5									
	6									
	7									
	8	ENROLLMENT								
	9	OF NOS. 1 2 and 3 HEREON APPROVED BY THE SECRETARY								
	10	OF INTERIOR DEC 12 1902								
	11									
	12									
	13									
	14									
	15									
	16									
	17									

TRIBAL ENROLLMENT OF PARENTS

	Name of Father	Year	County	Name of Mother	Year	County
1	Johnson Hochubbee	Dead	Skullyville	Con-che-he-ma	Dead	Skullyville
2	Tom Greenwood	"	Jacks Fork	No1		
3	" "	"	" "	No1		
4						
5						
6						
7						
8			No3 on 1896 roll as Myett Greenwood			
9						
10						
11						
12						
13						
14						
15						
16				Date of Application for Enrollment.	5/15/99	
17						

Choctaw By Blood Enrollment Cards 1898-1914

RESIDENCE: Kiamitia
POST OFFICE: Nelson, I.T.

COUNTY. **Choctaw Nation**

Choctaw Roll *(Not Including Freedmen)*

CARD NO.
FIELD NO. **1707**

Dawes' Roll No.	NAME	Relationship to Person	AGE	SEX	BLOOD	TRIBAL ENROLLMENT		
						Year	County	No.
4820	1 Colbert, Suckey 63	First Named	60	F	Full	1896	Kiamitia	2715
	2							
	3							
	4							
	5							
	6							
	7							
	8	ENROLLMENT OF NOS. 1 HEREON APPROVED BY THE SECRETARY OF INTERIOR Dec. 12, 1902						
	9							
	10							
	11							
	12							
	13							
	14							
	15							
	16							
	17							

TRIBAL ENROLLMENT OF PARENTS

	Name of Father	Year	County	Name of Mother	Year	County
1	Na-kish-noah	Dead	Towson		Dead	Towson
2						
3						
4						
5						
6						
7						
8						
9						
10						
11						
12						
13						
14				Date of Application for Enrollment.		
15						
16				5/15/99		
17						

207

Choctaw By Blood Enrollment Cards 1898-1914

RESIDENCE: Jacks Fork	COUNTY. Choctaw Nation	Choctaw Roll (Not Including Freedmen)	CARD No.
POST OFFICE: Antlers, I.T.			FIELD No. 1708

Dawes' Roll No.	NAME		Relationship to Person	AGE	SEX	BLOOD	TRIBAL ENROLLMENT		
							Year	County	No.
4821	1 Cole, Silas E	33	First Named	30	M	Full	1896	Jacks Fork	3015
4822	2 " Missie	22	Wife	19	F	"	1896	Kiamitia	360
4823	3 " Amanda	2	Dau	3mo	F	"			
	4								
	5								
	6								
	7	ENROLLMENT OF NOS. 1 2 and 3 HEREON APPROVED BY THE SECRETARY OF INTERIOR Dec 12, 1902							
	8								
	9								
	10								
	11								
	12								
	13								
	14								
	15								
	16								
	17								

TRIBAL ENROLLMENT OF PARENTS

	Name of Father	Year	County	Name of Mother	Year	County
1	Edmund Cole	Dead	Jacks Fork	Sarabel Cole	Dead	Jacks Fork
2	Solomon Adams	dead	Jackson	Siney Gibson	1896	Kiamitia
3	No 1			No 2		
4						
5						
6						
7			On 1896 roll as S E Cole			
8						
9			No 2 transferred from Choctaw card #1503 January 3, 1901			
10			No 3 Enrolled January 3, 1901.			
11			No 2 on 1896 Choctaw roll as Missie Adams.			
12						
13						
14						#1
15					Date of Application for Enrollment.	
16				Date of Application for Enrollment.	5/15/99	
17	P.O. Nelson I.T. 12/23/02					

Choctaw By Blood Enrollment Cards 1898-1914

RESIDENCE: Jacks Fork   COUNTY. **Choctaw Nation**   **Choctaw Roll** CARD NO.
POST OFFICE: Antlers, I.T   *(Not Including Freedmen)*   FIELD NO. 1709

Dawes' Roll No.	NAME	Relationship to Person First Named	AGE	SEX	BLOOD	TRIBAL ENROLLMENT		
						Year	County	No.
4824	1 Cole, Eastman ³⁰	First Named	27	M	Full	1896	Blue	2883
4825	2 " Susan ²⁷	Wife	24	F	"	1896	"	2884
	3							
	4							
	5							
	6							
	7							
	8							
	9							
	10							
	11							
	12							
	13							
	14							
	15							
	16							
	17							

ENROLLMENT
OF NOS. 1 and 2 HEREON
APPROVED BY THE SECRETARY
OF INTERIOR DEC 12 1902

TRIBAL ENROLLMENT OF PARENTS

	Name of Father	Year	County	Name of Mother	Year	County
1	Edmund Cole	Dead	Jacks Fork	Sarabel Cole	Dead	Jacks Fork
2	William May	"	Blue	Sibitee Scott	1896	Jackson
3						
4						
5						
6						
7						
8						
9						
10						
11						
12						
13						
14				Date of Application for Enrollment.		
15						
16				5/15/99		
17						

Choctaw By Blood Enrollment Cards 1898-1914

RESIDENCE: Jacks Fork   COUNTY. **Choctaw Nation**   **Choctaw Roll** *(Not Including Freedmen)*   CARD NO.

POST OFFICE: Antlers, I.T.   FIELD NO. 1710

Dawes' Roll No.	NAME		Relationship to Person	AGE	SEX	BLOOD	TRIBAL ENROLLMENT		
							Year	County	No.
4826	1 Perry, Selina	54	First Named	51	F	Full	1893	Kiamitia	850
	2								
	3								
	4								
	5								
	6	ENROLLMENT							
	7	OF NOS. 1 HEREON APPROVED BY THE SECRETARY							
	8	OF INTERIOR DEC 12 1902							
	9								
	10								
	11								
	12								
	13								
	14								
	15								
	16								
	17								

TRIBAL ENROLLMENT OF PARENTS

	Name of Father	Year	County	Name of Mother	Year	County
1	Cha-cubbee	Dead	Kiamitia	Rhoda	Dead	Kiamitia
2						
3						
4						
5						
6						
7			On 1893 Pay roll, Page 103, No. 850, Kiamitia County			
8						
9			No. 1 Died prior to September 25, 1902; not entitled to land or money			
10			See Indian Office Letter April 20, 1908 (I.T. 19329-1908)			
11						
12						
13						
14						
15						
16				Date of Application for Enrollment.	5/15/99	
17						

Choctaw By Blood Enrollment Cards 1898-1914

RESIDENCE: Jacks Fork COUNTY. **Choctaw Nation** **Choctaw Roll** CARD NO.
POST OFFICE: Antlers, I.T. (Not Including Freedmen) FIELD NO. 1711

Dawes' Roll No.	NAME	Relationship to Person	AGE	SEX	BLOOD	TRIBAL ENROLLMENT		
						Year	County	No.
4827	1 Nahomake — DIED PRIOR TO SEPTEMBER 25 1902	First Named	60	F	Full	1896	Jacks Fork	9871
	2							
	3							
	4							
	5							
	6							
	7							
	8							
	9							
	10							
	11	ENROLLMENT						
	12	OF NOS. 1 HEREON APPROVED BY THE SECRETARY						
	13	OF INTERIOR DEC 12 1902						
	14							
	15							
	16							
	17							

TRIBAL ENROLLMENT OF PARENTS

	Name of Father	Year	County	Name of Mother	Year	County
1	E-la-pin-tubbee	Dead	Jacks Fork	Ho-te-ma	Dead	Nashoba
2						
3						
4						
5						
6	No 1 died October 1900: Enrollment cancelled by Department May 2, 1901					
7						
8						
9						
10						
11						
12						
13						
14						
15						
16				Date of Application for Enrollment.	5/15/99	
17						

Choctaw By Blood Enrollment Cards 1898-1914

RESIDENCE: Kiamitia   COUNTY. **Choctaw Nation**   **Choctaw Roll**   CARD No.
POST OFFICE: Goodland, I.T.   *(Not Including Freedmen)*   FIELD No. **1712**

Dawes' Roll No.	NAME		Relationship to Person	AGE	SEX	BLOOD	TRIBAL ENROLLMENT		
							Year	County	No.
4828	1 Joe, Sampson	38	First Named	35	M	Full	1896	Kiamitia	7079
	2								
	3								
	4								
	5								
	6	ENROLLMENT							
	7	OF NOS. 1 HEREON APPROVED BY THE SECRETARY							
	8	OF INTERIOR DEC 12 1902							
	9								
	10								
	11								
	12								
	13								
	14								
	15								
	16								
	17								

TRIBAL ENROLLMENT OF PARENTS

	Name of Father	Year	County	Name of Mother	Year	County
1	Te-hok-lo-tubbee	Dead	Towson		Dead	Towson
2						
3						
4						
5						
6						
7						
8						
9						
10						
11						
12						
13						
14						
15						
16				Date of Application for Enrollment.	5/15/99	
17						

Choctaw By Blood Enrollment Cards 1898-1914

RESIDENCE: Jacks Fork　　COUNTY: **Choctaw Nation** Choctaw Roll CARD NO.
POST OFFICE: Antlers, I.T.　　　　　　(Not Including Freedmen)　FIELD NO. 1713

Dawes' Roll No.	NAME	Relationship to Person First Named	AGE	SEX	BLOOD	TRIBAL ENROLLMENT		
						Year	County	No.
4829	1 Anderson, Isaac ²⁷	First Named	24	M	Full	1896	Jacks Fork	454
4830	2 " George ⁶	Son	3	"	Full	1896	Jacks Fork	456
4831	3 " Impson ⁵	"	2	"	Full	1896	Jacks Fork	457
	4							
	5							
	6							
	7	ENROLLMENT						
	8	OF NOS. 1 2 and 3 HEREON APPROVED BY THE SECRETARY						
	9	OF INTERIOR DEC 12 1902						
	10							
	11							
	12							
	13							
	14							
	15							
	16							
	17							

TRIBAL ENROLLMENT OF PARENTS

	Name of Father	Year	County	Name of Mother	Year	County	
1	Anderson	Dead	Jacks Fork	Liney Impson	Dead	Jacks Fork	
2	No1			Sillen Anderson	"	" " "	
3	No1			" "	"	" " "	
4							
5							
6							
7							
8							
9							
10							
11							
12							
13							
14							
15	No1 P.O.						
16	Stratford, Okla			Date of Application for Enrollment.	5/15/99		
17	10-5-10						

213

Choctaw By Blood Enrollment Cards 1898-1914

RESIDENCE: Jacks Fork	COUNTY. **Choctaw Nation**	**Choctaw Roll**	CARD No.
POST OFFICE: Antlers, I.T.		*(Not Including Freedmen)*	FIELD No. **1714**

Dawes' Roll No.	NAME	Relationship to Person First Named	AGE	SEX	BLOOD	TRIBAL ENROLLMENT		
						Year	County	No.
4832	1 Nelson, Maulsey ⁶⁸	First Named	65	F	Full	1896	Jacks Fork	9887
	2							
	3							
	4							
	5							
	6							
	7	ENROLLMENT OF NOS. 1 HEREON APPROVED BY THE SECRETARY OF INTERIOR Dec 12, 1902						
	8							
	9							
	10							
	11							
	12							
	13							
	14							
	15							
	16							
	17							

TRIBAL ENROLLMENT OF PARENTS

	Name of Father	Year	County	Name of Mother	Year	County
1	Carn Underwood	Dead	Jacks Fork	Tennessee Underwood	Dead	Jacks Fork
2						
3						
4						
5						
6						
7			No 1 Died April 17, 1906 See inhereted[sic] land sale			
8						
9						
10						
11						
12						
13						
14						
15						
16						
17				Date of Application for Enrollment.	5/15/99	

RESIDENCE: Jacks Fork
POST OFFICE: Nelson, I.T.
COUNTY. **Choctaw Nation**
Choctaw Roll *(Not Including Freedmen)*
CARD No. FIELD No. **1715**

Dawes' Roll No.	NAME		Relationship to Person	AGE	SEX	BLOOD	TRIBAL ENROLLMENT		
							Year	County	No.
4833	1 Parish, Thomas		First Named	46	M	1/2	1896	Jacks Fork	10600
4834	2 " Eve		Wife	21	F	Full	1896	" "	10601
4835	3 " Elias	27	Son	24	M	3/4	1893	" "	621
4836	4 " Robert	24	"	21	"	3/4	1896	" "	10602
4837	5 " Rosie	15	Dau	12	F	3/4	1896	" "	10603
4838	6 Durant, Ellis	14	Ward	11	M	Full	1896	" "	10604
14691	7 Parish, Hattie	23	Dau in Law	23	F	Full	1896	Red River	309
	8								
	9	ENROLLMENT							
	10	OF NOS. 1 2 3 4 5 and 6 HEREON APPROVED BY THE SECRETARY							
	11	OF INTERIOR Dec. 12, 1902							

For child of No3 see N.B. (March 3, 19050 #1207

No 7 13 For information as to parents see
14 her letter of Jan. 19, 1903 filed
15 herein.
16
17

TRIBAL ENROLLMENT OF PARENTS

	Name of Father	Year	County	Name of Mother	Year	County
1	Toney Parish	Dead	Non Citz	Julie Parish	Dead	Jacks Fork
2	Mullen Underwood	1896	Jacks Fork	Aby Underwood	1896	" "
3	No 1			Siney Parish	Dead	" "
4	No 1			" "	" "	" "
5	No 1			" "	" "	" "
6	Winston	Dead	Jacks Fork	Betsey Winston	" "	" "
7	Louis Austin		Choctaw	Melvina Austin		Choctaw
8						
9						

10 For child of No4 see N.B. (Apr 26 '06) Card #1204
No 3 on 1893 Pay roll, Page 70, No 621, Jacks Fork as Elias Perish
11 No6 on 1896 roll as Elles Parish
12 No 3 is now the husband of Eliza Lewis on Choctaw Card #1694 Aug. 6, 1902
13 No.1 Died May 2, 1900: proof of death filed Dec. 5, 1902
14 No 2 " June 1901: " " " " " "
15 No 7 Enrolled December 2, 1902: See testimony of her husband Robert
16 Parish who is No 4 hereon, dated Dec. 2, 1901
17 No 7 also on 1896 Choctaw census roll page 8 #309 as Hattie Austin

Date of Application for Enrollment 5/15/99

ENROLLMENT OF NOS. 7 HEREON APPROVED BY THE SECRETARY OF INTERIOR May 20, 1903

No.1 died May 2,1900: No.2 died June – 1901: Enrollment cancelled by Department Sept. 16,1904

RESIDENCE: Jacks Fork	COUNTY.	**Choctaw Nation**	Choctaw Roll	CARD No.	
POST OFFICE: Antlers, I.T.			*(Not Including Freedmen)*	FIELD No.	**1716**

Dawes' Roll No.	NAME		Relationship to Person First Named	AGE	SEX	BLOOD	TRIBAL ENROLLMENT		
							Year	County	No.
4839	1 Hampton, Johnson	26	Named	23	M	Full	1896	Jacks Fork	6132
4840	2 " Frances	27	Wife	24	F	"	1896	" "	6133
4841	3 " Josephine	6	Dau	2	"	"			
4842	4 DIED PRIOR TO SEPTEMBER 25, 1902 Jack		Son	7mo	M	"			
4843	5 Wesley, Davis	12	S son	9	"	"	1896	Jacks Fork	14120
4844	6 Turner, Hattie	9	S Dau	6	F	"	1896	" "	12514
4845	7 Hampton, William	2	Son	2mo	M	"			
14692	8 " Ettaline	1	Dau	4mo	F	"			
	9								
	10	ENROLLMENT							
	11	OF NOS. 123456and7 HEREON							
	12	APPROVED BY THE SECRETARY OF INTERIOR Dec. 12. 1902							
	13								
	14	ENROLLMENT							
	15	OF NOS. 8 HEREON							
	16	APPROVED BY THE SECRETARY OF INTERIOR May 20, 1903							
	17								

TRIBAL ENROLLMENT OF PARENTS

Name of Father	Year	County	Name of Mother	Year	County
1 Willis Hampton	Dead	Sugar Loaf	Charity Hampton	Dead	Sugar Loaf
2 Stephen Noah	"	Jacks Fork	Isabelle Noah	"	Jacks Fork
3 No 1			No 2		
4 No 1			No 2		
5			No 2		
6 James Turner	1896	Jacks Fork	No 2		
7 No 1			No 2		
8 No 1			No 2		
9 No1 on 1896 roll as John Hampton					
10 No.4 died Aug. 2, 1899: Enrollment cancelled by Department July 8, 1904					
11 No 5 is an illegitimate child. Enrolled by step father who					
12 claims not to know father. For child of Nos 1&2 see N.B.(Mar 3'05)#1281					
13 No.7 Enrolled, Oct. 31st, 1900.					
13 No 4 died Aug. 2, 1899; proof of death filed Dec. 8, 1902					
14 No 8 Born Aug. 2, 1902: Enrolled Dec. 18, 1902.					
15				Date of Application for Enrollment.	#1 to 6
16					
17 P.O. Zorava I.T. 1/1/07					5/15/99

216

Choctaw By Blood Enrollment Cards 1898-1914

RESIDENCE: Jacks Fork	COUNTY.	CARD No.
POST OFFICE: Antlers, I.T.	**Choctaw Nation**	**Choctaw Roll** (Not Including Freedmen) FIELD No. **1717**

Dawes' Roll No.	NAME	Relationship to Person First Named	AGE	SEX	BLOOD	TRIBAL ENROLLMENT		
						Year	County	No.
4846	1 Lewis, Barefield 46	First Named	43	M	Full	1896	Jacks Fork	8370
4847	2 " Susan 31	Wife	38	F	"	1896	" "	8371
4848	3 " Sampson 17	Son	14	M	"	1896	" "	8372
4849	4 DIED PRIOR TO SEPTEMBER 25 1902 Eastman	"	12	"	"	1896	" "	8373
4850	5 " John 13	"	10	"	"	1896	" "	8374
4851	6 " Susianna 3	Dau	1wk	F	"			
4852	7 Harrison, Thomas 17	Ward	14	M	"	1896	Jacks Fork	6120
4853	8 " Louisa 9	"	6	F	"	1896	" "	6121
	9							
	10							
	11	ENROLLMENT OF NOS. 1234567and8 HEREON						
	12	APPROVED BY THE SECRETARY						
	13	OF INTERIOR Dec. 12, 1902						
	14							
	15							
	16							
	17							

TRIBAL ENROLLMENT OF PARENTS

	Name of Father	Year	County	Name of Mother	Year	County
1	Lewis	Dead	Jacks Fork	Miley Lewis	Dead	Jacks Fork
2	"	"	Red River	Tilley	"	Kiamitia
3	No 1			No 2		
4	No 1			No 2		
5	No 1			No 2		
6	No 1			No 2		
7	Lawson Harrison	Dead	Kiamitia	Rhoda Harrison	Dead	Kiamitia
8	" "	"	"	" "	"	"
9						
10						
11						
12						
13		No 3 on 1896 roll as Sam Lewis				
14		No 4 died July 6, 1899; proof of death filed Dec. 8, 1902.				Date of Application for Enrollment.
15		No.7 in Pen.				
16		No.3 is husband of Lizzie Miller No4 on Choctaw Card #1749.				
17		No 4 died July 6, 1899; Enrollment cancelled by Department July 8, 1904				5/15/99

Choctaw By Blood Enrollment Cards 1898-1914

RESIDENCE: Jacks Fork   COUNTY. **Choctaw Nation**   **Choctaw Roll** CARD No.
POST OFFICE: Antlers, I.T.   *(Not Including Freedmen)*   FIELD No. **1718**

Dawes' Roll No.	NAME		Relationship to Person First Named	AGE	SEX	BLOOD	TRIBAL ENROLLMENT		
							Year	County	No.
4854	1 Camp, Amos	53	First Named	50	M	Full	1896	Jacks Fork	3056
4855	2 " Jincy	47	Wife	44	F	"	1896	" "	3057
4856	3 " Neles	20	Dau	17	"	"	1896	" "	3059
4857	4 " Willis	17	Son	14	M	"	1896	" "	3061
4858	5 " Ellen	15	Dau	12	F	"	1896	" "	3062
4859	6 " Sallie	18	"	15	"	"	1896	" "	3060
4860	7 " Phoebe	11	"	8	"	"	1896	" "	3063
	8								
	9								
	10								
	11	ENROLLMENT							
	12	OF NOS. 123456and7 HEREON APPROVED BY THE SECRETARY							
	13	OF INTERIOR Dec 12, 1902							
	14								
	15								
	16								
	17								

TRIBAL ENROLLMENT OF PARENTS

	Name of Father	Year	County	Name of Mother	Year	County
1	E-la-po-tubbee	Dead	Jacks Fork	Tik-bom-tema	Dead	Sugar Loaf
2	Louis John	"	Skullyville	Mary Ann	"	Jacks Fork
3	No 1			Siney Camp	"	" " "
4	No 1			" "	"	" " "
5	No 1			" "	"	" " "
6	No 1			No 2		
7	No 1			No 2		
8						
9						
10						
11						
12						
13						
14						
15					Date of Application for Enrollment.	
16					5/15/99	
17						

RESIDENCE: Jacks Fork
COUNTY. **Choctaw Nation**
POST OFFICE: Antlers, [sic]

Choctaw Roll *(Not Including Freedmen)*

CARD No.
FIELD No. 1719

Dawes' Roll No.	NAME	Relationship to Person	AGE	SEX	BLOOD	TRIBAL ENROLLMENT		
						Year	County	No.
4861	1 William, Edmond	First Named	35	M	Full	1896	Jacks Fork	14102
4862	2 " Jincy 35	Wife	32	F	"	1896	" "	14103
	3							
	4							
	5							
	6	ENROLLMENT						
	7	OF NOS. 1 and 2 HEREON						
	8	APPROVED BY THE SECRETARY OF INTERIOR						
	9							
	10							
	11							
	12							
	13							
	14							
	15							
	16							
	17							

DIED PRIOR TO SEPTEMBER 23 1902

TRIBAL ENROLLMENT OF PARENTS

Name of Father	Year	County	Name of Mother	Year	County
1 William	Dead	Cedar	Sally Farlis	1896	Jacks Fork
2 Tomby Greenwood	"	Jacks Fork	Sibbey Greenwood	Dead	" "
3					
4					
5					
6		No1 Died January – 1900; proof of Death filed Dec. 5, 1902			
7		No.1 died Jan. – 1900: Enrollment cancelled by Department July 8, 1904			
8					
9					
10					
11					
12					
13					
14					
15			Date of Application for Enrollment	5/15/99	
16					
17					

Choctaw By Blood Enrollment Cards 1898-1914

RESIDENCE: Jacks Fork		COUNTY. **Choctaw Nation**			**Choctaw Roll** *(Not Including Freedmen)*		CARD No.	
POST OFFICE: Antlers I T.							FIELD No.	**1720**

Dawes' Roll No.	NAME		Relationship to Person	AGE	SEX	BLOOD	TRIBAL ENROLLMENT		
							Year	County	No.
4863	1 Tom, Montuna	53	First Named	50	F	Full	1893	Jacks Fork	P.R. 697
4864	2 " Simeon	23	Son	20	M	"	1893	" "	699
	3								
	4								
	5								
	6	ENROLLMENT							
	7	OF NOS. 1 and 2 HEREON APPROVED BY THE SECRETARY							
	8	OF INTERIOR Dec. 12, 1902							
	9								
	10								
	11								
	12								
	13								
	14								
	15								
	16								
	17								

TRIBAL ENROLLMENT OF PARENTS

	Name of Father	Year	County	Name of Mother	Year	County
1	O-tim-il-li	Ded	Bok-Tuk-lo	Lucy	Ded	Cedar
2	Missin Tom	"	Jacks Fork	No 1		
3						
4						
5			No 1 on 93 Pay Roll for Jacks Fork Co as			
6			Montana Tom			
7						
8			No 2 also on 1896 roll, Page 326, No 12515			
9			Jacks Fork			
10			No 2 is now married to Louisa Jones Choctaw Card #1702			
11		No 1 also on 1896 Choctaw Census roll, #8896 as Mantena.				
12		No.1 is a duplicate of Matona on Choctaw Card #4885				
13						
14					Date of Application for Enrollment.	
15						
16					5/15/99	
17						

Choctaw By Blood Enrollment Cards 1898-1914

RESIDENCE:	Jack's Fork	COUNTY.	Choctaw Nation		Choctaw Roll	CARD NO.	
POST OFFICE:	Antlers, IT				(Not Including Freedmen)	FIELD NO.	1721

Dawes' Roll No.	NAME	Relationship to Person	AGE	SEX	BLOOD	TRIBAL ENROLLMENT		
						Year	County	P.N.R.
4865	1 Hayes, Malissa DIED PRIOR TO SEPTEMBER 25, 1902	First Named	30	F	Full	1893	Kiamitia	272
	2							
	3							
	4							
	5							
	6 ENROLLMENT OF NOS. 1 HEREON							
	7 APPROVED BY THE SECRETARY OF INTERIOR Dec. 12, 1902							
	8							
	9							
	10							
	11							
	12							
	13							
	14							
	15							
	16							
	17							

TRIBAL ENROLLMENT OF PARENTS

	Name of Father	Year	County	Name of Mother	Year	County
1	Jesse Lewis	Ded	Kiamitia	Mary Lewis	Ded	Atoka
2						
3						
4						
5	No. 1 died in 1900. Enrollment cancelled by Department May 2, 1906.					
6						
7						
8						
9						
10						
11						
12						
13						
14						
15						
16				Date of Application for Enrollment.		5/15/99
17						

Choctaw By Blood Enrollment Cards 1898-1914

RESIDENCE: Jacks – Fork COUNTY. **Choctaw Nation** Choctaw Roll CARD No.
POST OFFICE: Antlers I.T. (Not Including Freedmen) FIELD No. **1722**

Dawes' Roll No.	NAME		Relationship to Person First Named	AGE	SEX	BLOOD	TRIBAL ENROLLMENT		
							Year	County	No.
4866	1	Tubbee, Raymon ~~DIED PRIOR TO SEPTEMBER 25 1902~~	First Named	38	M	Full	1896	Jack's Fork	12507
4867	2	" Silwee ⁴²	Wife	39	F	"	1896	" "	12508
4868	3	" Emeline ¹¹	Dau	8	"	"	1896	" "	12509
4869	4	" Levina ⁶	"	3	"	"	1896	" "	12510
	5								
	6								
	7								
	8								
	9								
	10								
	11	ENROLLMENT							
	12	OF NOS. 1 2 3 and 4 HEREON APPROVED BY THE SECRETARY							
	13	OF INTERIOR Dec. 12, 1902							
	14								
	15								
	16								
	17								

TRIBAL ENROLLMENT OF PARENTS

	Name of Father	Year	County	Name of Mother	Year	County
1	James Tubbee	Ded	Jack's Fork	Lucy Tubbee	Ded	Jack's Fork
2	Alfred Wade	"	Jackson	Susan Wade	"	Cedar
3	No 1			Eliza Williams	"	Jacks Fork
4	No 1			No 2		
5						
6						
7						
8						
9			No 2 on 1896 Roll as Silvy Tubbee			
10			No 1 died June – 1901· Enrollment cancelled by Department July 8, 1904			
11						
12						
13						
14						
15						
16				Date of Application for Enrollment	5/15/99	
17						

222

Choctaw By Blood Enrollment Cards 1898-1914

RESIDENCE:	Jacks Fork	COUNTY.		CARD No.	
POST OFFICE:	Kosoma I.T.	**Choctaw Nation**	**Choctaw Roll** (Not Including Freedmen)	FIELD NO.	**1723**

Dawes' Roll No.	NAME	Relationship to Person First Named	AGE	SEX	BLOOD	TRIBAL ENROLLMENT		
						Year	County	No.
4870	₁ Hudson, Culberson J. ³²	Named	29	M	Full	1896	Jacks Fork	6138
4871	₂ " Mary ³³	Wife	30	F	"	1896	" "	9882
4872	₃ Frazier, Sweny ¹⁶	S.Son	13	M	"	1896	" "	4545
4873	₄ " Cillen ¹³	S.Dau	10	F	"	1896	" "	4546
4874	₅ " Sibble ¹¹	"	8	"	"	1896	" "	4547
	₆							
	₇							
	₈							
	₉	ENROLLMENT OF NOS. 1 2 3 4 and 5 HEREON APPROVED BY THE SECRETARY OF INTERIOR Dec. 2, 1902						
	₁₀							
	₁₁							
	12							
	13							
	14							
	15							
	16							
	17							

TRIBAL ENROLLMENT OF PARENTS

	Name of Father	Year	County	Name of Mother	Year	County
₁	James Hudson	Ded	Jacks Fork	Siny Hudson	Ded	Jacks Fork
₂	Stephen Noah	"	" "	Isabell Noah	"	" "
₃	Dixon Frazier	1896	" "	No 2		
₄	" "	1896	" "	No 2		
₅	" "	1896	" "	No 2		
₆						
₇						
₈						
₉		No 1 on 1896 Roll as C J. Hudson				
10		No 2 " 1896 " " Mary Noah				
11						
12						
13						
14						Date of Application for Enrollment.
15						
16						5/15/99
17	P.O. Antlers I.T. 12/4/02					

223

Choctaw By Blood Enrollment Cards 1898-1914

RESIDENCE: Jack's Fork   COUNTY. **Choctaw Nation**   **Choctaw Roll** CARD NO.
POST OFFICE: Antlers I.T.   *(Not Including Freedmen)*   FIELD NO. 1724

Dawes' Roll No.	NAME	Relationship to Person First Named	AGE	SEX	BLOOD	TRIBAL ENROLLMENT		
						Year	County	No.
4875	1 Nelson, Rhoda DIED PRIOR TO SEPTEMBER 25 1902		68	F	Full	1896	Jacks Fork	9877
4876	2 Joel Solomon ³³	G.Son	30	M	"	1896	" "	7351
	3							
	4							
	5							
	6							
	7							
	8							
	9							
	10							
	11	ENROLLMENT						
	12	OF NOS. 1 and 2 HEREON APPROVED BY THE SECRETARY						
	13	OF INTERIOR DEC 12 1902						
	14							
	15							
	16							
	17							

TRIBAL ENROLLMENT OF PARENTS

	Name of Father	Year	County	Name of Mother	Year	County
1	Can Underwood	Ded	Jacks Fork	Maria Underwood	Ded	
2	John Jewell	"	" "	Suky Jewell	1896	Nashoba
3						
4						
5						
6						
7		No1 died January, 1901; proof of death filed Dec 5, 1902				
8		No.1 died Jan. – 1901: Enrollment cancelled by Department July 8 1904				
9						
10		No.2 is now husband of Mary Parsons, Choc #1611				
11						
12						
13						
14						
15				Date of Application for Enrollment.	5/15/99	
16						
17						

Choctaw By Blood Enrollment Cards 1898-1914

RESIDENCE: Jacks Fork   COUNTY. **Choctaw Nation**   **Choctaw Roll** *(Not Including Freedmen)*   CARD NO.
POST OFFICE: Antlers I.T.   FIELD NO.   1725

Dawes' Roll No.	NAME		Relationship to Person First Named	AGE	SEX	BLOOD	TRIBAL ENROLLMENT		
							Year	County	No.
4877	1 Willis, Ben	29	First Named	26	M	Full	1896	Jacks Fork	14125
4878	2 " Sallie	41	Wife	38	F	"	1896	" "	14126
4879	3 " John	7	Son	4	M	"	1896	" "	14127
	4								
	5								
	6								
	7								
	8								
	9								
	10								
	11	ENROLLMENT OF NOS. 1 2 and 3 HEREON							
	12	APPROVED BY THE SECRETARY							
	13	OF INTERIOR DEC 12 1902							
	14								
	15								
	16								
	17								

TRIBAL ENROLLMENT OF PARENTS

	Name of Father	Year	County	Name of Mother	Year	County
1	David Willis	Ded	Jacks Fork	Lydia Willis	Ded	Atoka
2	Charlie Fisher	"	Blue	"Annona"	"	Blue
3	No 1			No 2		
4						
5						
6						
7						
8						
9						
10						
11						
12						
13						
14					Date of Application for Enrollment.	
15						
16			Date of application for enrollment		5/15/99	
17						

Choctaw By Blood Enrollment Cards 1898-1914

RESIDENCE: Jackson COUNTY. **Choctaw Nation** Choctaw Roll CARD NO.
POST OFFICE: Mayhew I.T. (Not Including Freedmen) FIELD NO. 1726

Dawes' Roll No.	NAME		Relationship to Person First Named	AGE	SEX	BLOOD	TRIBAL ENROLLMENT		
							Year	County	No.
4880	1 James Sophia	19	First Named	16	F	1/4	1896	Jackson	7150
4881	2 " Noah	16	Bro.	13	M	1/4	1896	"	7151
	3								
	4								
	5								
	6								
	7	ENROLLMENT							
	8	OF NOS. 1 and 2 HEREON APPROVED BY THE SECRETARY							
	9	OF INTERIOR DEC 12 1902							
	10								
	11								
	12								
	13								
	14								
	15								
	16								
	17								

TRIBAL ENROLLMENT OF PARENTS

	Name of Father	Year	County	Name of Mother	Year	County
1	David James		Non Citz	Mary James	Ded	Jackson
2	" "		" "	" "	"	"
3						
4						
5						
6						
7						
8						
9						
10			No 1 on 1896 roll as Sophira James			
11			For child of No.1 see NB (March 3, 1905) #1478			
12						
13						
14					Date of Application for Enrollment.	
15						
16					5/15/99	
17						

Choctaw By Blood Enrollment Cards 1898-1914

RESIDENCE: Jacks Fork   COUNTY. **Choctaw Nation**   **Choctaw Roll** CARD No.
POST OFFICE: Antlers, I.T.   *(Not Including Freedmen)*   FIELD No. **1727**

Dawes' Roll No.	NAME		Relationship to Person First Named	AGE	SEX	BLOOD	TRIBAL ENROLLMENT		
							Year	County	No.
4882	1 Camp, Vinson	27	First Named	24	M	Full	1896	Jacks Fork	3064
4883	2 " , Selina	37	Wife	34	F	"	1896	" "	3065
*4884	3 Jefferson, Henry	9	Son	6	M	"	1896	" "	7369
4885	4 Fulsom, Johnson	17	Ward	14	"	"	1896	" "	4558
	5								
	6								
	7								
	8								
	9								
	10								
	11								
	12								
	13								
	14								
	15								
	16								
	17								

ENROLLMENT
OF NOS. 1 2 3 and 4 HEREON
APPROVED BY THE SECRETARY
OF INTERIOR Dec. 12, 1902

TRIBAL ENROLLMENT OF PARENTS

	Name of Father	Year	County	Name of Mother	Year	County
1	Amos Camp	1896	Jacks Fork	Sina Camp	Ded	Jacks Fork
2	Joseph Lowlin	Ded	Jackson	Hama Lowlin	"	Jackson
3	No 1			No 2		
4	Milton Folsom[sic]	Ded	Jack's Fork	Ickany Folsom	Ded	Jacks Fork
5						
6						
7						
8						
9	* Father of No3 is Charles Jefferson deceased. See testimony of No1 taken Aug. 5, 1903.					
10						
11						
12						
13						
14					Date of Application for Enrollment.	
15						
16					5/15/99	
17						

Choctaw By Blood Enrollment Cards 1898-1914

RESIDENCE: Jacks Fork   COUNTY. **Choctaw Nation**   **Choctaw Roll**   CARD No.
POST OFFICE: Antlers, I.T.   (Not Including Freedmen)   FIELD No. **1728**

Dawes' Roll No.	NAME	Relationship to Person	AGE	SEX	BLOOD	TRIBAL ENROLLMENT		
						Year	County	P.R.
4886	1 Gibson, Morris 21	First Named	18	M	Full	1893	Jacks Fork	114
	2							
	3							
	4							
	5							
	6							
	7							
	8							
	9							
	10							
	11	ENROLLMENT						
	12	OF NOS. 1 HEREON APPROVED BY THE SECRETARY						
	13	OF INTERIOR Dec. 12, 1902						
	14							
	15							
	16							
	17							

TRIBAL ENROLLMENT OF PARENTS

	Name of Father	Year	County	Name of Mother	Year	County
1	John Gibson	1896	Atoka	Ok-la-hona	Ded	Jacks Fork
2						
3						
4						
5						
6						
7			On 1893 Pay Roll as Melis Gibson			
8			For child of No.1 see NB (March 3, 1905) #1485.			
9						
10						
11						
12						
13						
14						
15				Date of Application for Enrollment.		
16					5/15/99	
17	P.O. Lehigh I.T.					

228

Choctaw By Blood Enrollment Cards 1898-1914

RESIDENCE: Jackson
POST OFFICE: Mayhew I.T.

COUNTY. **Choctaw Nation**

Choctaw Roll
(Not Including Freedmen)

CARD NO.
FIELD NO. 1729

Dawes' Roll No.	NAME		Relationship to Person First Named	AGE	SEX	BLOOD	TRIBAL ENROLLMENT Year	County	No.
4887	1 Drew Daniel	26	First Named	23	M	Full	1896	Jackson	3472
4888	2 " Susan	47	Wife	44	F	"	1896	"	8157
4889	3 Loring Solomon	15	S Son	12	M	"	1896	"	8158
4890	4 " Thomas	10	S "	7	"	"	1896	"	8159
4891	5 Jones Cornelius	5	S "	1	"	"			
	6								
	7								
	8								
	9								
	10								
	11	ENROLLMENT							
	12	OF NOS. 1 2 3 4 and 5 HEREON APPROVED BY THE SECRETARY							
	13	OF INTERIOR DEC 12 1902							
	14								
	15								
	16								
	17								

TRIBAL ENROLLMENT OF PARENTS

	Name of Father	Year	County	Name of Mother	Year	County
1	Lewis Drew	Ded	Jackson	Wicey Drew	Ded	Jackson
2	[This line blank on microfilm]					
3	Jess Loring	Dead	Cedar	No 2		
4	" "	"	"	No 2		
5	Davis Jones	1896	Jackson	No 2		
6						
7						
8						
9				No 2 on 1896 roll as Susan Loring		
10				For child of No 3 see NB (Apr 26/06) Card #25		
11						
12						
13						
14						
15				Date of Application for Enrollment.		
16				5/15/99		
17						

Choctaw By Blood Enrollment Cards 1898-1914

RESIDENCE: Cedar	COUNTY.		Choctaw Nation		Choctaw Roll (Not Including Freedmen)	CARD No.	
POST OFFICE: Kosoma I.T.						FIELD No. 1730	

Dawes' Roll No.	NAME		Relationship to Person	AGE	SEX	BLOOD	TRIBAL ENROLLMENT		
							Year	County	No.
4892	1 Wesley, Silvie	58	First Named	55	F	Full	1896	Cedar	13135
	2								
	3								
	4								
	5	ENROLLMENT							
	6	OF NOS. 1 HEREON							
	7	APPROVED BY THE SECRETARY OF INTERIOR DEC 12 1902							
	8								
	9								
	10								
	11								
	12								
	13								
	14								
	15								
	16								
	17								

TRIBAL ENROLLMENT OF PARENTS

	Name of Father	Year	County	Name of Mother	Year	County
1	Yim-mi-ha-bi	Ded	Jackson	Kauchihona	Ded	Bok Tuklo
2						
3						
4						
5						
6						
7						
8						
9						
10						
11						
12		No.1 is now the wife of Edward Horner Choc. #1996				
13						
14						
15					Date of Application for Enrollment:	5/15/99
16						
17	P.O. Dexter, I.T.					

230

Choctaw By Blood Enrollment Cards 1898-1914

RESIDENCE:	Jacks Fork	COUNTY.					CARD NO.	
POST OFFICE:	Antlers I.T.		Choctaw Nation			Choctaw Roll (Not Including Freedmen)	FIELD NO.	1731

Dawes' Roll No.	NAME		Relationship to Person Named	AGE	SEX	BLOOD	TRIBAL ENROLLMENT		
							Year	County	No.
4893	1 Moore, Thomas G	10	First Named	7	M	1/16	1893	Atoka	787
4894	2 " John R	14	Bro	11	M	1/16	1893	"	788
I.W. 1526	3 Young, Elizabeth A		Mother	31	F	I.W.			
	4								
	5								
	6								
	7	ENROLLMENT							
	8	OF NOS. 1 and 2 HEREON APPROVED BY THE SECRETARY							
	9	OF INTERIOR DEC 12 1902							
	10								
	11								
	12	ENROLLMENT							
	13	OF NOS. ~~ 3 ~~ HEREON APPROVED BY THE SECRETARY							
	14	OF INTERIOR MAR 14 1906							
	15								
	16								
	17								

TRIBAL ENROLLMENT OF PARENTS

	Name of Father	Year	County	Name of Mother	Year	County
1	Jacob Moore	Ded	Atoka	Lizzie Moore	1896	Atoka
2	" "	"	"	" "	1896	"
3	Oliver Van	"	non citizen	Amanda Van		non citizen
4						
5						
6						
7						
8	No.3 placed on this card September 28th, 1905, in accordance with order of the Commissioner					
9	to the Five Civilized Tribes of that date holding application was made within time prescribed					
10	by act of Congress approved July 1, 1902 (32 Stat 641)					
11						
12	Nos 1 and 2 live with H.H. Young, a non-citizen – 12/5 '02					
13						
14	No 3 GRANTED					#1&2
15	NOV 6 1905					Date of Application for Enrollment.
16						5/15/99
17						

231

Choctaw By Blood Enrollment Cards 1898-1914

RESIDENCE: Kiamitia   COUNTY. **Choctaw Nation**   **Choctaw Roll**   CARD NO.
POST OFFICE: Antlers I.T.   *(Not Including Freedmen)*   FIELD NO. **1732**

Dawes' Roll No.	NAME		Relationship to Person First Named	AGE	SEX	BLOOD	TRIBAL ENROLLMENT		
							Year	County	No.
4895	₁ Hickman Sarah	43	First Named	40	F	Full	1893	Cedar	207
4896	₂ McAlister William	21	Son	18	M	"	1893	"	208
4897	₃ Hickman Taylor	20	"	17	"	"	1893	"	209
4898	₄ " Nancy	19	Dau	16	F	"	1893	"	210
4899	₅ " Mary	15	"	12	"	"	1893	"	211
15571	₆ " William	3	Son	4	M	"			
	7								
	8								
	9								
	10								
	11	ENROLLMENT							
	12	OF NOS. 1,2,3,4 and 5 HEREON APPROVED BY THE SECRETARY							
	13	OF INTERIOR DEC 12 1902							
	14	ENROLLMENT							
	15	OF NOS. ~ 6 ~ HEREON APPROVED BY THE SECRETARY							
	16	OF INTERIOR SEP 22 1904							
	17								

TRIBAL ENROLLMENT OF PARENTS

	Name of Father	Year	County	Name of Mother	Year	County
₁	George Clover	Ded	Towson	Mary Clover	Ded	Cedar
₂	McAlister	"	"	No 1		
₃	John Hickman	"	Cedar	No 1		
₄	" "	"	"	No 1		
₅	" "	"	"	No 1		
₆	" "	"	"	Nº1		
₇	No3 Died prior to September 25, 1902; not entitled to land or money [illegible]					
₈						
₉	No 2 on 1896 roll Page 239 No 9471 as Wᵐ McColister					
₁₀	Jacks Fork Co.					
₁₁						
₁₂	Nº6 Born Feby 14, 1900. Application received Dec 2, 1902 and returned for identification of the					
₁₃	parents. Received with necessary information and Nº6 Enrolled Aug 3, 1904.					
₁₄	No6 Son of Jonas Watkins (See testimony Apr 20, 1905) 7/6/11 ONB			Date of Application for Enrollment. #1 to 5		
₁₅						
₁₆				5/15/99		
₁₇						

| RESIDENCE: Jacks Fork | COUNTY: | Choctaw Nation | Choctaw Roll | CARD NO. |
| POST OFFICE: Antlers I.T. | | | (Not Including Freedmen) | FIELD NO. 1733 |

Dawes' Roll No.	NAME			Relationship to Person Named	AGE	SEX	BLOOD	TRIBAL ENROLLMENT		
								Year	County	No.
I.W. 88	1	Ennis Robert A	48	First Named	45	M	I.W.	1896	Jacks Fork	14504
4900	2	" Maggie F	26	Wife	23	F	1/8	1896	" "	3820
4901	3	" Mary L.	5	Dau	2	"	1/16			
4902	4	" Henry D	4	Son	1	M	1/16			
DEAD.	5	~~" Tulli H.~~ DEAD.		~~"~~	~~2mo~~	~~"~~	~~1/16~~			
DEAD.	6	" Alice Marche		Dau	2mo	F	1/16			
	7									
	8	No. 5 and 6 HEREON DISMISSED UNDER								
	9	ORDER OF THE COMMISSION TO THE FIVE CIVILIZED TRIBES OF MARCH 31, 1905.								
	10									
	11									
	12	ENROLLMENT OF NOS 2 3 and 4 HEREON								
	13	APPROVED BY THE SECRETARY OF INTERIOR DEC 12 1902								
	14	ENROLLMENT								
	15	OF NOS. 1 HEREON APPROVED BY THE SECRETARY								
	16	OF INTERIOR JUN 13 1903								
	17									

TRIBAL ENROLLMENT OF PARENTS

	Name of Father	Year	County	Name of Mother	Year	County
1	John Ennis	Ded	Non Citz	Parthena Ennis	1896	Alabama
2	Lawson Spigel	1896	Jacks Fork	Lou Spigel	1896	Jacks Fork
3	No 1			No 2		
4	No 1			No 2		
5	~~No. 1~~			~~No. 2~~		
6	No. 1			No. 2		
7						
8	For child of Nos 1&2 see NB (Mar 3rd 1905) Card No 68.					
9						
10				No1 enrolled as R.A. Ennis and in		
11				like manner by Dawes Commission		
12				#845. No appeal		
13	No.6 Died Dec. 28, 1901, proof[sic] death filed April 9, 1902.					
14	No3 [sic]				#1 to 4	
15	No5 Died Oct. 24, 1900. Evidence of death			Date of Application for Enrollment.		
16	filed Feby. 23, 1901.			5/15/99		
17	2/23/02 PO McAlister	No.6 Enrolled May 21, 1901.		No5 enrolled Dec 14/99		

Choctaw By Blood Enrollment Cards 1898-1914

Dawes' Roll No.	NAME	Relationship to Person First Named	AGE	SEX	BLOOD	TRIBAL ENROLLMENT		
						Year	County	No.
4903	1 Underwood, Kennedy 47	First Named	44	M	Full	1896	Kiamitia	12576
4904	2 DIED PRIOR TO SEPTEMBER 25, 1902 Annie	Wife	43	F	1/2	1896	"	12577
4905	3 " Alexander 27	Son	24	M	3/4	1896	"	12578
4906	4 " Silas 23	"	20	"	3/4	1896	"	12579
4907	5 " Ella 18	Dau	15	F	3/4	1896	"	12580
4908	6 " Jesse 15	Son	12	M	3/4	1896	"	12581
4909	7 DIED PRIOR TO SEPTEMBER 25, 1902 Lonn	"	10	"	3/4	1896	"	12582
4910	8 " Elizabeth 11	Dau	8	F	3/4	1896	"	12583
4911	9 " Siveeny 8	Son	5	M	3/4	1896	"	12584
	10							
	11 ENROLLMENT							
	12 OF NOS. 12345678and9 HEREON APPROVED BY THE SECRETARY							
	13 OF INTERIOR Dec. 12, 1902							
	14 No2 died June 20, 1900: No7							
	15 died June 6, 1900: Enrollment							
	16 cancelled by Department July 8, 1904.							
	17							

TRIBAL ENROLLMENT OF PARENTS

	Name of Father	Year	County	Name of Mother	Year	County
1	Pe-le-chi	Ded	Jacks Fork	Tennessee	Ded	Jacks Fork
2	Jesse McKinney	"	" "	Elsie McKinney	"	Cedar
3	No 1			No 2		
4	No 1			No 2		
5	No 1			No 2		
6	No 1			No 2		
7	No 1			No 2		
8	No 1			No 2		
9	No 1			No 2		
10			No2 on 1896 roll as Emma Underwood			
11			No7 " " " " Lula A. "			
12			No2 died June 20, 1900; Proof of death filed Dec 5, 1902			
13			No7 " June 6, 1900; " " " " 5, 1902			
14			For child of No3 see NB (March 3, 1905) #1338.			
15						Date of Application for Enrollment.
16						5/15/99
17						

RESIDENCE: Jacks Fork	COUNTY. **Choctaw Nation**		**Choctaw Roll**	CARD No.
POST OFFICE: Antlers, I.T.			*(Not Including Freedmen)*	FIELD No. **1735**

Dawes' Roll No.	NAME	Relationship to Person	AGE	SEX	BLOOD	TRIBAL ENROLLMENT		
						Year	County	No.
4912	₁ Locke, Victor M. Jr. ²⁶	First Named	23	M	1/4	1896	Jacks Fork	8358
4913	₂ Archer, Mary A. ²³	Sis	20	F	1/4	1896	" "	8359
4914	₃ Locke, Ben D. ²⁰	Bro	17	M	1/4	1896	" "	8360
4915	₄ " , Jesse N. ¹⁷	"	14	"	1/4	1896	" "	8361
4916	₅ " , Edwin S. ¹⁵	"	12	"	1/4	1896	" "	8362
4917	₆ " , Curtis ¹	Son of 3	7mo	"	1/8	ENROLLMENT OF NOS. ___7___ HEREON APPROVED BY THE SECRETARY OF INTERIOR Jun. 13, 1903		
I.W. 180	₇ " , Mattie B.	Wife of No 3	20	F	I.W.			
	₈							

No 1 Evidence of divorce from Mattie B Locke on Choctaw Card #D560 filed July 16-1902
No 3 Now the Husband of Mattie B Locke on Choctaw card #D560. Evidence of marriage filed July 16ᵗʰ 1902
No 6 Born Dec. 12ᵗʰ 1901. Enrolled July 16ᵗʰ 1902.
No.2 is now the Wife of Charles E. Archer on
Choctaw Card #D.811.5906 Sept 29, 1902
No.2 is also called "Daellye"

```
          ENROLLMENT
OF NOS. 12345and6 HEREON
APPROVED BY THE SECRETARY
OF INTERIOR  Dec. 12, 1902
```

TRIBAL ENROLLMENT OF PARENTS

Name of Father	Year	County	Name of Mother	Year	County
₁ V. M. Locke Sr.	1896	Jacks Fork	Susan P. Locke	Ded	Jacks Fork
₂ " " " "	1896	" "	" " "	"	" " "
₃ " " " "	1896	" "	" " "	"	" " "
₄ " " " "	1896	" "	" " "	"	" " "
₅ No. 3			Mattie B. Locke on Choctaw Card #D560		
₆ W. M. Keith		Non-Citz	Bettie Keith		Non-Citz
₇					
₈					
₉					
₁₀		No.1 Enrolled on 1896 roll as V.M. Locke Jr.			
₁₁		No.2 " " " " " M.E. " .			
₁₂		No.3 " " " " " D.D. " .			
		No.4 " " " " " J.N. " .			
₁₃		No.5 " " " " " E.S. "			
₁₄					
₁₅		Wife of No.1 on White Card No. 560.			2/21/1900.
₁₆		No.7 transferred from Choctaw Card #D.560. See decision of April 20, 1903.		Date of Application Enrollment.	5/15/99 ↓1 to 5
₁₇					

Choctaw By Blood Enrollment Cards 1898-1914

RESIDENCE: Kiamitia   COUNTY.   **Choctaw Nation**   **Choctaw Roll**   CARD NO.

POST OFFICE: Nelson I.T.   *(Not Including Freedmen)*   FIELD NO. **1736**

Dawes' Roll No.	NAME	Relationship to Person First Named	AGE	SEX	BLOOD	TRIBAL ENROLLMENT Year	County	No.
4918	1 Homer, Mayles 51		48	F	Full	1896	Kiamitia	4250
	2							
	3							
	4	ENROLLMENT						
	5	OF NOS. 1 HEREON APPROVED BY THE SECRETARY						
	6	OF INTERIOR DEC 12 1902						
	7							
	8							
	9							
	10							
	11							
	12							
	13							
	14							
	15							
	16							
	17							

TRIBAL ENROLLMENT OF PARENTS

Name of Father	Year	County	Name of Mother	Year	County
1 Chubbee Homer	Ded	Jacks Fork	In-lan-tim-ana	De'd	Jacks Fork
2					
3					
4					
5					
6			On 1896 roll as Mayles Frazier		
7					
8					
9					
10					
11	No 1	For Brother See Card 1466			
12					
13					
14				Date of Application for Enrollment	
15					
16				5/15/99	
17					

Choctaw By Blood Enrollment Cards 1898-1914

RESIDENCE:	Jacks Fork	COUNTY.							
POST OFFICE:	Antlers I.T.		**Choctaw Nation**				**Choctaw Roll** (Not Including Freedmen)	CARD NO. FIELD NO.	1737

Dawes' Roll No.		NAME		Relationship to Person First Named	AGE	SEX	BLOOD	TRIBAL ENROLLMENT		
								Year	County	No.
4919	1	Gibson Ellis	43	Named	40	M	Full	1896	Jacks Fork	5000
1920	2	DIED PRIOR TO SEPTEMBER 25 1902 Lizzie		Wife	38	F	"	1896	" "	5001
VOID.	3	" Agnees[sic]		Dau	16	"	"	1896	Atoka	4974
4921	4	" Martha	17	Dau	14	"	"	1896	"	4975
4922	5	" Lena	12	"	9	"	"	1896	"	4976
	6									
	7									
	8	ENROLLMENT								
	9	OF NOS. 1 2 4 and 5 HEREON APPROVED BY THE SECRETARY								
	10	OF INTERIOR DEC 12 1902								
	11									
	12									
	13									
	14									
	15									
	16									
	17									

TRIBAL ENROLLMENT OF PARENTS

	Name of Father	Year	County	Name of Mother	Year	County
1	John Gibson	1896	Jacks Fork	Malissa Gibson	1896	Jacks Fork
2	Forbis Nak hi la bi	Ded	Atoka	Oklemahona	De'd	Cedar
3	No 1			Celina Wright	"	Atoka
4	No 1			" "	"	"
5	No 1			" "	"	"
6						
7						
8						
9						
10				No 3 on 1896 roll as Agnes Gipson		
11				No 4 " " " " Martha "		
12	No 3 transferred to Card #4807					
13	Sept 15th 1899					
14	No 2 died March 9, 1900; proof of death filed Dec 5, 1902					
15	No. 2 died March 9, 1900: Enrollment cancelled by Department July 8, 1904				Date of Application for Enrollment.	
16	No.1 is Husband of No.2 on Choctaw Card #1819.				5/15/99	
17	For child of No.4 see NB (March 3, 1905) #1274					

Choctaw By Blood Enrollment Cards 1898-1914

RESIDENCE:	Jacks Fork	COUNTY.	Choctaw Nation		Choctaw Roll	CARD NO.	
POST OFFICE:	Antlers, I.T.				(Not Including Freedmen)	FIELD NO.	1738

Dawes' Roll No.	NAME	Relationship to Person	AGE	SEX	BLOOD	TRIBAL ENROLLMENT		
						Year	County	No.
4923	1 Forrest, Sallie Ann 68	First Named	60	F	Full	1896	Jacks Fork	4542
	2							
	3							
	4							
	5	ENROLLMENT						
	6	OF NOS. 1 HEREON APPROVED BY THE SECRETARY						
	7	OF INTERIOR Dec. 12, 1902						
	8							
	9							
	10							
	11							
	12							
	13							
	14							
	15							
	16							
	17							

TRIBAL ENROLLMENT OF PARENTS

	Name of Father	Year	County	Name of Mother	Year	County
1			Dead in Mississippi	En-tune-la-e-ma	Dead	Atoka
2						
3						
4						
5						
6			On 1896 roll as Silly Ann Forrest			
7						
8						
9						
10						
11						
12						
13						
14						
15						
16				Date of Application for Enrollment	5/15/99	
17						

238

Choctaw By Blood Enrollment Cards 1898-1914

RESIDENCE: Cedar   COUNTY.   **Choctaw Nation**   **Choctaw Roll** (*Not Including Freedmen*)   CARD NO.

POST OFFICE: Kosoma, I.T.   FIELD NO. 1739

Dawes' Roll No.	NAME	Relationship to Person	AGE	SEX	BLOOD	Year	County	No.
4924	1 Homer, Sinwe DIED PRIOR TO SEPTEMBER 26 1902	First Named	63	F	Full	1896	Cedar	5426
	2							
	3							
	4							
	5							
	6	ENROLLMENT						
	7	OF NOS. 1 HEREON APPROVED BY THE SECRETARY						
	8	OF INTERIOR DEC 12 1902						
	9							
	10							
	11							
	12							
	13							
	14							
	15							
	16							
	17							

TRIBAL ENROLLMENT OF PARENTS

	Name of Father	Year	County	Name of Mother	Year	County
1	Yak-ma-tubbee	Dead	Bok Tuklo	Ish-te-ma-haya	Dead	Kiamitia
2						
3						
4						
5						
6						
7						
8	No1 died April 10, 1902; proof of death filed Dec 5, 1902					
9	No.1 died April 10, 1902; Enrollment cancelled by Department July 8, 1904					
10						
11						
12						
13						
14						
15						
16				Date of Application for Enrollment.	5/15/99	
17						

Choctaw By Blood Enrollment Cards 1898-1914

RESIDENCE: Cedar   COUNTY. **Choctaw Nation**   **Choctaw Roll** (Not Including Freedmen)   CARD NO.

POST OFFICE: Rodney, I.T.   FIELD NO. 1740

Dawes' Roll No.	NAME	Relationship to Person First Named	AGE	SEX	BLOOD	TRIBAL ENROLLMENT		
						Year	County	No.
4925	1 Camp, Betsy 71	First Named	68	F	Full	1893	Cedar	78
	2							
	3							
	4							
	5							
	6	ENROLLMENT OF NOS. 1 HEREON						
	7	APPROVED BY THE SECRETARY OF INTERIOR DEC 12 1902						
	8							
	9							
	10							
	11							
	12							
	13							
	14							
	15							
	16							
	17							

TRIBAL ENROLLMENT OF PARENTS

	Name of Father	Year	County	Name of Mother	Year	County
1	Ta-lo-pa	Dead	Red River	Sallie	Dead	Kiamitia
2						
3						
4						
5						
6						
7		On 1893 Pay roll Page 7, No 78, Cedar Co				
8						
9						
10						
11						
12						
13						
14						
15						
16				Date of Application for Enrollment.	5/15/99	
17						

RESIDENCE: Kiamitia	COUNTY.		CARD NO.	
POST OFFICE: Antlers, I.T.	Choctaw Nation	Choctaw Roll (Not Including Freedmen)	FIELD NO.	1741

Dawes' Roll No.	NAME	Relationship to Person First Named	AGE	SEX	BLOOD	TRIBAL ENROLLMENT		
						Year	County	No.
DEAD.	1 Lewis, Battiest	Named	48	M	Full	1896	Kiamitia	8096
4926	2 " Nancy ⁴⁸	Wife	45	F	"	1896	"	8097
4927	3 DIED PRIOR TO SEPTEMBER 25 1902 Mary	Dau	14	"	"	1896	"	8099
	4							
	5							
	6							
	7	ENROLLMENT OF NOS. 2 and 3 HEREON						
	8	APPROVED BY THE SECRETARY OF INTERIOR DEC 12 1902						
	9							
	10							
	11	No. 1 HEREON DISMISSED UNDER ORDER OF THE COMMISSION TO THE FIVE						
	12	CIVILIZED TRIBES OF MARCH 31, 1905.						
	13							
	14							
	15							
	16							
	17							

TRIBAL ENROLLMENT OF PARENTS

Name of Father	Year	County	Name of Mother	Year	County
1 Ola-lin-tubbee	Dead	Jacks Fork	Alh-pe-sa-hona	Dead	Towson
2 Edmund Cole	"	" "	Sabile Cole	"	Jacks Fork
3 Alfred Nelson	"	" "	No 2		
4					
5					
6					
7					
8					
9					
10					
11					
12	Nº1 Died May 26, 1899, proof of death filed Oct. 16, 1902				
13	No2 is now wife of William H. Anderson on Choctaw card #4219: evidence of marriage filed Dec. 6, 1902				
14	No. 3 died Aug. 15, 1900; proof of death filed Dec 8, 1902			Date of Application for Enrollment.	
15	No. 3 died Aug. 15, 1900: Enrollment cancelled by Department July 8, 1904				
16				5/15/99	
17					

Choctaw By Blood Enrollment Cards 1898-1914

RESIDENCE:	Cedar	COUNTY.	**Choctaw Nation**			**Choctaw Roll**		CARD NO.	
POST OFFICE:	Kosoma, I.T.					*(Not Including Freedmen)*		FIELD NO.	1742

Dawes' Roll No.		NAME		Relationship to Person First Named	AGE	SEX	BLOOD	TRIBAL ENROLLMENT		
								Year	County	No.
4928	1	Nelson, Palama	DIED PRIOR TO SEPTEMBER 25 1902	Named	65	F	Full	1896	Cedar	9651
4929	2	" Isham	38	Son	35	M	"	1893	"	365
	3									
	4									
	5	ENROLLMENT								
	6	OF NOS. 1 and 2 HEREON								
	7	APPROVED BY THE SECRETARY OF INTERIOR DEC 12 1902								
	8									
	9									
	10									
	11									
	12									
	13									
	14									
	15									
	16									
	17									

TRIBAL ENROLLMENT OF PARENTS

	Name of Father	Year	County	Name of Mother	Year	County
1	Ho-shin-she-homa	Dead	in Mississippi	Man-che-ho-ya	Dead	Mississippi
2	Jimson Nelson	"	Cedar	No 1		
3						
4						
5						
6						
7						
8						
9	No2 on 1893 Pay roll Page 34, No 365, Cedar Co. as Isom Nelson					
10	No2 also on 1896 Choctaw census roll, page 244, No. 9640 as					
11	Isham Noalabbe.					
12	No1 died January 2, 1901; proof of death filed Dec 5, 1902					
13	Nº1 Died Jany 2, 1901; Enrollment cancelled by Department (illegible)					
14						
15						
16				Date of Application for Enrollment.	5/15/99	
17						

Choctaw By Blood Enrollment Cards 1898-1914

RESIDENCE:	Cedar	COUNTY.	**Choctaw Nation**	Choctaw Roll	CARD NO.	
OFFICE:	Antlers, I.T.			(Not Including Freedmen)	FIELD NO.	1743

Res' No.	NAME	Relationship to Person First Named	AGE	SEX	BLOOD	TRIBAL ENROLLMENT Year	County	No.
30	1 Harkin, William ⁴⁷	First Named	44	M	Full	1896	Cedar	5452
31	2 " Betsy ⁴³	Wife	40	F	"	1896	"	5453
32	3 ~~Isham~~ DIED PRIOR TO SEPTEMBER 25 1902	~~Son~~	~~7~~	~~M~~	~~"~~	~~1896~~	~~"~~	~~5454~~
33	4 Frazier, Sam ²¹	S.Son	18	"	"	1896	"	4109
45	5 " Sammy	S.Son	15	M	Full	1895[sic]		218
	6							
	7							
	8	ENROLLMENT OF NOS. 1 2 3 and 4 HEREON						
	9	APPROVED BY THE SECRETARY						
	10	OF INTERIOR DEC 12 1902						
	11	ENROLLMENT OF NOS. 5 HEREON						
	12	APPROVED BY THE SECRETARY OF INTERIOR						
	13							
	14							
	15							
	16							
	17							

TRIBAL ENROLLMENT OF PARENTS

	Name of Father	Year	County	Name of Mother	Year	County
1	Ka-la-bee	Dead	Cedar	Siley Kalabee	Dead	Cedar
2	Gibson	"	Kiamitia	Nawee Gibson	"	"
3	~~No 1~~			~~No 2~~		
4	John Frazier	Dead	Cedar	No 2		
5	John Frazier	Dead	Cedar	No 2		
6						
7						
8	No 3 died Oct. 6, 1900; proof of death filed Dec 9, 1902					
9	No.3 died Oct. 6, 1900 Enrollment cancelled by Department July 8, 1904					
10	Application was made for the enrollment of No.5 at Antlers, I.T. May 15, 1899					
11	but his name was omitted from this card. Name of No.5 placed on this					
12	card April 27, 1905.					
13	No. 5 on 1893 Choctaw roll as Siemmy Frazier					
14						
15					#1 to 4	
16				Date of Application for Enrollment.	5/15/99	
17						

Choctaw By Blood Enrollment Cards 1898-1914

RESIDENCE: Cedar COUNTY.								
POST OFFICE: Kosoma, I.T.	Choctaw Nation			Choctaw Roll (Not Including Freedmen)		CARD NO. FIELD NO. 1744		

Dawes' Roll No.	NAME	Relationship to Person First Named	AGE	SEX	BLOOD	TRIBAL ENROLLMENT		
						Year	County	No.
4934	1 Sherred, Wesley 54	First Named	51	M	Full	1896	Cedar	11354
4935	2 " Martha 40	Wife	37	F	"	1896	"	11355
4936	3 " Ida 7	S.Dau	4	"	"	1896	"	11356
4937	4 Cole, James 17	Ward	14	M	"	1896	"	2422
	5							
	6							
	7	ENROLLMENT						
	8	OF NOS. 1 2 3 and 4 HEREON APPROVED BY THE SECRETARY						
	9	OF INTERIOR DEC 12 1902						
	10							
	11							
	12							
	13							
	14							
	15							
	16							
	17							

TRIBAL ENROLLMENT OF PARENTS

Name of Father	Year	County	Name of Mother	Year	County
1 Tick-ba-tubbee	Dead	Cedar	Ka-na-ha-ma	Dead	Jacks Fork
2 James Homer	"	Kiamitia	Silwee Homer	11896	Cedar
3 Harrison Cole	1896	Cedar	No 2		
4 Nicholas Cole	Dead	Cedar	Jennie Cole	Dead	Cedar
5					
6					
7					
8					
9					
10					
11					
12					
13					
14					
15					
16			Date of Application for Enrollment.	5/15/99	
17 P.O. Finley, Okla 9/1/08					

244

Choctaw By Blood Enrollment Cards 1898-1914

RESIDENCE: Jacks Fork
POST OFFICE: Antlers, I.T.

COUNTY. **Choctaw Nation**

Choctaw Roll
(Not Including Freedmen)

CARD NO.
FIELD NO. 1745

Dawes' Roll No.		NAME		Relationship to Person First Named	AGE	SEX	BLOOD	TRIBAL ENROLLMENT		
								Year	County	No.
4938	1	Gibson, John	68	First Named	65	M	Full	1896	Jacks Fork	5002
4939	2	" Melissa	53	Wife	50	F	"	1896	" "	5003
4940	3	" Ella	9	G.Dau	6	"	"	1896	" "	5004
	4									
	5									
	6									
	7	ENROLLMENT								
	8	OF NOS. 1 2 and 3 HEREON APPROVED BY THE SECRETARY								
	9	OF INTERIOR DEC 12 1902								
	10									
	11									
	12									
	13									
	14									
	15									
	16									
	17									

TRIBAL ENROLLMENT OF PARENTS

	Name of Father	Year	County	Name of Mother	Year	County
1	Peh-le-tubbee	Dead in Mississippi		Ho-yo-kee	Dead	Cedar
2	Kan-che-tubbee	"	" "	In-tun-la-hema	"	Atoka
3	Ellis Gibson	1896	Jacks Fork	Ellen	1896	"
4						
5						
6						
7						
8						
9		No2 on 1896 roll as Melissa Gibson				
10						
11						
12						
13						
14						
15						
16				Date of Application for Enrollment.	5/15/99	
17						

245

Choctaw By Blood Enrollment Cards 1898-1914

RESIDENCE: Jacks Fork   COUNTY **Choctaw Nation**   **Choctaw Roll**   CARD NO.
POST OFFICE: Antlers, I.T.   *(Not Including Freedmen)*   FIELD NO. 1746

Dawes' Roll No.	NAME	Relationship to Person	AGE	SEX	BLOOD	TRIBAL ENROLLMENT Year	County	No.
I.W. 89 ₁	Bedford, Bennett S. ³¹	First Named	28	M	I.W.			
4941 ₂	" Florence ²³	Wife	20	F	Full	1896	Skullyville	6434
4942 ₃	" Thelma Ellen ²	Dau	1mo	F	1/2			
4943 ₄	" Raymond B. ¹	Son	7wks	M	1/2			
₅								
₆								
₇	ENROLLMENT							
₈	OF NOS. 2 3 and 4 HEREON APPROVED BY THE SECRETARY							
₉	OF INTERIOR DEC 12 1902							
₁₀								
₁₁	ENROLLMENT							
₁₂	OF NOS. 1 ~~~~ HEREON APPROVED BY THE SECRETARY							
₁₃	OF INTERIOR JUN 13 1903							
₁₄								
₁₅								
₁₆								
₁₇								

TRIBAL ENROLLMENT OF PARENTS

	Name of Father	Year	County	Name of Mother	Year	County
₁	S. H. Bedford	1896	Non Citz	America C. Bedford	Dead	Non Citz
₂	Jacob Jackson	1896	Skullyville	Levicey Jackson	"	Skullyville
₃	No 1			No 2		
₄	No 1			No 2		
₅						
₆						
₇			No2 on 1896 roll as Florence Jackson			
₈			No 3 enrolled December 3, 1900			
₉			Nº4 Born July 25, 1902: enrolled Sept. 12, 1902			
₁₀						
₁₁						
₁₂						
₁₃						
₁₄				#1&2		
₁₅						
₁₆				Date of Application for Enrollment	5/15/99	
₁₇						

RESIDENCE:	Jacks Fork	COUNTY.							

RESIDENCE: Jacks Fork
POST OFFICE: Antlers, I.T.
COUNTY. **Choctaw Nation** (Not Including Freedmen)
Choctaw Roll
CARD NO.
FIELD NO. **1747**

Dawes' Roll No.	NAME	Relationship to Person First Named	AGE	SEX	BLOOD	TRIBAL ENROLLMENT		
						Year	County	No.
4944	1 Fletcher, William F ⁵⁶	Named	53	M	Full	1896	Jacks Fork	4518
4945	2 " , Eliza ⁴⁷	Wife	44	F	"	1896	" "	4519
4946	3 " , Emiline ²⁷	Dau	23	"	"	1896	" "	4520
4947	4 " , Tillis ¹²	Son	9	M	"	1896	" "	4523
4948	5 " , Emma ⁹	Dau	6	F	"	1896	" "	4524
4949	6 " , Amos ²⁰	Ward	17	M	"	1896	" "	4521
4950	7 " , Jim ¹⁹	"	16	"	"	1896	" "	4522
	8							
	9							
	10							
	11	ENROLLMENT						
	12	OF NOS. 1 2 3 4 5 6 and 7 HEREON APPROVED BY THE SECRETARY						
	13	OF INTERIOR Dec 12, 1902.						
	14							
	15							
	16							
	17							

TRIBAL ENROLLMENT OF PARENTS

	Name of Father	Year	County	Name of Mother	Year	County
1	Jim Fletcher	Dead	Jacks Fork	Jincy Fletcher	Dead	Cedar
2	Josiah Impson	"	" " "		"	Jacks Fork
3	No 1			No 2		
4	No 1			No 2		
5	No. 1			No. 2		
6	Noel Harris	Dead	Atoka	Susan Harris	Dead	Jacks Fork
7	" "	"	"	" "	"	" "
8						
9						
10			No.1 on 1896 roll as Wᵐ F. Fletcher			
11			No 5 " 1896 " " Emily "			
12			No.7 " 1896 " " Jennie "			
13						
14			No 3 is Wife of No.3 on Choc. #1597.			
15						
16				Date of Application for Enrollment.	5/15/99	
17						

Choctaw By Blood Enrollment Cards 1898-1914

RESIDENCE: Kiamitia   COUNTY. **Choctaw Nation**   **Choctaw Roll**   CARD No.
POST OFFICE: Antlers, I.T. Tushkahomma[sic]   *(Not Including Freedmen)*   FIELD No. **1748**

Dawes' Roll No.	NAME	Relationship to Person First Named	AGE	SEX	BLOOD	TRIBAL ENROLLMENT		
						Year	County	No.
4951	1 Williams, Louisiana 26		23	F	Full	1896	Kiamitia	13783
4952	2 Isabelle DIED PRIOR TO SEPTEMBER 25, 1902	Dau	1	"	"			
	3							
	4							
	5							
	6							
	7 ENROLLMENT OF NOS. 1 and 2 HEREON							
	8 APPROVED BY THE SECRETARY OF INTERIOR Dec. 2, 1902							
	9							
	10							
	11							
	12							
	13							
	14							
	15							
	16							
	17							

TRIBAL ENROLLMENT OF PARENTS

	Name of Father	Year	County	Name of Mother	Year	County
1	Jacob Fulsom	Dead	Jacks Fork	Isabelle Fulsom	Dead	Kiamitia
2	Forbis Williams	1896	Kiamitia	No 1		
3						
4						
5						
6						
7						
8		No.2 died Nov. 5, 1901: Proof of death filed Dec 15, 1902				
9		No.2 died Nov. 5, 1901: Enrollment cancelled by Department July 8, 1904				
10						
11						
12						
13						
14						
15						
16				Date of Application for Enrollment.	5/15/99	
17						

Choctaw By Blood Enrollment Cards 1898-1914

RESIDENCE: Jacks Fork   COUNTY. **Choctaw Nation**   **Choctaw Roll** CARD NO.
POST OFFICE: Antlers, I.T.   (Not Including Freedmen)   FIELD NO. **1749**

Dawes' Roll No.	NAME	Relationship to Person First Named	AGE	SEX	BLOOD	TRIBAL ENROLLMENT Year	County	No.
4953	₁ Miller, Daniel ⁴⁶	First Named	43	M	Full	1896	Jacks Fork	8879
4954	₂ " , Sallie ⁴⁷	Wife	44	F	"	1896	" "	8880
4955	₃ " , Davis ²³	Son	20	M	"	1896	" "	8881
4956	₄ " , Lizzie ¹³	Dau	10	F	"	1896	" "	8882
4957	₅ " , Caroline ¹⁰	"	7	"	"	1896	" "	8883
	6							
	7							
	8							
	9							
	10							
	11							
	12							
	13							
	14							
	15							
	16							
	17							

ENROLLMENT
OF NOS. 1 2 3 4 and 5 HEREON
APPROVED BY THE SECRETARY
OF INTERIOR Dec. 12, 1902.

TRIBAL ENROLLMENT OF PARENTS

Name of Father	Year	County	Name of Mother	Year	County
₁ E-bi-a-tubbee	Dead	Cedar	Fa-la-ma	1896	Cedar
₂ Ish-to-po-na	"	Kiamitia		Dead	Kiamitia
₃ No 1			No 2		
₄ No 1			No 2		
₅ No 1			No 2		
6					
7					
8	No. 3 is husband of Elsie Carnes Choc #368.				
9	No.4 ' Wife " No3 on Choc# 1717.				
10					
11					
12					
13					
14					
15					
16			Date of Application for Enrollment.	5/15/99	
17					

249

Choctaw By Blood Enrollment Cards 1898-1914

RESIDENCE: Jacks Fork
POST OFFICE: Antlers, I.T.

COUNTY. **Choctaw Nation**

Choctaw Roll
(Not Including Freedmen)

CARD No.
FIELD No. 1750

Dawes' Roll No.	NAME	Relationship to Person First Named	AGE	SEX	BLOOD	TRIBAL ENROLLMENT		
						Year	County	No.
4958	1 Locke, James S 31	First Named	28	M	1/4	1896	Jacks Fork	8364
	2							
	3							
	4							
	5							
	6							
	7							
	8							
	9							
	10							
	11							
	12							
	13							
	14							
	15							
	16							
	17							

ENROLLMENT OF NOS. 1 HEREON APPROVED BY THE SECRETARY OF INTERIOR DEC 12 1902

TRIBAL ENROLLMENT OF PARENTS

Name of Father	Year	County	Name of Mother	Year	County
1 V.M. Locke	1896	Non Citz	Susan Locke	Dead	Jacks Fork
2					
3					
4					
5		On 1896 roll as J. S. Locke.			
6					
7		Wife and children on Chickasaw Card No 1428			
8					
9					
10					
11					
12					
13					
14					
15					
16			Date of Application for Enrollment.	5/15/99	
17					

Choctaw By Blood Enrollment Cards 1898-1914

RESIDENCE: Jacks Fork	COUNTY.	Choctaw Nation	Choctaw Roll (Not Including Freedmen)	CARD NO.
POST OFFICE: Antlers, I.T.				FIELD NO. 1751

Dawes' Roll No.	NAME	Relationship to Person Named	AGE	SEX	BLOOD	TRIBAL ENROLLMENT Year	TRIBAL ENROLLMENT County	TRIBAL ENROLLMENT No.
4959	1 Durant, Gleason 31	First Named	28	M	Full	1896	Cedar	3353
4960	2 ", Kingsby DIED PRIOR TO SEPTEMBER 25, 27-02	Wife	24	F	"	PK 1893	Red River	276
14889	3 ", Lyazien 3	Dau	3	F	"			
	4							
	5							
	6							
	7	ENROLLMENT						
	8	OF NOS. 1 and 2 HEREON APPROVED BY THE SECRETARY						
	9	OF INTERIOR Dec 12, 1902						
	10							
	11							
	12	ENROLLMENT						
	13	OF NOS. 3 HEREON APPROVED BY THE SECRETARY						
	14	OF INTERIOR May 21, 1903						
	15							
	16							
	17							

TRIBAL ENROLLMENT OF PARENTS

	Name of Father	Year	County	Name of Mother	Year	County
1	Wallace Durant	Dead	Jacks Fork	Julia Durant	Dead	Atpla
2	Elija Homma	1896	Towson	Phena Homma	Dead	Red River
3	No 1			No 2		
4						
5	No. 1 enrolled as Clayson Durant					
6	No. 2 " " Kingsby Homma on Red River Co Pay Rolls Page 33, No. 276.					
7						
8	No.2 died Nov. 15, 1901: Proof of death filed Dec 2, 1902					
9	No.2 died Nov. 13[sic], 1901; Enrollment cancelled by Department July 8, 1904					
10	Nos.1&2 have a child Larsean[sic] Durant Affidavit of birth to be supplied No3 Born Oct. 22, 1899; application made March 15, 1900. 11/25/02.					
11	" 3 Proof of birth filed March 10, 1903.					
12						
13						
14						
15						
16				Date of Application for Enrollment.	5-15-99	
17						

251

Choctaw By Blood Enrollment Cards 1898-1914

RESIDENCE: Jacks Fork	COUNTY.							
POST OFFICE: Antlers I.T.								

Choctaw Nation

Choctaw Roll *(Not Including Freedmen)*

CARD NO.
FIELD NO. 1752

Dawes' Roll No.	NAME	Relationship to Person First Named	AGE	SEX	BLOOD	TRIBAL ENROLLMENT		
						Year	County	No.
4961	1 Noah, Abel 50	First Named	47	M	Full	1896	Jacks Fork	9866
5962	2 " Bessie 51	Wife	48	F	"	1896	" "	9867
4963	3 " Alexander 21	Son	18	M	"	1896	" "	9868
4964	4 " Louisa 14	Dau	11	F	"	1896	" "	9869
4965	5 " Joses[sic] 9	Son	6	M	"	1896	" "	9870
	6							
	7							
	8							
	9							
	10							
	11	ENROLLMENT OF NOS. 1 2 3 4 and 5 HEREON						
	12	APPROVED BY THE SECRETARY						
	13	OF INTERIOR DEC 12 1902						
	14							
	15							
	16							
	17							

TRIBAL ENROLLMENT OF PARENTS

	Name of Father	Year	County	Name of Mother	Year	County
1	Ayokatabi	Dead	Nashoba	Ishtahoke	Dead	Nashoba
2	Aynkpachitabi	"	Jacks Fork	Oklashtima	"	Gaines
3	No 1			No 2		
4	No 1			No 2		
5	No 1			No 2		
6						
7			No 4 enrolled as Levisey Noah			
8						
9						
10						
11						
12						
13						
14						
15				Date of Application for Enrollment.		
16				5-15-99		
17						

Choctaw By Blood Enrollment Cards 1898-1914

RESIDENCE: Jacks Fork
POST OFFICE: Antlers, I.T.

COUNTY. **Choctaw Nation**

Choctaw Roll
(Not Including Freedmen)

CARD NO.
FIELD NO. 1753

Dawes' Roll No.	NAME		Relationship to Person First Named	AGE	SEX	BLOOD	TRIBAL ENROLLMENT		
							Year	County	No.
4966	1 Gibson, Harrison	32	First Named	29	M	Full	1896	Jacks Fork	5005
4967	2 " Emma	26	Wife	23	F	"	1896	" "	5006
4968	3 " Tina	5	Dau	1 1/2	"	"			
4969	4 " Ida	3	"	3mo	"	"			
4970	5 " Edmun[sic]	1	Son	1mo	M	"			
	6								
	7								
	8								
	9								
	10								
	11	ENROLLMENT OF NOS. 1 2 3 4 and 5 HEREON							
	12	APPROVED BY THE SECRETARY							
	13	OF INTERIOR DEC 12 1902							
	14								
	15								
	16								
	17								

TRIBAL ENROLLMENT OF PARENTS

	Name of Father	Year	County	Name of Mother	Year	County
1	John Gibson	1896	Jacks Fork	Melissie Gibson	1896	Jacks Fork
2	Alfred Nelson	Dead	Kiamitia	Nancy Lewis	1896	Kiamitia
3	No1			No2		
4	No1			No2		
5	Nº1			Nº2		
6						
7						
8			Nº5 Born April 29, 1902, enrolled June 2, 1902.			
9			Annie Matthews on Choc. Card #3878 now lives with No.1			
10			For child of Nos 1&2 see N.B (Apr. 26, 1906) Card No. 111.			
11			" " " " " " " (March 3, 1905) " " 1246			
12						
13						
14						
15				#1 to 3		
16				DATE OF APPLICATION FOR ENROLLMENT.	5/15/99	
17				No 4 enrolled Nov. 1/99		

Choctaw By Blood Enrollment Cards 1898-1914

RESIDENCE: Kiamitia COUNTY. **Choctaw Nation** **Choctaw Roll** CARD NO.
POST OFFICE: Grant I.T. *(Not Including Freedmen)* FIELD NO. **1754**

Dawes' Roll No.	NAME	Relationship to Person	AGE	SEX	BLOOD	TRIBAL ENROLLMENT		
						Year	County	No.
4971	1 Woods, Elijah 59	First Named	56	M	Full	1896	Nashoba	13298
4972	2 " Samuel 19	Son	16	M	"	1896	"	13299
	3							
	4							
	5							
	6	ENROLLMENT						
	7	OF NOS. 1 and 2 HEREON						
	8	APPROVED BY THE SECRETARY OF INTERIOR Dec 12 1902						
	9							
	10							
	11							
	12							
	13							
	14							
	15							
	16							
	17							

TRIBAL ENROLLMENT OF PARENTS

	Name of Father	Year	County	Name of Mother	Year	County
1	Bradford Woods	Dead	Kiamitia	Halbihoka	Dead	Kiamitia
2	No. 1			Sinie Woods	"	Blue
3						
4						
5						
6	Nº2 carried off by white man, Frank Nelmar, to Okla.					
7						
8						
9						
10						
11						
12						
13						
14						
15				Date of Application for Enrollment.		
16	P.O. Hugo, 12/2/02				5-15-99	
17						

Choctaw By Blood Enrollment Cards 1898-1914

RESIDENCE: Kiamitia   COUNTY: **Choctaw Nation**   **Choctaw Roll** *(Not Including Freedmen)*   CARD NO.
POST OFFICE: Nelson I.T.   FIELD NO. 1755

Dawes' Roll No.		NAME	Relationship to Person Named	AGE	SEX	BLOOD	TRIBAL ENROLLMENT		
							Year	County	No.
4973	1	Devenport, Narcissa S ²⁸	First Named	25	F	3/4	1896	Kiamitia	3454
4974	2	DIED PRIOR TO SEPTEMBER 25, 1902 Dora B.	Dau	3	"	3/8	1896	"	3455
4975	3	" Henry E. ⁵	Son	2	M	3/8			
4976	4	" Lena O. ³	Dau.	5mo	F.	3/8			
I.W. 181	5	" George A.	husband	34	M	I.W.	1896	Kiamitia	14473
	6								
	7								
	8	ENROLLMENT							
	9	OF NOS. 1 2 3 and 4 HEREON APPROVED BY THE SECRETARY							
	10	OF INTERIOR DEC 12 1902							
	11								
	12	ENROLLMENT							
	13	OF NOS. ___ 5 ___ HEREON APPROVED BY THE SECRETARY							
	14	OF INTERIOR JUN 13 1903							
	15								
	16								
	17								

TRIBAL ENROLLMENT OF PARENTS

	Name of Father	Year	County	Name of Mother	Year	County
1	Jno. Wilson	1896		Emily Wilson	1896	Kiamitia
2	Geo. A Devenport	1896	Kiamitia	No 1		
3	"	1896	"	No 1		
4	"	"	"	No. 1		
5	G. W. Devenport		non-citz	Sarah K Devenport		non-citz
6						
7			No.1 enrolled Narcissa Devenport			
8			Husband of No 1 on Card D-161			
9			Affidavit to cover No.3 to be supplied. Recd May 16/99			
			No. 2 died Feb. 14, 1900. Enrollment cancelled by Department July 8, 1904			
10			Husband of No1 on Card No D.161			
11			No.4 Enrolled June 26, 1900			
			No2 died Feb. 30[sic], 1900; proof of death filed Dec 5, 1902			
12			N⁰5 transferred from Choctaw card ᵗD.161. See decision of May 5, 1903.			
13			For child of Nos 1 &5 see NB (Apr 26 '06) Card No. 160.			
14	" "	"	" " "	" (March 5, 1906) "	" 1306	
15						#1 to 3 Date of Application for Enrollment:
16						5-15-99
17						

255

Choctaw By Blood Enrollment Cards 1898-1914

RESIDENCE: Jacks Fork	COUNTY. **Choctaw Nation**	**Choctaw Roll** *(Not Including Freedmen)*	CARD NO.
POST OFFICE: Antlers, I.T.			FIELD NO. **1756**

Dawes' Roll No.	NAME	Relationship to Person First Named	AGE	SEX	BLOOD	TRIBAL ENROLLMENT		
						Year	County	No.
4977	1 Thompson, Cephus 24	First Named	21	M	Full	1896	Jacks Fork	12499
	2							
	3							
	4							
	5							
	6							
	7							
	8							
	9							
	10							
	11	ENROLLMENT OF NOS. 1 HEREON APPROVED BY THE SECRETARY OF INTERIOR Dec 12 1902						
	12							
	13							
	14							
	15							
	16							
	17							

TRIBAL ENROLLMENT OF PARENTS

	Name of Father	Year	County	Name of Mother	Year	County
1	Jacob Thompson	Dead	Red River	Melissa Thompson	1896	Jacks Fork
2						
3						
4						
5			No 1 is husband of Lucy Morris, Choctaw card #1786			
6						
7						
8						
9						
10						
11						
12						
13						
14						
15						
16				Date of Application for Enrollment	5/15/99	
17						

Choctaw By Blood Enrollment Cards 1898-1914

RESIDENCE: Jacks Fork COUNTY.
POST OFFICE: Stringtown, I.T.

Choctaw Nation

Choctaw Roll
(Not Including Freedmen)

CARD NO.
FIELD NO. 1757

Dawes' Roll No.	NAME		Relationship to Person Named	AGE	SEX	BLOOD	TRIBAL ENROLLMENT		
							Year	County	No.
4978	1 Impson, Daniel	32	First Named	29	M	Full	1896	Jacks Fork	6337
4979	2 " Sokey	29	Wife	26	F	"	1896	" "	6338
4980	3 " Sophia	4	Dau	1	"	"			
4981	4 " Minerva	9	S.Dau	6	"	"	1896	Jacks Fork	6339
	5								
	6								
	7	ENROLLMENT OF NOS. 1 2 3 and 4 HEREON							
	8	APPROVED BY THE SECRETARY OF INTERIOR DEC 12 1902							
	9								
	10								
	11								
	12								
	13								
	14								
	15								
	16								
	17								

TRIBAL ENROLLMENT OF PARENTS

	Name of Father	Year	County	Name of Mother	Year	County
1	Morris Impson	1896	Jacks Fork	Selina Impson	Dead	Jacks Fork
2	Gibson Lewis	Dead	" "	Latie Allen	1896	" "
3	No 1			No 2		
4	David Bon	1896	Jacks Fork	No 2		
5						
6						
7						
8						
9						
10						
11						
12						
13						
14				Date of Application for Enrollment		
15						
16				5/15/99		
17	P.O. Redden, Okla 10/2/09					

Choctaw By Blood Enrollment Cards 1898-1914

RESIDENCE:	Jacks Fork	COUNTY.						CARD No.	
POST OFFICE:	Antlers I.T.	**Choctaw Nation**				Choctaw Roll *(Not Including Freedmen)*		FIELD No. 1758	

Dawes' Roll No.	NAME		Relationship to Person	AGE	SEX	BLOOD	TRIBAL ENROLLMENT		
							Year	County	No.
4982	1 Lewis Johnson	24	First Named	21	M	Full	P R 1893	Jacks Fork	335
	2								
	3								
	4								
	5								
	6	ENROLLMENT OF NOS. 1 HEREON							
	7	APPROVED BY THE SECRETARY OF INTERIOR DEC 12 1902							
	8								
	9								
	10								
	11								
	12								
	13								
	14								
	15								
	16								
	17								

TRIBAL ENROLLMENT OF PARENTS

	Name of Father	Year	County	Name of Mother	Year	County
1	David Lewis	Dead	Atoka	Susan Lewis	1896	Jacks Fork
2						
3						
4						
5						
6	No 1 enrolled on Page 36 No 335 1893 Pay Rolls					
7	Jacks Fork County as John Louis					
8	No.1 is now the husband of Mary Palmer on Choctaw Card 1816. Aug 20, 1901					
9	For child of No 1 see NB (Mar 3 1905) #647					
10						
11						
12						
13						
14					Date of Application for Enrollment.	
15						
16					5-15-99	
17						

Choctaw By Blood Enrollment Cards 1898-1914

Choctaw By Blood Enrollment Cards 1898-1914

| RESIDENCE: Jacks Forks | COUNTY. | Choctaw Nation | Choctaw Roll | CARD NO. |
| POST OFFICE: Antlers I.T. | | | (Not Including Freedmen) | FIELD NO. 1759 |

Dawes' Roll No.	NAME	Relationship to Person Named	AGE	SEX	BLOOD	TRIBAL ENROLLMENT		
						Year	County	No.
4983	1 Anowatubbi Stephenson 33	First Named	30	M	Full	1896	Jacks Fork	458
4984	2 " Sissy 43	Wife	40	F	"	1896	" "	459
4985	3 DIED PRIOR TO SEPTEMBER 25 1902 Joe	Son	10	M	"	1896	" "	460
	4							
	5							
	6							
	7							
	8	ENROLLMENT						
	9	OF NOS. 1 2 and 3 HEREON APPROVED BY THE SECRETARY						
	10	OF INTERIOR DEC 12 1902						
	11							
	12							
	13							
	14							
	15							
	16							
	17							

TRIBAL ENROLLMENT OF PARENTS

	Name of Father	Year	County	Name of Mother	Year	County
1	Anderson Anowatubbi	De'd	Cedar	Mary Anowatubbi	De'd	Jacks Fork
2	William Ashohpai	"	Atoka		"	Atoka
3	No 1			No 2		
4						
5						
6			No 1 on 96 roll as Stephen Anowatubbi			
7						
8			No.3 died July 11, 1900; proof of death filed Dec 9, 1902			
9			No.3 died July 11, 1900. Enrollment cancelled by Department July 8, 1904			
10						
11						
12						
13						
14					Date of Application for Enrollment.	
15						
16					5-15-99	
17						

259

Choctaw By Blood Enrollment Cards 1898-1914

RESIDENCE: Jacks Fork   COUNTY. **Choctaw Nation**   **Choctaw Roll** CARD NO.
POST OFFICE: ~~Kiowa, I.T.~~   (Not Including Freedmen)   FIELD NO. 1760

Dawes' Roll No.	NAME	Relationship to Person First Named	AGE	SEX	BLOOD	TRIBAL ENROLLMENT		
						Year	County	No.
4986	1 Impson, William C 29	First Named	26	M	Full	1896	Jacks Fork	6324
I.W. **964**	2 " , Eveline 24	Wife	24	F	IW			
DEAD.	3 ~~" , May~~	~~Dau~~	~~4~~	~~F~~	~~1/2~~			
	4							
	5							
	6	~~ENROLLMENT~~						
	7	OF NOS. 1 HEREON						
	8	~~APPROVED BY THE SECRETARY OF INTERIOR~~ DEC 12 1902						
	9							
	10	ENROLLMENT						
	11	OF NOS. ~~~ 2 ~~~ HEREON APPROVED BY THE SECRETARY						
	12	OF INTERIOR SEP 22 1904						
	13							
	14	No.3 DISMISSED						
	15	JUL 19 1904						
	16	Present P.O. address Stringtown I.T. Jany 24, 1901						
	17							

TRIBAL ENROLLMENT OF PARENTS

Name of Father	Year	County	Name of Mother	Year	County
1 Morris Impson	1896	Jacks Fork	Salina Impson	Dead	Jacks Fork
2 Wm. Flinchem		noncitizen	Susan Flinchem		noncitizen
3	~~No 1~~		~~No 2~~		
4					
5					
6	On 1896 roll as Wm C. Impson				
7					
8	~~Wife of William C. Impson on Doubtful Card Choctaw D #462~~				
9	No 2 transferred from Choctaw card D 462 August 4, 1904				
10	See decision of July 19, 1904				
11	~~No.3 born May 24, 1898: died Feby. 26, 1901: dismissed July 19, 1904~~				
12	~~For child of No1 see NB (Apr 26 06) Card #414~~				
13	3/4/1916 Above notation is an error; See Choctaw				
14	Card No. 3592. WHA				
15					Date of Application for Enrollment.
16					5/15/99
17 P. O. Antlers					

260

RESIDENCE:	Jacks Fork	COUNTY:							
POST OFFICE:	Kosoma, I.T.		**Choctaw Nation**				**Choctaw Roll** (Not Including Freedmen)	CARD NO. FIELD NO.	1761

Dawes' Roll No.	NAME		Relationship to Person	AGE	SEX	BLOOD	TRIBAL ENROLLMENT		
							Year	County	No.
I.W. 90	1 Miller, John C	32	First Named	29	M	I.W			
4987	2 " Fannie	24	Wife	21	F	3/4	1896	Kiamitia	4248
4988	3 " Leo Victor	2	Son	2mo	M	3/8	New born		
	4								
	5								
	6	ENROLLMENT							
	7	OF NOS. 2 and 3 HEREON							
	8	APPROVED BY THE SECRETARY OF INTERIOR DEC 12 1902							
	9								
	10	ENROLLMENT							
	11	OF NOS. 1 HEREON APPROVED BY THE SECRETARY							
	12	OF INTERIOR JUN 13 1903							
	13								
	14								
	15								
	16								
	17								

	TRIBAL ENROLLMENT OF PARENTS					
	Name of Father	Year	County	Name of Mother	Year	County
1	John U. Miller	Dead	Non Citz	Martha Miller	1896	Non Citz
2	John Fowler	"	Kiamitia	Elizabeth Fowler	Dead	Kiamitia
3	No.1			No.2		
4						
5						
6						
7		No2 on 1896 roll as Fannie Fowler				
8						
9		No.3 Enrolled June 8, 1900				
10						
11		For child of Nos 1&2 see NB (Apr 26-06) Card #646				
12						
13						
14						
15						
16				Date of Application for Enrollment.	5/15/99	
17						

261

Choctaw By Blood Enrollment Cards 1898-1914

RESIDENCE: Jacks Fork   COUNTY: **Choctaw Nation**   **Choctaw Roll**   CARD NO.

POST OFFICE: Atoka, I.T.   *(Not Including Freedmen)*   FIELD NO. 1762

Dawes' Roll No.		NAME		Relationship to Person First Named	AGE	SEX	BLOOD	TRIBAL ENROLLMENT		
								Year	County	No.
I.W. 91	1	Rogers, Benjamin F	49	Named	46	M	I.W	1896	Jacks Fork	15000
4989	2	" Mary M	47	Wife	44	F	3/16	1896	" "	11016
4990	3	" Mary I.	24	Dau	21	"	3/32	1896	" "	11018
4991	4	" Isaac L	22	Son	19	M	3/32	1896	" "	11019
	5									
	6									
	7									
	8									
	9									
	10									
	11	ENROLLMENT								
	12	OF NOS. 2 3 and 4 HEREON APPROVED BY THE SECRETARY								
	13	OF INTERIOR DEC 12 1902								
	14	ENROLLMENT								
	15	OF NOS. 1 ~~~~~~ HEREON APPROVED BY THE SECRETARY								
	16	OF INTERIOR JUN 13 1903								
	17									

TRIBAL ENROLLMENT OF PARENTS

	Name of Father	Year	County	Name of Mother	Year	County
1	William Rogers	Dead	Non Citz	Matilda Rogers	Dead	Non Citz
2	S.P. Passons	"	" "	Sophia Passons	"	
3	No1			No2		
4	No1			No2		
5						
6	No1 on 1896 roll as B.F. Rogers. Was also admitted by Dawes Commission					
7	as an intermarried citizen December 3, 1896, Case No 649. Was married to					
8	wife before she was admitted by Choctaw Council in 1881.					
9	"That Mary M. Rogers, and her husband B.F. Rogers and their children					
	William F. Rogers, Mary I. Rogers and Isaac L. Rogers, and					
10	Sophia A. Flint, daughter of said Mary M. Rogers by a former					
11	husband" were admitted by Act of Council, Approver November 1, 1881.					
12						
13						
14						
15						
16				Date of Application for Enrollment.	5/16/99	
17						

Choctaw By Blood Enrollment Cards 1898-1914

RESIDENCE: Jacks Fork   COUNTY. **Choctaw Nation**   **Choctaw Roll** CARD NO.
POST OFFICE: Antlers, I.T.   *(Not Including Freedmen)*   FIELD NO. 1763

Dawes' Roll No.		NAME		Relationship to Person First Named	AGE	SEX	BLOOD	TRIBAL ENROLLMENT		
								Year	County	No.
I.W.709	1	Farr, John G.	⁴⁵	First Named	52	M	I.W	1896	Jacks Fork	14545
DEAD.	2	" Anna E	35	Wife	38	F	1/8	1896	" "	4531
14313	3	" Arthur T.	23	Son	20	M	1/16	1896	" "	4532
14314	4	" George C	18	"	15	"	1/16	1896	" "	4533
14315	5	" Inez E	15	Dau	12	F	1/16	1896	" "	4536
14316	6	" Estelle M	11	"	8	"	1/16	1896	" "	4635
14317	7	" John G. Jr	9	Son	6	M	1/16	1896	" "	4534
14318	8	" Arthur G.	1	Gr Son	6mo	M	1/32			
I.W.760	9	" Lena Eliza	²²	Wife of Nº3	22	F	I.W.			
	10	No 2 3 4 5 6 and 7 admitted by Dawes Com								
	11	in 1896 Case No 448, no appeal								
No 1	12	See Decision of March 2 '04.								
	13	Nº8 Born March 13, 1902, enrolled Sept. 24, 1902.								
	14	No2 died Feb 22, 1902; proof of death filed Dec 9, 1902.								

ENROLLMENT OF NOS. ~~ 9 ~~ HEREON APPROVED BY THE SECRETARY OF INTERIOR MAY -7 1904

15
ENROLLMENT OF NOS. 34567and8 HEREON APPROVED BY THE SECRETARY OF INTERIOR APR 11 1903

No 2 HEREON DISMISSED UNDER ORDER OF THE COMMISSION TO THE FIVE CIVILIZED TRIBES OF MARCH 31, 1905.

TRIBAL ENROLLMENT OF PARENTS

	Name of Father	Year	County	Name of Mother	Year	County
1	Thos. G. Farr	Dead	Non Citz	Jane C. Farr	Dead	Non Citz
2	William Harris	"	" "	Eliza Harris	"	Eagle
3	No 1			No 2		
4	No 1			No 2		
5	No 1			No 2		
6	No 1			No 2		
7	No 1			No 2		
8	Nº3			Lena Eliza Farr		intermarried
9	T.B. Poulter		noncitizen	Teck Poulter		non-citizen

ENROLLMENT OF NOS. ~~ 1 ~~ HEREON APPROVED BY THE SECRETARY OF INTERIOR MAY -7 1904

10 No1 on 1896 roll as Jno. G. Farr. Was also admitted as an Intermarried
11 Citizen by Dawes Commission, Case No 448. No appeal
12 No2 on 1896 roll as A. E. Farr
13 No3 " 1896 " " A. L. "   Nº9 transferred from Choctaw card #D798. See
14 No4 " 1896 " " J. C. "   decision of Feby 27, 1904
15 No5 " 1896 " " Inezie "
16 No6 " 1896 " " Estella "
17 No7 " 1896 " " Jno. G. "
16 Nº3 is now the husband of Lena Eliza Farr on Choctaw Card #D798   5/16/99
17 For child of Nos 3 and 9 see NB (March 3,1905) #1250 Sept. 22,1902

Choctaw By Blood Enrollment Cards 1898-1914

RESIDENCE: Towson	COUNTY.				
POST OFFICE: Doaksville, I.T.	**Choctaw Nation**		Choctaw Roll (Not Including Freedmen)	CARD NO. FIELD NO. 1764	

Dawes' Roll No.	NAME		Relationship to Person First Named	AGE	SEX	BLOOD	TRIBAL ENROLLMENT		
							Year	County	No.
I.W. 92	1 Swink, David R	53	First Named	50	M	I.W.	1896	Towson	15046
4992	2 " Lena B	30	Wife	27	F	1/16	1896	"	11384
4993	3 " Florence	9	Dau	6	"	1/32	1896	"	11385
4994	4 " Henry D	7	Son	4	M	1/32	1896	"	11386
4995	5 " Bert R.	5	"	1	"	1/32			
4996	6 " J. W.	3	Son	6mo	M	1/32			
	7								
	8								
	9	ENROLLMENT OF NOS. 1 ~~~~ HEREON APPROVED BY THE SECRETARY OF INTERIOR							
	10								
	11								
	12								
	13	ENROLLMENT OF NOS. 2,3,4,5,6 HEREON APPROVED BY THE SECRETARY OF INTERIOR JAN 16 1903							
	14								
	15								
	16								
	17								

TRIBAL ENROLLMENT OF PARENTS

	Name of Father	Year	County	Name of Mother	Year	County
1	Wilburn Swink	1896	Non Citz	Mary E. Swink	Dead	Non Citz
2	H. C. Harris	1896	Red River	Maggie Harris	1896	" "
3	No 1			No 2		
4	No 1			No 2		
5	No 1			No 2		
6	No.1			No.2		
7						
8	No4 on 1896 roll as David Swink					
9						
10	See Card of H.C. Harris for evidence of marriage					
11	of parents of No2					
12						
13	No5 Affidavit of birth to be supplied. Recd May 24/99				#1 to 5 inc	
14					Date of Application for Enrollment.	
15	No.6 Enrolled May 24, 1900					
16	For child of Nos 1&2 see NB (March 3, 1905) #1399				5/16/99	
17	P O Swink, I.T. 11/28/02					

Choctaw By Blood Enrollment Cards 1898-1914

RESIDENCE: Kiamitia		COUNTY.				Choctaw Roll		CARD NO.	
POST OFFICE: Nelson, I.T		**Choctaw Nation**				(Not Including Freedmen)		FIELD NO. 1765	

Dawes' Roll No.	NAME	Relationship to Person Named	AGE	SEX	BLOOD	TRIBAL ENROLLMENT		
						Year	County	No.
4997	1 Ashford, Thomas 35	First Named	32	M	1/4	1896	Kiamitia	353
I.W. 93	2 " Mary 28	Wife	25	F	I.W.	1896	"	14259
4998	3 " Elizabeth 8	Dau	5	"	1/8	1896	"	354
4999	4 ~~" Caroline~~ DIED PRIOR TO SEPTEMBER 25 1902	"	3	"	1/8	1896	"	355
5000	5 " Dora M 4	"	4mo	"	1/8			
5001	6 " Sim 2	Son	7wks	M	1/8			
	7							
	8							
	9	ENROLLMENT						
	10	OF NOS. 1, 3 4, 5, 6 HEREON APPROVED BY THE SECRETARY						
	11	OF INTERIOR JAN 16 1903						
	12	ENROLLMENT						
	13	OF NOS. 2 HEREON APPROVED BY THE SECRETARY						
	14	OF INTERIOR JUN 13 1903						
	15							
	16							
	17							

TRIBAL ENROLLMENT OF PARENTS

	Name of Father	Year	County	Name of Mother	Year	County
1	King Ashford	Dead	Non Citz	Elizabeth Perkins	1896	Kiamitia
2	John Owens	"	" " "	Matilda Owens	1896	Non Citz
3	No1			No2		
4	~~No1~~			~~No2~~		
5	No1			No2		
6	No1			No2		
7						
8						
9						
10	For evidence of marriage see testimony of No1 – No2 and					
11	Isaac Simpson					
12	~~No3 on 1896 roll as Lizzie Ashford~~					
13	No.4 died Aug 2 1900: Enrollment cancelled by Department July 8, 1904					
14	No5 Affidavit of birth to be supplied. Recd May 24/99				#1 to 5 inc	
15	No.6 Enrolled March 16, 1901. ~~No.4 died Aug 2 1900; proof of death filed Dec 6, 1902~~				Date of Application for Enrollment.	
16	For child of Nos 1&2 see NB (Mar 3rd 1905) Card No 64				5/16/99	
17						

Choctaw By Blood Enrollment Cards 1898-1914

RESIDENCE: Cedar
POST OFFICE: Kosoma, I.T.

COUNTY. **Choctaw Nation**

Choctaw Roll (Not Including Freedmen)

CARD NO.

FIELD NO. **1766**

Dawes' Roll No.	NAME	Relationship to Person First Named	AGE	SEX	BLOOD	TRIBAL ENROLLMENT		
						Year	County	No.
DEAD	1 Davenport, Betsie	Named	35	F	1/2	1896	Cedar	3361
5002	2 " George 16	Son	12	M	1/4	1896	"	3362
5003	3 " Eliza 13	Dau	9	F	1/4	1896	"	3363
5004	4 " Pearlie 11	"	7	"	1/4	1896	"	3364
5005	5 " Vena 7	"	3	"	1/4	1896	"	3365
5006	6 DIED PRIOR TO SEPTEMBER 25, 1902 Ivy	"	2	"	1/4			
5007	7 DIED PRIOR TO SEPTEMBER 25, 1902 Mattie	"	3mo	"	1/4			
5008	8 Everidge, Susan F. 9	"	6	"	3/4	1896	Kiamitia	3773
5009	9 Davenport, Mack Arthur	Son	1/2	M				
	10							
	11 No 6 died July - 1900: proof of							
	12 death filed Dec 6, 1902.							
	13 No 7 died Dec 15, 1899: proof of death filed Dec 6, 1902.							
	14 No.8 has always lived with and been cared for by Edward M Everedge Choctaw Card #1769 He is her legal guardian.							
	15 ENROLLMENT							
	16 OF NOS. 2,3,4,5,6,7,8,9 HEREON APPROVED BY THE SECRETARY							
	17 OF INTERIOR Jan 16 1903							

	TRIBAL ENROLLMENT OF PARENTS					
	Name of Father	Year	County	Name of Mother	Year	County
1	Ya kam bey	Dead	Chick Roll	Liza Norman	1896	Cedar
2	Geo. Davenport	"	" "	No 1		
3	" "	"	" "	No 1		
4	" "	"	" "	No 1		
5	" "	"	" "	No 1		
6	" "	"	" "	No 1		
7	" "	"	" "	No 1		
8	Ed Everidge	1896	Kiamitia	No 1	Check Card 1334	
9	Unknown			No 1		
10						
11						
12	No4 on 1896 roll as Pollie Devenport.			No.1 hereon dismissed under order of the		
13	No5 " 1896 " " Emily "			Commission to the Five Civilized Tribes		
14	Surname on 1896 roll as " Husband of No.1 is George Davenport on Chickasaw card #1334.			of March 31, 1905		
15	All but Nos 7-8 were enrolled Nov. 22/98, Card No 454.				Date of Application for Enrollment.	
16	No.9 born Aug. 22, 1901: Enrolled Mch. 3, 1902.				5/16/99	
17	N°1 Died March 21, 1902, proof of death filed Oct. 16, 1902					

No.6 died July – 1900: No.7 died Dec. 15,1899: Enrollment cancelled by Department July 8, 1904.

RESIDENCE: Cedar   COUNTY. **Choctaw Nation**   **Choctaw Roll**   CARD NO.
POST OFFICE: Kosoma, I.T.   *(Not Including Freedmen)*   FIELD NO. **1767**

Dawes' Roll No.	NAME	Relationship to Person	AGE	SEX	BLOOD	TRIBAL ENROLLMENT Year	County	No.
5010	1 Nelson, Ellen 61	First Named	58	F	Full	1896	Cedar	9633
5011	2 Davenport, Rebecca 23	Dau	19	"	1/2	1896	"	3366
5012	3 " Joe 10	Ward	6	M	1/2	1896	"	3367
	4							
	5							
	6							
	7							
	8							
	9							
	10							
	11							
	12							
	13							
	14							
	15							
	16							
	17							

ENROLLMENT
OF NOS. 1, 2, 3 HEREON
APPROVED BY THE SECRETARY
OF INTERIOR Jan 16, 1903

TRIBAL ENROLLMENT OF PARENTS

	Name of Father	Year	County	Name of Mother	Year	County
1	John Nelson	Dead	Cedar	Eliza McKinney	Dead	Gaines
2	Geo Davenport	"	Chick Roll	No 1		
3	" "	"	" "	Eliza Cole	Dead	Cedar
4						
5						
6			No2 on 1896 roll as Beckie Devenport			
7			No3 " 1896 " " Joe "			
8						
9						
10			Nos 2 – 3 were enrolled Nov 22/98 Card No. 454			
11						
12						
13						
14						
15				Date of Application for Enrollment.	5/16/99	
16						
17						

Choctaw By Blood Enrollment Cards 1898-1914

RESIDENCE: Kiamitia   COUNTY. **Choctaw Nation**   **Choctaw Roll** *(Not Including Freedmen)*   CARD NO.
POST OFFICE: Antlers, I.T.   FIELD NO. **1768**

Dawes' Roll No.	NAME	Relationship to Person First Named	AGE	SEX	BLOOD	TRIBAL ENROLLMENT Year	County	No.
	1 Perkins, John C		53	M	I.W.			
5013	2 " Elizabeth 57	Wife	54	F	1/2	1896	Kiamitia	4246
5014	3 Roebuck, Carrie 21	S.Dau	18	"	3/4	1896	"	4247
5015	4 Jones, Harrison 9	Ward	6	M	Full	1896	Red River	7-34
5016	5 Roebuck, Inez DIED PRIOR TO SEPTEMBER 25, 1902	Dau of No 3	2mo	F	5/8			
	6							
	7							
	8							
	9							
	10							
	11							
	12 ENROLLMENT							
	13 OF NOS. 2, 3, 4, 5 HEREON APPROVED BY THE SECRETARY							
	14 OF INTERIOR Jan 16 1903							
	15							
	16 No.5 died Jan. 4, 1902: Enrollment							
	17 cancelled by Department July 8, 1904.							

TRIBAL ENROLLMENT OF PARENTS

Name of Father	Year	County	Name of Mother	Year	County
1 Simeon Perkins	Dead	Non-Citz	Nancy Perkins	Dead	Non-Citz
2 LeRoy Griggs	"	" "	Lizzie Griggs	"	Kiamitia
3 John Fowler	"	Kiamitia	No 2		
4 Harmon Jones	"	Red River	Nancy Jones	Dead	Red River
5 David E Roebuck	1896	Kiamitia	No 3		
6					
7					
8 Oct. 16,1906 Dept affirms decision of this office Apr. 19, 1906, denying					
9 enrollment of No1					
10 No2 on 1896 roll as Elizabeth Fowler					
11 No3 is now the wife of David E Roebuck on Choctaw Card #1681 Evidence of					
12 marriage requested. See affidavit of No3 filed July 20, 1901.					
13 No.5 Enrolled July 20 1901. See letter and evidence of marriage filed Aug. 10, 1901 For child of No.3 see NB (March 3, 1905) #1173					
14 No5 died January 4, 1902: proof of death filed Dec 5, 1902					
15 Notify Riley & Cotner Tishomingo I.T. of decision				Date of Application for Enrollment.	
16 No1 Further evidence requested 3/20/04		No 1 Refused		5/16/99	
17			Apr 19 1906		

(over) [no other information given]   April 19, 1906 Record as to No.1 forwarded Dept.

Choctaw By Blood Enrollment Cards 1898-1914

RESIDENCE:	Kiamitia	COUNTY.							
POST OFFICE:	Grant, I.T.	**Choctaw Nation**			Choctaw Roll *(Not Including Freedmen)*		CARD NO. FIELD NO.	**1769**	

Dawes' Roll No.	NAME		Relationship to Person Named	AGE	SEX	BLOOD	TRIBAL ENROLLMENT		
							Year	County	No.
5017	1 Everidge, Edward M	50	First Named	47	M	3/8	1896	Kiamitia	3771
5018	2 " Ezra Dora	2	Dau	1mo	F	3/16			
5019	3 " Joel	1	Son	3wks	M	3/16			
I.W. 642	4 " Lula	21	Wife	21	F	I.W.			
5									
6	ENROLLMENT								
7	OF NOS. 4 HEREON								
8	APPROVED BY THE SECRETARY OF INTERIOR Mar 26 1904								
9									
10									
11									
12									
13									
14	ENROLLMENT								
15	OF NOS. 1, 2, 3 HEREON APPROVED BY THE SECRETARY								
16	OF INTERIOR Jan 16 1903								
17									

TRIBAL ENROLLMENT OF PARENTS

	Name of Father	Year	County	Name of Mother	Year	County
1	J. W. Everidge	1896	Kiamitia	Sophia Everidge	Dead	Kiamitia
2	No.1			Lula Everidge		non-citizen
3	No 1			" "		" "
4	Sandy Williams		non citizen	Sarah Williams		" "
5						
6	No4 transferred from Choctaw card D619 January 21, 1904.					
7	See decision of January 4 1904.					
8						
9						
10	On 1896 roll as E. M. Everidge					
11	Evidence of marriage of No.1 and Lula Everidge filed Feby. 15,1901 in Jacket D619					
12	No.2 Enrolled Feby. 15th, 1901					
13	No.1 is now the husband of Lula Everidge on Choctaw card #D-619.					
14	N°3 Born May 3, 1902; enrolled May 28, 1902 Feb. 23, 1901					
15	No1 is legal guardian of Susan F. Everidge on Choctaw Card #1766 #1					
16	For child of Nos 1&4 see N.B. (Apr. 26, 1906) Card No. 85. Date of Application for Enrollment:					
17	" " " " " " (March 3, 1905) " " 1189 5/16/99					

Choctaw By Blood Enrollment Cards 1898-1914

Dawes' Roll No.	NAME		Relationship to Person	AGE	SEX	BLOOD	TRIBAL ENROLLMENT		
							Year	County	No.
DEAD	₁ Herman, Susan	DEAD.	First Named	33	F	Full	1896	Kiamitia	3783
5020	₂ Loman, Eliza	13	Dau	10	"	3/4	1896	"	8104
	₃								
	₄								
	₅								
	₆ No. 1 HEREON DISMISSED UNDER								
	₇ ORDER OF THE COMMISSION TO THE FIVE CIVILIZED TRIBES OF MARCH 31, 1905.								
	₈								
	₉								
	₁₀								
	₁₁								
	₁₂								
	₁₃								
	₁₄								
	₁₅ ENROLLMENT OF NOS. 2 HEREON								
	₁₆ APPROVED BY THE SECRETARY OF INTERIOR JAN 16 1903								
	₁₇								

TRIBAL ENROLLMENT OF PARENTS

	Name of Father	Year	County	Name of Mother	Year	County
₁	Robert Wahee	Dead	Kiamitia	Mollie Wahee	Dead	Kiamitia
₂	Albert Loman	"	"	No 1		
₃						
₄						
₅						
₆	No1 on 1896 roll as Susan Harmon.					
₇	No2 " 1896 " " Elza Loman					
₈						
₉						
₁₀	Husband of No1 on Card D 163					
₁₁	No.1 died April 21, 1900. Evidence of death filed March 19, 1901.					
₁₂						
₁₃						
₁₄						
₁₅				Date of Application for Enrollment.		
₁₆				5/16/99		
₁₇						

270

Choctaw By Blood Enrollment Cards 1898-1914

RESIDENCE: Kiamitia	COUNTY.								
POST OFFICE: Nelson, I.T.	Choctaw Nation					Choctaw Roll (Not Including Freedmen)	CARD NO. FIELD NO. 1771		

Dawes' Roll No.	NAME	Relationship to Person First Named	AGE	SEX	BLOOD	TRIBAL ENROLLMENT		
						Year	County	No.
5021	1 Willis, Susan 28	First Named	25	F	Full	1896	Kiamitia	13766
5022	2 " Lymon 6	Son	3	M	"	1896	"	13767
5023	3 DIED PRIOR TO SEPTEMBER 25 1902 George	"	1 1/2	"	"			
	4							
	5							
	6							
	7							
	8							
	9							
	10							
	11							
	12							
	13							
	14	ENROLLMENT OF NOS. 1, 2, 3						
	15	APPROVED BY THE SECRETARY HEREON						
	16	OF INTERIOR Jan 16 1903						
	17							

TRIBAL ENROLLMENT OF PARENTS

	Name of Father	Year	County	Name of Mother	Year	County
1	Davis Lobbee	1896	Kiamitia	Hannah Lobbee	Dead	Jackson
2	William Willis	1896	Jacks Fork	No 1		
3	" "	1896	" "	No 1		
4						
5						
6						
7	No.3 died Feb. – 1901: Enrollment cancelled by Department July 8, 1904					
8						
9	No 1 is the mother of Solomon Sanders on Choctaw card #3867:					
10	see affidavit as to birth of Solomon Sanders filed with that card.					
11					Dec. 9, 1904	
12	For child of No.1 see NB (March 3, 1905) #1079.					
13						
14						
15				Date of Application for Enrollment.		
16				5/16/99		
17						

Choctaw By Blood Enrollment Cards 1898-1914

RESIDENCE: Jacks Fork   COUNTY. **Choctaw Nation**   **Choctaw Roll**   CARD NO.
POST OFFICE: Kosoma I.T.   *(Not Including Freedmen)*   FIELD NO.   1772

Dawes' Roll No.		NAME		Relationship to Person	AGE	SEX	BLOOD	TRIBAL ENROLLMENT		
								Year	County	No.
~~5024~~	1	~~Simply~~ ~~Nancy~~ DIED PRIOR TO SEPTEMBER 25 1902		~~First Named~~	~~50~~	~~F~~	~~Full~~	~~1896~~	~~Jack's Fork~~	~~11704~~
~~5025~~	2	~~Susan~~ DIED PRIOR TO SEPTEMBER 25 1902		~~Dau~~	~~18~~	~~"~~	~~"~~	~~1896~~	~~" "~~	~~11705~~
5026	3	" Lafit	17	Son	14	M	"	1896	" "	11706
5027	4	" Narcissa	15	Dau	12	F	"	1896	" "	11707
	5									
	6									
	7									
	8									
	9									
	10									
	11									
	12									
	13									
	14									
	15	ENROLLMENT OF NOS. 1,2,3,4 HEREON								
	16	APPROVED BY THE SECRETARY								
	17	OF INTERIOR JAN 16 1903								

TRIBAL ENROLLMENT OF PARENTS

	Name of Father	Year	County	Name of Mother	Year	County
1		~~Dead~~	~~Cedar~~		~~Dead~~	~~Cedar~~
2	~~Lamon Simply~~	"	~~Jack's Fork~~	~~No 1~~		
3	" "	"	" " "	No 1		
4	" "	"	" " "	No 1		
5						
6						
7	No 3 Enrolled on 1896 roll as Louie Simply					
8						
9	~~No 1 died May 8, 1901; proof of death filed Dec 5, 1902~~					
10	No 2 " April – 1901; " " " " " "					
11	No.1 died May 8, 1901; No.2 died April–1901; Enrollment cancelled by Department July 8, 1904					
12						
13						
14						
15						
16				Date of Application for Enrollment.	5-16-99	
17						

Choctaw By Blood Enrollment Cards 1898-1914

RESIDENCE: Kiamitia   COUNTY. **Choctaw Nation**   **Choctaw Roll** CARD No.
POST OFFICE: Nelson I.T.   *(Not Including Freedmen)*   FIELD No. 1773

Dawes' Roll No.	NAME	Relationship to Person	AGE	SEX	BLOOD	TRIBAL ENROLLMENT Year	County	No.
5028	1 Watkins, Charles ~~DIED PRIOR TO SEPTEMBER 25, 1902~~	First Named	20	M	Full	1896	Kiamitia	13763
5029	2 " Lena 44	Wife	41	F	"	1896	"	10457
	3							
	4							
	5							
	6							
	7							
	8							
	9							
	10							
	11							
	12							
	13							
	14							
	15	ENROLLMENT OF NOS. 1,2 APPROVED BY THE SECRETARY HEREON OF INTERIOR JAN 16 1903						
	16							
	17							

TRIBAL ENROLLMENT OF PARENTS

	Name of Father	Year	County	Name of Mother	Year	County
1	~~John Watkins~~	~~1896~~	~~Kiamitia~~	~~Malis Homa~~	~~1896~~	~~Kiamitia~~
2	Davis Oklabe	1896	"	Hannah Oklabe	Dead	"
3						
4						
5						
6						
7						
8						
9						
10	No 2 on 1896 roll as Lena Pisso					
11	No 1 " 1896 " " Charlie Watkins					
12	No 1 died Oct 1899; proof of death filed Dec 6, 1902					
	N°2 is now the wife of Sim Folsom, Choctaw card #1571					
13	~~No 1 died Oct — 1899. Enrollment cancelled by Department July 8, 1904~~					
14	For child of No.1 see NB (March 3, 1905) #1080					
15	~~PO Soper IT 4/17/05~~			Date of Application for Enrollment	5-16-99	
16						
17	P.O. Soper, I.T. 10/20/06					

273

Choctaw By Blood Enrollment Cards 1898-1914

RESIDENCE: Jack's Fork
POST OFFICE: Atoka I.T.
COUNTY. **Choctaw Nation**
Choctaw Roll (Not Including Freedmen)
CARD NO.
FIELD NO. 1774

Dawes' Roll No.	NAME	Relationship to Person Named	AGE	SEX	BLOOD	TRIBAL ENROLLMENT		
						Year	County	No.
5030	1 Rogers, William F. 28	First Named	25	M	3/32	1896	Jack's Fork	11017
I.W. 94	2 " Kittie D 22	Wife	19	F	I.W.			
5031	3 " William F, Jr. 4	Son	6mo	M	3/64			
5032	4 " Florence Mary 2	Dau	2mo	F	3/64			
	5							
	6							
	7							
	8							
	9							
	10							
	11	ENROLLMENT						
	12	OF NOS. 2 HEREON APPROVED BY THE SECRETARY						
	13	OF INTERIOR JUN 13 1903						
	14							
	15	ENROLLMENT						
	16	OF NOS. 1, 3, 4 HEREON APPROVED BY THE SECRETARY						
	17	OF INTERIOR JAN 16 1903						

TRIBAL ENROLLMENT OF PARENTS

	Name of Father	Year	County	Name of Mother	Year	County
1	B.F. Rogers	1896	Adopted	Mary M. Rogers	1896	Adopted
2	T.P. Gregg	1896	Non-Citizen	Florence Gregg	1896	Non-Citizen
3	No 1			No 2		
4	No 1			No 2		
5						
6						
7		No 3 Affidavit of birth to be supplied. Recd May 24/99				
8		No 1 on 1896 Roll as Willie F. Rogers				
9		For child of Nos. 1&2 see NB (Mar 3 1905) #538				
10						
11		See note on card 1762				
12		No.4 Enrolled March 5th, 1901				
13						
14						
15						
16			Date of Application for Enrollment.	5-16-99		
17						

RESIDENCE: Jack's Fork   COUNTY. **Choctaw Nation**   **Choctaw Roll**   CARD NO.
POST OFFICE: Kosoma I.T.   _(Not Including Freedmen)_   FIELD NO. **1775**

Dawes' Roll No.	NAME	Relationship to Person	AGE	SEX	BLOOD	TRIBAL ENROLLMENT		
						Year	County	No.
5033	DIED PRIOR TO SEPTEMBER 25 1902 ₁ Simply, James	First Named	28	M	Full	1896	Jack's Fork	11708
5034	₂ " Cillin ⁴⁵	Wife	42	F	"	1896	" "	11709
	3							
	4							
	5							
	6							
	7							
	8							
	9							
	10							
	11							
	12							
	13							
	14	ENROLLMENT						
	15	OF NOS. 1,2 HEREON APPROVED BY THE SECRETARY						
	16	OF INTERIOR Jan 16 1903						
	17							

	TRIBAL ENROLLMENT OF PARENTS					
Name of Father	Year	County	Name of Mother	Year	County	
₁ Lamon Simply	Dead	Jack's Fork	Nancy Simply	1896	Jack's Fork	
₂ Simon Makabe	"	Red River	Elsie Makabe	Dead	Red River	
3						
4						
5						
6						
7	No1 died April 1901; proof of death filed Dec 6 1902					
8	No.1 died April – 1901: Enrollment cancelled by Department July 8, 1904					
9						
10						
11						
12						
13				Date of Application for Enrollment.		
14						
15				5-16-99		
16						
17	P.O. Antlers, I.T. 12/2/02					

Choctaw By Blood Enrollment Cards 1898-1914

RESIDENCE: Kiamitia   COUNTY. **Choctaw Nation**   **Choctaw Roll**   CARD NO.
POST OFFICE: Antlers I.T.   (Not Including Freedmen)   FIELD NO. 1776

Dawes' Roll No.	NAME	Relationship to Person	AGE	SEX	BLOOD	TRIBAL ENROLLMENT		
						Year	County	No.
5035	1 Billy, Agnes 26	First Named	23	F	Full	1893	Cedar	35
	2							
	3							
	4							
	5							
	6							
	7							
	8							
	9							
	10							
	11							
	12							
	13							
	14							
	15	ENROLLMENT						
	16	OF NOS. 1 HEREON APPROVED BY THE SECRETARY						
	17	OF INTERIOR JAN 16 1903						

TRIBAL ENROLLMENT OF PARENTS

	Name of Father	Year	County	Name of Mother	Year	County
1	Ayo Kaltabe	Dead	Jack's Fork	Betey Billy	Dead	Jack's Fork
2						
3						
4						
5						
6		On 1893 Pay Roll, page 4 No. 35 Cedar County				
7						
8						
9						
10						
11						
12						
13						
14						
15						
16						
17	P.O. Hamden, Okla 1/20/08			Date of Application for Enrollment.	5/16/99	

RESIDENCE:	Jack's Fork	COUNTY.	Choctaw Nation		Choctaw Roll	CARD No.	
POST OFFICE:	Antlers I.T.				*(Not Including Freedmen)*	FIELD No.	1777

Dawes' Roll No.	NAME		Relationship to Person	AGE	SEX	BLOOD	TRIBAL ENROLLMENT		
							Year	County	No.
5036	1 Willis, William	27	First Named	24	M	Full	1896	Jack's Fork	14128
5037	2 " Emily	32	Wife	29	F	"	1893	Kiamitia	396
5038	3 Loman Annie	12	S.Dau.	9	F	"	1893	"	397
	4								
	5								
	6								
	7								
	8								
	9								
	10								
	11								
	12								
	13								
	14								
	15	ENROLLMENT							
	16	OF NOS. 1,2,3 HEREON APPROVED BY THE SECRETARY							
	17	OF INTERIOR JAN 16 1903							

TRIBAL ENROLLMENT OF PARENTS

	Name of Father	Year	County	Name of Mother	Year	County
1	Simon Willis	Dead	Cedar	Montona Willis	1896	Jack's Fork
2	Joslin Lewis	"	Kiamitia	Selina Lewis	Dead	Kiamitia
3	Joe Loman	"	"	No. 2		
4						
5						
6				No 2 On page 50, No 396, 1893 Pay Roll Kiamitia Co as Emily Loman		
7				No 3 On Page 50 No 397, 1893 Pay Roll Kiamitia Co.		
8						
9				No1 on 1896 roll as Wilburn Willis		
10						
11				Nos 1 & 2 have separated		
12						
13						
14				Date of Application for Enrollment.		
15				5-16-99		
16						
17						

Choctaw By Blood Enrollment Cards 1898-1914

RESIDENCE: Jack's Fork   COUNTY. **Choctaw Nation**   **Choctaw Roll** CARD No.
POST OFFICE: Antlers I.T.   *(Not Including Freedmen)* FIELD No. 1778

Dawes' Roll No.	NAME	Relationship to Person First Named	AGE	SEX	BLOOD	TRIBAL ENROLLMENT Year	County	No.
I.W.710	1 Speegle David L.H. 57		53	M	I.W.	1896	Jack's Fork	15071
5039	2 " Lucy P. M. 45	Wife	42	F	1/8	1896	" "	11724
5040	3 Byrne, Alice M. 20	Dau	17	F	1/16	1896	" "	11725
5041	4 Speegle, John F. 14	Son	11	M	1/16	1896	" "	11726
5042	5 " Lion E. 3	"	4mo	"	1/16			
5043	6 Byrne Dalton R.S. 1	Gr Son	1mo	M	1/32			
	7							
	8							
	9							
	10	ENROLLMENT OF NOS. ~~~ 1 ~~~ HEREON APPROVED BY THE SECRETARY OF INTERIOR MAY 7 1904						
	11							
	12							
	13							
	14							
	15	ENROLLMENT OF NOS. 2,3,4,5,6 HEREON APPROVED BY THE SECRETARY OF INTERIOR JAN 16 1903						
	16							
	17							

TRIBAL ENROLLMENT OF PARENTS

Name of Father	Year	County	Name of Mother	Year	County
1 J.D.W. Speegle	Dead	Non Citz.	Nancy Speegle	1896	Non Citz
2 Robert Harris	"	" "	Eliza Harris	Dead	Eagle
3	No 1		No 2		
4	No 1		No 2		
5	No 1		No 2		
6 Albert E. Byrne		non-citizen	Nº3		
7					
8					

9 No1 See Decision of March 2, '04.
10 No1 Admitted as intermarried citizen by Dawes Com. Dec 2nd 1896
Case No 843 enrolled on 1896 Roll as T.L. Speegles[sic]
11 No 2 on 1896 Roll as Lucy Speagle
12 No 3 On 1896 Roll as Alice Speagle
13 No 4 On 1896 Roll as Frank Speagle
No.3 is now the wife of A.E. Byrne a non citizen Feby. 24, 1902
14 Evidence of marriage requested. Received and filed April 29, 1902   #1 to 4
15 Nº3 is also called Alice M   Date of Application for Enrollment: 5-16-99
16 Nº6 Born July 29, 1902: enrolled Sept. 3, 1902.   No 5 enrolled Oct 6/99
17

Choctaw By Blood Enrollment Cards 1898-1914

RESIDENCE: Jack's Fork
POST OFFICE: Antlers I.T.

COUNTY.
Choctaw Nation

Choctaw Roll
(Not Including Freedmen)

CARD NO.
FIELD NO. 1779

Dawes' Roll No.	NAME	Relationship to Person First Named	AGE	SEX	BLOOD	TRIBAL ENROLLMENT Year	County	No.
15043	1 Nelson, Susan	43 Named	40	F	Full	1893	Jack's Fork	334
5044	2 Gibson, Laymon	6 Son	3	M	"			
	3							
	4							
	5							
	6							
	7							
	8							
	9							
	10							
	11							
	12							
	13							
	14							
	15							
	16							
	17							

ENROLLMENT
OF NOS. 2 HEREON
APPROVED BY THE SECRETARY
OF INTERIOR JAN 16 1903

ENROLLMENT
OF NOS. ~~ 1 ~~ HEREON
APPROVED BY THE SECRETARY
OF INTERIOR FEB 16 1904

TRIBAL ENROLLMENT OF PARENTS

	Name of Father	Year	County	Name of Mother	Year	County
1	John Gibson	1896	Jack's Fork	Melina Gibson	1896	Jack's Fork
2	Gabriel Nelson	1896	Kiamatia[sic]	No 1		
3						
4						
5						
6						
7		No 1 is now wife of Gabriel Nelson 7-1567				
8		No 1 On page 36, No 334. 1893 Pay Roll Jack's Fork Co.				
9						
10		No 1 Died June 12 1900. Evidence of death filed May 1, 1901				
11		Notation as to death of No.1 is erroneous.				
12						
13						
14					Date of Application for Enrollment.	
15						
16					5-26-1899	
17						

279

Choctaw By Blood Enrollment Cards 1898-1914

Dawes' Roll No.	NAME		Relationship to Person	AGE	SEX	BLOOD	TRIBAL ENROLLMENT		
							Year	County	No.
5045	1 Harris, Paul C.	30	First Named	27	M	1/8	1896	Jack's Fork	6115
5046	2 " Susie	23	Wife	20	F	3/8	1896	" "	6116
5047	3 " Emma	7	Dau	4	F	1/4	1896	" "	6117
5048	4 " Robert L	3	Son	1mo	M	1/4			
5049	5 " Elizabeth M	2	Dau	1mo	F	1/4			
	6								
	7								
	8								
	9								
	10								
	11								
	12								
	13								
	14								
	15	ENROLLMENT OF NOS. 1,2,3,4,5 HEREON							
	16	APPROVED BY THE SECRETARY							
	17	OF INTERIOR JAN 16 1903							

TRIBAL ENROLLMENT OF PARENTS

	Name of Father	Year	County	Name of Mother	Year	County
1	Frank Harris	Dead	Non Citz	Freda Harris	Dead	Red River
2	Joe Everidge	1896	Kiamitia	Susie Everidge	Dead	Kiamitia
3	No 1			No 2		
4	No 1			No 2		
5	No 1			No 2		
6						
7			No 5 Enrolled April 13, 1902			
8						
9			For child of Nos 1&2 see NB (Mar 3-1905) Card No 60.			
10						
11						
12						
13						
14					#1 to 3 inc	
15				Date of Application for Enrollment.	5-16-99	
16				No 4 enrolled Nov 1/99		
17						

280

Choctaw By Blood Enrollment Cards 1898-1914

RESIDENCE: Jack's Fork
POST OFFICE: Rodney I.T.

COUNTY. **Choctaw Nation**

Choctaw Roll CARD NO.
(Not Including Freedmen) FIELD NO. **1781**

Dawes' Roll No.	NAME		Relationship to Person Named	AGE	SEX	BLOOD	TRIBAL ENROLLMENT		
							Year	County	No.
5050	1 Everidge, Edgar	7	First Named	4	M	3/32	1896	Kiamitia	3783
5051	2 " Earl	5	Bro	2	M	3/32			
I.W. 1103	3 " Minnie	24	Mother	24	F	I.W.	1896	Kiamitia	14497
	4								
	5								
	6								
	7								
	8								
	9								
	10								
	11								
	12								
	13								
	14								
	15								
	16								
	17								

ENROLLMENT
OF NOS. 1, 2 HEREON
APPROVED BY THE SECRETARY
OF INTERIOR Jan 16 1903

ENROLLMENT
OF NOS. 3 HEREON
APPROVED BY THE SECRETARY
OF INTERIOR Nov. 16 1904

TRIBAL ENROLLMENT OF PARENTS

	Name of Father	Year	County	Name of Mother	Year	County
1	Will Everidge	1896	Kiamitia	Minnie Everidge	1896	Non Citz
2	" "	1896	"	" "	1896	" "
3	David Pierce	Dead	non-citizen	Rosa M. Pierce	1896	non citz.
4						
5						
6						
7			Mother of Nos. 1 and 2 on card D 164			
8						
9			No2 affidavit of birth to be supplied. Rec'd May 17/99			
10						
11			Father of Nos. 1 & 2 on Choctaw card #1443			
12	No 3 transferred from Choctaw card #D-164, Oct. 31, 1904: See decision of Oct. 15, 1904					
13						
14					Date of Application for Enrollment.	
15					5-16-99	
16						
17						

No.3 P.O. Antlers I.T. 12/1/02

281

Choctaw By Blood Enrollment Cards 1898-1914

RESIDENCE: Jack's Fork   COUNTY. **Choctaw Nation**   **Choctaw Roll**   CARD NO.
POST OFFICE: Antlers I.T.   *(Not Including Freedmen)*   FIELD NO. 1782

Dawes' Roll No.	NAME	Relationship to Person	AGE	SEX	BLOOD	TRIBAL ENROLLMENT		
						Year	County	No.
5052	1 Bond Redmond 32	First Named	29	M	Full	1896	Atoka	1754
	2							
	3							
	4							
	5							
	6							
	7							
	8							
	9							
	10							
	11							
	12							
	13							
	14							
	15							
	16							
	17							

ENROLLMENT
OF NOS. 1 HEREON
APPROVED BY THE SECRETARY
OF INTERIOR JAN 16 1903

TRIBAL ENROLLMENT OF PARENTS

	Name of Father	Year	County	Name of Mother	Year	County
1	Jessie Bond	Dead	Atoka	Sophie Bond	Dead	Atoka
2						
3						
4						
5	No 1 Enrolled Richmond Bond on 1896 Roll					
6	Nº1 is the husband of Sallie Lewis on Choctaw card #3829, Oct. 22, 1902.					
7	For children of No.1 see NB (Mar. 3, 1905) #528					
8						
9						
10						
11						
12						
13						
14						Date of Application for Enrollment.
15						
16						5/16/99
17		P. O. Dunc				

Choctaw By Blood Enrollment Cards 1898-1914

Choctaw Nation
Choctaw Roll
(Not Including Freedmen) FIELD NO. **1783**

Dawes' Roll No.	NAME	Relationship to Person Named	AGE	SEX	BLOOD	TRIBAL ENROLLMENT Year	County	No.
5053	1 Davenport Jimpson 32	First Named	29	M	Full	1896	Cedar	3357
5054	2 " Lina 33	Wife	30	F	"	1896	Kiamitia	3772
14693	3 Frazier, Sarah 19	Ward	16	F	"	1896	Kiamitia	7086
15784	4 " , Harriet 1	Dau of No 3	1	F	"			
	5							
	6							
	7							
	8							
	9							
	10							
	11							
	12							
	13							
	14							
	15							
	16							
	17							

ENROLLMENT
OF NOS. 4 HEREON
APPROVED BY THE SECRETARY
OF INTERIOR Mar. 15, 1905

ENROLLMENT
OF NOS. 1, 2 HEREON
APPROVED BY THE SECRETARY
OF INTERIOR Jan. 16, 1903

ENROLLMENT
OF NOS. 3 HEREON
APPROVED BY THE SECRETARY
OF INTERIOR May 20 1903

TRIBAL ENROLLMENT OF PARENTS

	Name of Father	Year	County	Name of Mother	Year	County
1	Barnard Davenport	Dead	Cedar	Selina Baldwin	1896	Jack's Fork
2	Gibson Eyakambe	"	Kiamatia[sic]	Eliza Norman	1896	Cedar
3	Johnson Bobb	1896	Towson	Louisa Le-flore	Ded	Kiamatia[sic]
4	Eli Bohannon			No 3		
5						
6						
7						
8						
9						
10						
11	No 1 Jimpson Devenport[sic] on 1896 Roll					
12	No 2 On 1896 Roll as Sina Everidge					
13	No 3 is now the wife of Jackson Frazier on Choctaw Card #1908. See					
14	copy of letter from No 1 filed Oct. 15 1902. Evidence of marriage					
	requested Oct. 15, 1902.					
15	No.4 application for enrollment made Sept. 13, 1902 #1 to 3					
16	Proof of birth filed Nov. 19, 1904			Date of Application for Enrollment.		
17				5/16/99		

No.3 P.O. Keota 11/26/07

Choctaw By Blood Enrollment Cards 1898-1914

RESIDENCE: Jacks – Fork   COUNTY. **Choctaw Nation**   **Choctaw Roll**   CARD NO.
POST OFFICE: Kosoma I.T.   *(Not Including Freedmen)*   FIELD NO.   1784

Dawes' Roll No.	NAME		Relationship to Person First Named	AGE	SEX	BLOOD	TRIBAL ENROLLMENT		
							Year	County	No.
5055	1 Cole, Allen	44	First Named	41	M	Full	1896	Jacks Fork	3004
5056	2 DIED PRIOR TO SEPTEMBER 25 1902 Jincey		Wife	35	F	"	1896	" "	3005
5057	3 " Peter	10	Son	7	M	"	1896	" "	3006
5058	4 " Eligh	3	Son	6mo	M	"			
	5								
	6								
	7								
	8								
	9								
	10								
	11								
	12								
	13								
	14								
	15	ENROLLMENT OF NOS 1,2,3,4 HEREON APPROVED BY THE SECRETARY OF INTERIOR JAN 16 1903							
	16								
	17								

TRIBAL ENROLLMENT OF PARENTS

	Name of Father	Year	County	Name of Mother	Year	County
1	Peter Cole	Ded	Cedar	Mulsy Cole	De'd	Jack Fork
2	Achilitubbi	"	Kiamatia[sic]	Lucy Achilitubbi	"	Kiamatia[sic]
3	No 1			No 2		
4	No. 1			No. 2		
5						
6						
7						
8			No.4 Enrolled Aug. 22d, 1900.			
9						
10			No 2 died July 30 1902; proof of death filed Dec 6, 1902			
11			No.2 died July 30, 1902; Enrollment cancelled by Department July 8, 1904			
12						
13						
14						
15						
16				Date of Application for Enrollment.		5-16-99
17						

284

RESIDENCE: Jacks Fork
POST OFFICE: Antlers IT
COUNTY. **Choctaw Nation**
Choctaw Roll *(Not Including Freedmen)*
CARD No.
FIELD No. 1785

Dawes' Roll No.	NAME		Relationship to Person	AGE	SEX	BLOOD	TRIBAL ENROLLMENT		
							Year	County	No.
5058	1 Colbert, Vina	39	First Named	36	F	Full	1896	Jacks Fork	2990
5060	2 Frazier Mike	15	Ward	12	M	"	1893	" "	P.B.267
5061	3 Billy Elsie	DIED PRIOR TO SEPTEMBER 25 1902	"	10	F	"	1893	" "	172
	4								
	5								
	6								
	7								
	8								
	9								
	10								
	11								
	12								
	13								
	14								
	15	ENROLLMENT OF NOS. 1, 2, 3 APPROVED BY THE SECRETARY OF INTERIOR JAN 16 1903 HEREON								
	16								
	17								

TRIBAL ENROLLMENT OF PARENTS

	Name of Father	Year	County	Name of Mother	Year	County
1	Simon Patterson	Ded	Jacks Fork	Haklotinima	Ded	Jacks Fork
2	Isom Frazier	"	Kiamatia[sic]	Sallie Frazier	"	Kiamatia[sic]
3	Peter Billy	"	Jacks Fork	Jinnie Billy	"	Jacks Fork
4						
5						
6		No 1 on 1896 Roll as Margaret Colbert				
7		'No 3 " 1893 Pay roll as Elzie Billy				
8						
9		No2 on 1896 roll Page 72 No 3050 as				
10		Mike Colbert Jacks Fork Co				
11	No 3 died Nov 10 1899 – proof of death filed Dec 6, 1902. No 1 wife of Lamon Colbert, Chickasaw card #1241					
12	No.3 died Nov. 10. 1899: Enrollment cancelled by Department July 8, 1904					
13						
14						
15					Date of Application for Enrollment.	
16					5-16-99	
17						

Choctaw By Blood Enrollment Cards 1898-1914

RESIDENCE: Jacks Fork COUNTY. **Choctaw Nation** **Choctaw Roll** *(Not Including Freedmen)* CARD No.
POST OFFICE: Stringtown, I.T. FIELD No. **1786**

Dawes' Roll No.	NAME	Relationship to Person First Named	AGE	SEX	BLOOD	Year	County	No.
5062	1 Morris, James ~~DIED PRIOR TO SEPTEMBER 25,32902~~		29	M	Full	1896	Jacks Fork	8874
5063	2 " Lucy 32	Wife	29	F	"	1896	" "	8875
5064	3 " Emma 10	Dau	7	"	"	1896	" "	8877
5065	4 " Joseph 4	S.son	6mo	M	"			
5066	5 " Abner 19	"	16	"	"	1896	Jacks Fork	8876
5067	6 " Winnie 15	S Dau	12	F	"	1896	Jacks Fork	10596
	7							
	8							
	9							
	10							
	11							
	12							
	13							
	14	ENROLLMENT OF NOS. 1,2,3,4,5,6 HEREON						
	15	APPROVED BY THE SECRETARY						
	16	OF INTERIOR Jan. 16, 1903						
	17							

TRIBAL ENROLLMENT OF PARENTS

	Name of Father	Year	County	Name of Mother	Year	County
1	Geo Morris	1896	Red River	Betsy Morris	Dead	Red River
2	Benj Wade	Dead	Tobucksy	Selote Wade	"	Jacks Fork
3	No 1			No 2		
4	Cornelius Bond	1896	Jacks Fork	No 2		
5	No 1			No 2		
6	No 1			No 2		
7						
8						
9						
10	No 2 on 1896 roll as Luthie Morris					
11	No 6 " 1896 " " Winnie Peter					
12	No 3 living with Culberson J. Hudson Choctaw card #1723					
13	No 2 is now wife of Cephus Thompson Choctaw card #1756					
14	No.1 died March –, 1900: Enrollment cancelled by Department July 8, 1904			#1 to 4 inc		
15				Date of Application for Enrollment.		
16				5/16/99		
17				Nos. 5-6 Enrolled Sept 1/99		

286

Choctaw By Blood Enrollment Cards 1898-1914

POST OFFICE: Antlers, I.T.　COUNTY. **Choctaw Nation**　**Choctaw Roll** *(Not Including Freedmen)*　CARD NO. FIELD NO. 1787

Dawes' Roll No.	NAME	Relationship to Person	AGE	SEX	BLOOD	TRIBAL ENROLLMENT		
						Year	County	No.
5068	DIED PRIOR TO SEPTEMBER 25,1902 ₁ Henderson, Selina	First Named	48	F	Full	1893	Atoka	415
5069	₂ Jones, Wilson ¹⁹	Ward	16	M	"	1893	Kiamitia	2
	₃							
	₄							
	₅							
	₆							
	₇							
	₈							
	₉							
	10							
	11							
	12							
	13							
	14							
	15	ENROLLMENT						
	16	OF NOS. 1, 2　HEREON APPROVED BY THE SECRETARY						
	17	OF INTERIOR　JAN 16 1903						

TRIBAL ENROLLMENT OF PARENTS

Name of Father	Year	County	Name of Mother	Year	County
₁ Un-tush-wa	Dead	Kiamitia	Lucy	Dead	Kiamitia
₂ Solomon Jones	"	"	Sophie Jones	"	"
₃					
₄					
₅	No.1 died before Sept 25 1902: Enrollment cancelled by Department May 2, 1906				
₆					
₇	No1 on 1893 Pay roll, Page 40, No 415, Atoka County				
₈	No2 " 1893 " " " 114 " 2 Kiamitia County (List in back of				
₉	book)				
10					
11	No1 on 1896 roll, Page 12 No 453 as Selina				
12	Anderson, Atoka Co.				
13					
14					
15					
16			Date of Application for Enrollment.	5/17/99	
17					

RESIDENCE:	Jacks Fork	COUNTY.	**Choctaw Nation**	**Choctaw Roll**	CARD No.	
POST OFFICE:	Atoka, I.T.			*(Not Including Freedmen)*	FIELD No.	**1788**

Dawes' Roll No.	NAME		Relationship to Person First Named	AGE	SEX	BLOOD	TRIBAL ENROLLMENT		
							Year	County	No.
5070	1	McGahey, John H. 26		23	M	1/8	1896	Jacks Fork	9467
5071	2	" Alexander J 23	Bro	19	"	1/8	1896	" "	9468
5072	3	" Luther L. 16	"	13	"	1/8	1896	" "	9469
5073	4	" Martha 14	Sister	11	F	1/8	1896	" "	9770
5074	5	" Florence 2	Dau	3mo	F	1/8			
5075	6	" Frances 1	Dau	2mo	F	1/8			
	7								
	8								
	9	Nos 5&6 are duplicate							
	10	of Nos 2&3 on Choctaw card #4292							
	11	For child of No2 see NB(March 3, 1905)#817							
	12								
	13								
	14	ENROLLMENT							
		OF NOS. 1,2,3,4,5,6 HEREON							
		APPROVED BY THE SECRETARY							
	16	OF INTERIOR Jan. 16, 1903							
	17								

TRIBAL ENROLLMENT OF PARENTS

	Name of Father	Year	County	Name of Mother	Year	County
1	J. F. McGahey	Dead	Jacks Fork	Martha J McGahey	1896	Non Citz
2	" "	"	" " "	" "	1896	" "
3	" "	"	" " "	" "	1896	" "
4	" "	"	" " "	" "	1896	" "
5	No 1			Minnie McGahey		Court Citizen
6	No 1			" " "		" "
7						
8						
9						
10	No1 on 1896 roll as J.H. McGahey					
11	No2 " 1896 " " A.J. "					
12	No3 " 1896 " " Lutha "					
13	No1 is the husband of Minnie McGahey on Choctaw card #4292.					
14	Nos. 1-2 were admitted as J.H. and A.J. McGahey by an					
15	Act of Council approved Nov. 5, 1880. The father of					
	all these, J.F. McGahey, admitted by same Act.					
	No.5 enrolled Dec. 7, 1900					
16	No.6 born July 17, 1902: enrolled Sep. 27, 1902.			Date of Application for Enrollment.		5/16/99
17	No1 is husband of Minnie McGahey Choctaw Card #D983 5910					

Choctaw By Blood Enrollment Cards 1898-1914

RESIDENCE: Atoka COUNTY.

POST OFFICE: Atoka, I.T.

Choctaw Nation

Choctaw Roll (Not Including Freedmen)

CARD NO. FIELD NO. 1789

Dawes' Roll No.		NAME	Relationship to Person	AGE	SEX	BLOOD	TRIBAL ENROLLMENT		
							Year	County	No.
5076	1	Anderson, MᶜCasson ²⁵	First Named	22	M	Full	1896	Atoka	440
	2								
	3								
	4								
	5								
	6								
	7								
	8								
	9								
	10								
	11								
	12								
	13								
	14								
	15								
	16								
	17								

ENROLLMENT
OF NOS. 1 HEREON
APPROVED BY THE SECRETARY
OF INTERIOR JAN 16 1903

TRIBAL ENROLLMENT OF PARENTS

	Name of Father	Year	County	Name of Mother	Year	County
1	Arlis Anderson	Dead	Atoka	Makale Anderson	Dead	Atoka
2						
3						
4						
5						
6						
7			On 1896 roll as Carson Anderson			
8						
9			No 1 now husband of Sillis Ben Choctaw card #1882			
10						
11						
12						
13						
14						
15						
16				Date of Application for Enrollment	5/16/99	
17			P O Antlers I T			

12/2/02

289

Choctaw By Blood Enrollment Cards 1898-1914

RESIDENCE: Cedar   COUNTY. **Choctaw Nation**   **Choctaw Roll**   CARD NO.
POST OFFICE: Kosoma, I.T.   (Not Including Freedmen)   FIELD NO. 1790

Dawes' Roll No.	NAME	Relationship to Person	AGE	SEX	BLOOD	TRIBAL ENROLLMENT		
						Year	County	No.
5077	1 Sherred, Josephus ³¹	First Named	28	M	Full	1896	Cedar	1357
	2							
	3							
	4							
	5							
	6							
	7							
	8							
	9							
	10							
	11							
	12							
	13							
	14							
	15	ENROLLMENT						
	16	OF NOS. 1 HEREON APPROVED BY THE SECRETARY						
	17	OF INTERIOR JAN 16 1903						

TRIBAL ENROLLMENT OF PARENTS

	Name of Father	Year	County	Name of Mother	Year	County
1	John Sherred	1896	Cedar	Rebecca Sherred	1896	Cedar
2						
3						
4						
5						
6			Wife and child on Chickasaw Card No 1429			
7						
8						
9						
10						
11						
12						
13						
14						
15						
16				Date of Application for Enrollment.	5/16/99	
17						

Choctaw By Blood Enrollment Cards 1898-1914

RESIDENCE: Kiamitia
POST OFFICE: Nelson, I.T.

COUNTY. **Choctaw Nation**

Choctaw Roll
(Not Including Freedmen)

CARD NO.
FIELD NO. 1791

Dawes' Roll No.	NAME	Relationship to Person	AGE	SEX	BLOOD	TRIBAL ENROLLMENT		
						Year	County	No.
5078	1 Smallwood, Robert 51	First Named	48	M	1/2	1896	Kiamitia11524	
	2							
	3							
	4							
	5							
	6							
	7							
	8							
	9							
	10							
	11							
	12							
	13							
	14							
	15							
	16							
	17							

ENROLLMENT
OF NOS. 1 HEREON
APPROVED BY THE SECRETARY
OF INTERIOR JAN 16 1903

TRIBAL ENROLLMENT OF PARENTS

	Name of Father	Year	County	Name of Mother	Year	County
1	John Smallwood	Dead	Kiamitia	Nancy Smallwood	Dead	Kiamitia
2						
3						
4						
5						
6						
7						
8						
9						
10						
11						
12						
13						
14						
15						
16			Date of Application for Enrollment.	5/16/99		
17						

Choctaw By Blood Enrollment Cards 1898-1914

RESIDENCE: Jacks Fork   COUNTY. **Choctaw Nation**   **Choctaw Roll**   CARD NO.
POST OFFICE: Abbott, I.T.   (Not Including Freedmen)   FIELD NO. 1792

Dawes' Roll No.	NAME		Relationship to Person First Named	AGE	SEX	BLOOD	TRIBAL ENROLLMENT		
							Year	County	No.
5079	₁ John, Dickson	49	First Named	46	M	Full	1896	Jacks Fork	7363
5080	₂ " Sophia	41	Wife	38	F	"	1896	" "	7364
5081	₃ " George	24	Son	21	M	"	1896	" "	7367
5082	₄ " Paul	13	"	10	"	"	1896	" "	7365
5083	₅ " Helen	8	Dau	5	F	"	1896	" "	7366
	₆								
	₇								
	₈								
	₉								
	10								
	11								
	12								
	13 P.O. Kosoma, I.T.								
	14 12/8/02								
	15 ENROLLMENT								
	16 OF NOS. 1,2,3,4,5 HEREON APPROVED BY THE SECRETARY								
	17 OF INTERIOR JAN 16 1903								

TRIBAL ENROLLMENT OF PARENTS

	Name of Father	Year	County	Name of Mother	Year	County
₁	Amos John	Dead	Jacks Fork	Mollie John	Dead	Nashoba
₂	Simon McCann	"	" " "	Sallie Turner	"	Jacks Fork
₃	No 1			Susana John	"	" " "
₄	No 1			No 2		
₅	No 1			No 2		
₆						
₇						
₈			For child of Nos 1&2 see N.B. (Apr. 26-06) Card #716			
₉			" " " No 3 " " (Mar. 3-05) " #717			
10			" " " " " " " " " " " #853			
11						
12						
13						
14						
15						
16				Date of Application for Enrollment.	5/16/99	
17						

Choctaw By Blood Enrollment Cards 1898-1914

RESIDENCE: Cedar   COUNTY. **Choctaw Nation**   **Choctaw Roll**   CARD NO.
POST OFFICE: Kosoma, I.T.   *(Not Including Freedmen)*   FIELD NO. 1793

Dawes' Roll No.	NAME		Relationship to Person Named	AGE	SEX	BLOOD	TRIBAL ENROLLMENT		
							Year	County	No.
5084	1 Bohanan, Eli	21	First Named	18	M	3/4	1896	Cedar	1074
I.W. 1293	2 " Ada	27	W=ife	27	F	I.W.			
	3								
	4								
	5								
	6								
	7								
	8								
	9								
	10								
	11	ENROLLMENT OF NOS. ~~~ 2 ~~~ HEREON APPROVED BY THE SECRETARY OF INTERIOR MAR 14 1905							
	12								
	13								
	14								
	15	ENROLLMENT OF NOS. 1 HEREON APPROVED BY THE SECRETARY OF INTERIOR JAN 16 1903							
	16								
	17								

TRIBAL ENROLLMENT OF PARENTS

	Name of Father	Year	County	Name of Mother	Year	County
1	Isom Bohanan	Dead	Red River	Liza Ann	Dead	Red River
2	John McKeever	dead	non citizen	Phoebe McKeever	dead	non citizen
3						
4						
5						
6	No1 is now husband of Ada Bohanan on Choctaw card D850					
7	Nos 1 and 2 were married Jan. 5, 1902.					
8	No.2 originally listed for enrollment on Choctaw Card D-850 Dec. 3, 1902; transferred to this card Jan. 29 1905. See decision of Jan 13, 1905.					
9	For child of Nos 1&2 see N.B. (Apr. 26, 1906) Card No. 76					
10	" " " " " " (Mar 3-1905) " " 108.					
11						
12						
13						
14						
15						
16				Date of Application for Enrollment.	5/16/99	
17		P.O. Antlers, I.T.				

P.O. Hugo IT 2/19/04   12/2/02

293

Choctaw By Blood Enrollment Cards 1898-1914

RESIDENCE:	Jacks Fork	COUNTY.	Choctaw Nation	Choctaw Roll	CARD No.	
POST OFFICE:	Antlers, I.T.			(Not Including Freedmen)	FIELD NO.	1794

Dawes' Roll No.	NAME		Relationship to Person	AGE	SEX	BLOOD	TRIBAL ENROLLMENT		
							Year	County	No.
5085	1 Hapotubbee, Susan	49	First Named	46	F	Full	1896	Jacks Fork	6345
5086	2 " Sallie	15	Dau	12	"	"	1896	" "	6346
5087	3 " Lubbin	9	Son	6	M	"	1896	" "	6347
	4								
	5								
	6								
	7								
	8								
	9								
	10								
	11								
	12								
	13								
	14								
	15	ENROLLMENT OF NOS. 1,2,3 HEREON							
	16	APPROVED BY THE SECRETARY							
	17	OF INTERIOR Jan. 16, 1903							

TRIBAL ENROLLMENT OF PARENTS

	Name of Father	Year	County	Name of Mother	Year	County
1	Joseph Loring	Dead	Atoka	Louisiana Loring	Dead	Atoka
2	Flan-so-na	"	Jacks Fork	No 1		
3	Hapotubbee	"	" "	No 1		
4						
5						
6						
7						
8						
9						
10	*					
11						
12						
13						
14				Date of Application for Enrollment.		
15						
16				5/16/99		
17						

294

RESIDENCE: Jacks Fork	COUNTY.							
POST OFFICE: Antlers, I.T.	**Choctaw Nation**					Choctaw Roll *(Not Including Freedmen)*	CARD No. FIELD No. **1795**	

Dawes' Roll No.	NAME	Relationship to Person	AGE	SEX	BLOOD	TRIBAL ENROLLMENT		
						Year	County	No.
5088	1 Jefferson Wallace ~DIED PRIOR TO SEPTEMBER 27 1902~	First Named	70	M	Full	1896	Jacks Fork	7357
5089	2 " Mary 47	Wife	44	F	"	1896	" "	7358
5090	3 " Benjamin 18	Son	15	M	"	1896	" "	7360
5091	4 " Katie ~DIED PRIOR TO SEPTEMBER 25, 1902~	G.Dau	6	F	"	1896	" "	7356
14932	5 Camp, Helen 1	Dau of No2	1	F	"			
	6							
	7							
	8	ENROLLMENT						
	9	OF NOS. ~~ 5 ~~ HEREON APPROVED BY THE SECRETARY						
	10	OF INTERIOR Oct. 15, 1903						
	11							
	12							
	13	ENROLLMENT						
	14	OF NOS. 1,2,3,4 HEREON						
	15	APPROVED BY THE SECRETARY						
	16	OF INTERIOR Jan. 16, 1903						
	17							

TRIBAL ENROLLMENT OF PARENTS

Name of Father	Year	County	Name of Mother	Year	County
1 Isaac Jefferson	Dead	in Mississippi	Pearlie Jefferson	Dead	Cedar
2 Co-le-by	"	Cedar	Siley	"	"
3 No 1			No 2		
4 Joe Jefferson	Dead	Jacks Fork	Betsy Jefferson	Dead	Cedar
5 Martin Camp		Choctaw card 1704	No 2		
6					
7		No 4 on 1896 roll as Kittie Jefferson			
8					
9		No 2 wife of No 1 on Choctaw card #1704			
10		No 1 died Dec. 3, 1900: proof of death filed Dec 10, 1902			
11		No 4 " in 1900. " " " " " " "			
		No 5 Born Sept. 24, 1901, enrolled Dec. 22, 1902			
12		~No 1 died Dec. 3, 1900; No 4 died __ 1900; Enrollment cancelled by Department July 8, 1904~			
13					
14					
15			Date of Application for Enrollment	5/16/99	
16					
17			↙ 1 to 4		

Choctaw By Blood Enrollment Cards 1898-1914

RESIDENCE: Cedar   COUNTY. **Choctaw Nation**   **Choctaw Roll**   CARD No.

POST OFFICE: Kosoma, I.T.   *(Not Including Freedmen)*   FIELD No. **1796**

Dawes' Roll No.	NAME	Relationship to Person	AGE	SEX	BLOOD	TRIBAL ENROLLMENT		
						Year	County	No.
5092	1 Felihkatabbee, Sallie 41	First Named	38	F	Full	1896	Cedar	4107
5093	2 McKinzie, Mack 20	Son	17	M	"	1896	"	9259
5094	3 Felihkatabbee, Vina 10	Dau	7	F	"	1896	"	4108
5095	4 " Johnson 5	Son	2	M	"			
14890	5 Cole, Caroline 1	Dau	4mo	F	"			
	6							
	7							
	8							
	9							
	10							
	11							
	12							
	13							

14

ENROLLMENT OF NOS. 1,2,3,4 HEREON APPROVED BY THE SECRETARY OF INTERIOR Jan. 16, 1903

ENROLLMENT OF NOS. 5 HEREON APPROVED BY THE SECRETARY OF INTERIOR May 21, 1903

TRIBAL ENROLLMENT OF PARENTS

Name of Father	Year	County	Name of Mother	Year	County
1 Felihkatabbee	Dead	Cedar	Lucy	Dead	Cedar
2 Goodman McKinzie	1896	"	No 1		
3 James Simply	1896	Jacks Fork	No 1		
4 Logan Cole	1896	Cedar	No 1		
5 " "	1896	"	No 1		
6					
7					
8					
9	No 3 on 1896 roll as Fannie Felihkatabbee				
10	No 1 wife of Logan Cole, Choctaw Card #1839			12/5/02	
11	No 5 Born Aug. 8, 1902 application made Dec. 5, 1902				
	" 5 Proof of birth filed Feb. 5, 1903				
12					
13					
14					
15				#1 to 4	
16			Date of Application for Enrollment.	5/16/99	
17					

296

Choctaw By Blood Enrollment Cards 1898-1914

RESIDENCE: Jacks Fork COUNTY. **Choctaw Nation** **Choctaw Roll** (Not Including Freedmen) CARD NO.
POST OFFICE: Kosoma, I.T. FIELD NO. **1797**

Dawes' Roll No.	NAME	Relationship to Person Named	AGE	SEX	BLOOD	Year	County	No.
I.W. 95	1 Napier, Thomas B ²⁶	First Named	23	M	I.W.			
5096	2 " Lucinda ³⁴	Wife	31	F	Full	1896	Jacks Fork	8383
5097	3 " Wyly ⁵	Son	1 1/2	M	1/2			
5098	4 " Fannie ²	Dau	7wks	F	1/2			
5099	5 Lewis Isom ⁸	S.Son	5	M	Full	1896	Jacks Fork	8384
5100	6 Cole, John ¹³	S.Son	10	"	"	1896	" "	3017
5101	7 Napier Mary ⁴	Dau	1mo	F	1/2			
	8							
	9							
	10							
	11							
	12							
	13	ENROLLMENT OF NOS. 2,3,4,5,6,7 HEREON APPROVED BY THE SECRETARY OF INTERIOR Jan. 16, 1903				ENROLLMENT OF NOS. 1 HEREON APPROVED BY THE SECRETARY OF INTERIOR Jun 13, 1903			

TRIBAL ENROLLMENT OF PARENTS

	Name of Father	Year	County	Name of Mother	Year	County
1	H. L. Napier	1896	Non Citz	Fannie Napier	Dead	Non Citz
2	Nat Fulsom	Dead	Jacks Fork	Susan Impson	"	Jacks Fork
3	No 1			No 2		
4	No 1			No 2		
5	Jesse Lewis	Dead	Jacks Fork	No 2		
6	Roebuck Cole	"	" "	No 2		
7	No 1			No 2		

No 2 on 1896 roll as Lucinda Lewis

Evidence of marriage to be supplied. Recd June 16/99.
No. 7 Enrolled April 25, 1901.

Date of Application for Enrollment. 5/16/99

For child of Nos 1&2 see N.B. (Mar 3rd 1905) Card #110
P.O. Antlers, I.T. 12/4/02

297

Choctaw By Blood Enrollment Cards 1898-1914

RESIDENCE:	Cedar	COUNTY.								
POST OFFICE:	Kosoma, I.T.									

Choctaw Nation — **Choctaw Roll** *(Not Including Freedmen)* — CARD NO. FIELD NO. **1798**

Dawes' Roll No.	NAME	Relationship to Person First Named	AGE	SEX	BLOOD	TRIBAL ENROLLMENT Year	County	No.
5102	1 Pecamontubbee, Frances 59	Named	56	F	Full	1896	Cedar	10328
5013	2 William, [illegible] DIED PRIOR TO SEPTEMBER 25, 1902	Ward	16	W [sic]	"	1896	"	13140
	3							
	4							
	5							
	6							
	7							
	8							
	9							
	10							
	11							
	12							
	13							
	14	ENROLLMENT OF NOS. 1, 2 HEREON APPROVED BY THE SECRETARY OF INTERIOR Jan 16, 1903						
	15							
	16							
	17							

TRIBAL ENROLLMENT OF PARENTS

	Name of Father	Year	County	Name of Mother	Year	County
1	Me-sha-ya	Dead	Towson	Maley Ann	Dead	Towson
2	Byington Cobat	"	Jacks Fork	Viney Cobat	"	Cedar
3						
4						
5						
6	No.1 is duplicate of Frances Pismotubby, Choctaw Card Nº 5621					
7	Approved roll of Choctaws by blood, No. 13480					
8	Enrolment of No.1 cancelled by Secretary of Interior Aug. 25-1904 See Department letter of that date (I.T.D. #6712-1904) D.C. #31482-1904					
9	No.2 died Jan – 1900: Enrollment cancelled by Department Sept. 16 - 1904					
10						
11						
12						
13						
14						
15						
16			Date of Application for Enrollment.	5/16/99		
17						

Choctaw By Blood Enrollment Cards 1898-1914

RESIDENCE: Cedar   COUNTY. **Choctaw Nation**   **Choctaw Roll** *(Not Including Freedmen)*   CARD NO.

POST OFFICE: Kosoma, I.T.   FIELD NO. **1799**

Dawes' Roll No.	NAME	Relationship to Person First Named	AGE	SEX	BLOOD	TRIBAL ENROLLMENT		
						Year	County	No.
5104	1 Billy, Siney 48		45	F	Full	1896	Cedar	1053
5105	2 " Allen DIED PRIOR TO SEPTEMBER 25 1902	Son	19	M	"	1896	"	1054
5106	3 " Emma 14	Dau	11	F	"	1896	"	1055
5107	4 Gibson, Sulena 17	Ward	14	"	"	1896	Towson	4730
	5							
	6							
	7							
	8							
	9							
	10							
	11							
	12							
	13	ENROLLMENT						
	14	OF NOS. 1, 2, 3, 4 HEREON						
		APPROVED BY THE SECRETARY						
	15	OF INTERIOR Jan. 16, 1903						
	16							
	17							

TRIBAL ENROLLMENT OF PARENTS

	Name of Father	Year	County	Name of Mother	Year	County
1	Moses Gibson	Dead	Kiamitia	Nawee Gibson	Dead	Kiamitia
2	Jackson Billy	"	Cedar	No 1		
3	" "	"	"	No 1		
4	Jackson Gibson	"	Kiamitia	Manda Thomas	Dead	Towson
5						
6						
7			No 2 died in 1896, proof of death filed Dec 9, 1902			
8						
9			No 2 died March 10, 1901; Enrollment cancelled by Department Dec. 24, 1904			
10			No.4 Dead G.F. 7300 – 1912			
11						
12						
13						
14						
15						
16					Date of Application for Enrollment.	
17					5/16/99	

P.O. Finley I.T. 8/15/04

Choctaw By Blood Enrollment Cards 1898-1914

RESIDENCE: Gaines	COUNTY.	Choctaw Nation	Choctaw Roll (Not Including Freedmen)	CARD No.
POST OFFICE: Hartshorne, I.T.				FIELD No. 1800

Dawes' Roll No.	NAME	Relationship to Person First Named	AGE	SEX	BLOOD	TRIBAL ENROLLMENT Year	County	No.
I.W. 96	1 Cowen, John R 36	First Named	33	M	I.W.			
5108	2 " Frances 19	Wife	16	F	1/2	1896	Gaines	11249
5109	3 " Charles 2	Son	2mo	M	1/4			
	4							
	5							
	6							
	7							
	8							
	9							
	10							
	11							
	12							
	13							
	14							
	15							
	16							
	17							

ENROLLMENT
OF NOS. 2, 3 HEREON
APPROVED BY THE SECRETARY
OF INTERIOR Jan. 16, 1903

ENROLLMENT
OF NOS. 1 ~~~ HEREON
APPROVED BY THE SECRETARY
OF INTERIOR Jun. 13, 1903

TRIBAL ENROLLMENT OF PARENTS

	Name of Father	Year	County	Name of Mother	Year	County
1	George Cowen	Dead	Non Citz	Margaret Cowen	1896	Non Citz
2	Chas Stewart	"	" "	Lottie Stewart	Dead	Jacks Fork
3	No 1			No 2		
4						
5						
6						
7			No 2 on 1896 roll as Frances Stewart.			
8						
9			See testimony of S. E. Cole.			
10						
11			No. 3 Enrolled September 20th 1900			
12						
13			For child of Nos 1&2 see N.B. (Apr. 26-06) Card #498			
14			" " " " " " " (Mar. 3-05) " #821			
15					#1 & 2	
16				Date of Application for Enrollment	5/16/99	
17						

P.O. Durant I.T. 4/7/05

300

313

www.ingramcontent.com/pod-product-compliance
Lightning Source LLC
Chambersburg PA
CBHW030236030426
42336CB00009B/120